Computer Forensics
JumpStart™

Michael G. Solomon
Diane Barrett
Neil Broom

San Francisco ◆ London

SYBEX

Associate Publisher: Neil Edde
Acquisitions and Developmental Editor: Maureen Adams
Production Editor: Lori Newman
Technical Editor: Warren G. Kruse
Copyeditor: Kathy Grider-Carlyle
Compositor: Jeff Wilson, Happenstance Type-O-Rama
Graphic Illustrator: Jeff Wilson, Happenstance Type-O-Rama
Proofreaders: Ian Golder, Amy Rasmussen, Nancy Riddiough
Indexer: Nancy Guenther
Book Designer: Judy Fung
Cover Designer: Richard Miller, Calyx Design
Cover Illustrator: Richard Miller, Calyx Design

Library of Congress Card Number: 2004113397

ISBN: 0-7821-4375-X

SYBEX and the SYBEX logo are either registered trademarks or trademarks of SYBEX Inc. in the United States and/or other countries.

JumpStart is a trademark of SYBEX Inc.

Screen reproductions produced with FullShot 99. FullShot 99 © 1991-1999 Inbit Incorporated. All rights reserved.
FullShot is a trademark of Inbit Incorporated.

Internet screen shot(s) using Microsoft Internet Explorer 6 reprinted by permission from Microsoft Corporation.

TRADEMARKS: SYBEX has attempted throughout this book to distinguish proprietary trademarks from descriptive terms by following the capitalization style used by the manufacturer.

The author and publisher have made their best efforts to prepare this book, and the content is based upon final release software whenever possible. Portions of the manuscript may be based upon pre-release versions supplied by software manufacturer(s). The author and the publisher make no representation or warranties of any kind with regard to the completeness or accuracy of the contents herein and accept no liability of any kind including but not limited to performance, merchantability, fitness for any particular purpose, or any losses or damages of any kind caused or alleged to be caused directly or indirectly from this book.

Manufactured in the United States of America

10 9 8 7 6 5 4 3 2

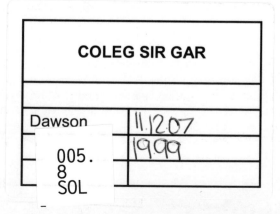

About the Authors

Michael G. Solomon is a full-time security speaker, consultant (http://www.solomonconsulting.com/), trainer, and a former college instructor who specializes in development and assessment security topics. As an IT professional and consultant since 1987, he has worked on projects or trained for more than 60 major companies and organizations, including EarthLink, Nike Corporation, Lucent Technologies, BellSouth, UPS, the U.S. Coast Guard, and Norrell.

From 1998 until 2001, Michael was an instructor in the Kennesaw State University's Computer Science and Information Sciences (CSIS) department, where he taught courses on software project management, C++ programming, computer organization and architecture, and data communications. Michael has an M.S. in mathematics and computer science from Emory University (1998) and a B.S. in computer science from Kennesaw State University (1987).

Michael has also contributed to various security certification books for LANWrights/iLearning, including *TICSA Training Guide* and an accompanying Instructor Resource Kit (Que, 2002), *CISSP Study Guide* (Sybex, 2003), as well as *Security+ Training Guide* (Que, 2003). Michael co-authored *Information Security Illuminated* (Jones and Bartlett, 2005), *Security+ Lab Manual Exam Cram 2* (Que, 2005), and authored and provided the on-camera delivery of LearnKey's CISSP Prep e-Learning course.

Michael's certifications include Certified Information Security Manager (CISM), Certified Information Systems Security Professional (CISSP), and TruSecure ICSA Certified Security Associate (TICSA).

Diane Barrett has been involved in the IT industry since 1993. She works at Remington College where she taught in the computer networking program for two years before becoming a director. She teaches online classes that include networking, security, and virus protection, and she is the president of a security awareness corporation that specializes in training.

Diane has co-authored several security and networking books, including *MCSA/MCSE 70-299 Exam Cram 2: Implementing and Administering Security in a Windows Server 2003 Network* (Que, 2004) and *Computer Networking Illuminated* (Jones and Bartlett, 2005). She is currently volunteering for ISSA's Generally Accepted Information Security Principles Project in the ethical practices working group.

Diane's certifications include Microsoft Certified Systems Engineer (MCSE) on Windows 2000, MCSE+I on Windows NT 4.0, Certified Information Systems Security Professional (CISSP), Cisco Certified Network Associate (CCNA), A+, Network+, i-Net+, and Security+.

Neil Broom is the President of the Technical Resource Center (http://www.trcglobal.com) in Atlanta, Georgia. As a speaker, trainer, course director, and consultant in the fields of Computer Forensics, Information Assurance, and Professional Security Testing, he has over 14 years of experience providing technical education and security services to the military, law enforcement, the health care industry, financial institutions, and government agencies.

Neil is the Lead Instructor and Developer of the Computer Forensics and Cyber Investigations course and the Certified Cyber Crime Examiner (C^3E) certification and provides Computer Forensics services to clients in the Metro Atlanta area and the Southeast United States.

Neil is currently the Vice President of the Atlanta Chapter of the International Information Systems Forensics Association, and he is a professional member of the National Speakers Association. His past employment includes the U.S. Navy as a submariner, the Gainesville, Florida Police Department as a law enforcement officer, and Internet Security Systems (ISS) as a security trainer.

Neil has multiple certifications including Certified Information Systems Security Professional (CISSP), Certified Computer Examiner (CCE), Certified Ethical Hacker (CEH), Computer Hacking Forensic Investigator (CHFI), National Security Agency's INFOSEC Assessment Methodology (IAM), Microsoft Certified Systems Engineer (MCSE 4.0 and 2000), Microsoft Certified Trainer (MCT), and TruSecure ICSA Certified Security Associate (TICSA).

About the Technical Editor

Warren G. Kruse II, CISSP, CFCE, is the co-author of *Computer Forensics: Incident Response Essentials*, published by Addison-Wesley. Warren has conducted forensics globally in support of cases involving some of the largest law firms and corporations in the world. He is a member of the New York and European Electronic Crimes Task Forces of the U.S. Secret Service. He was elected President of the High Tech Crime Investigation Association's (www.htcia.org) 2005 International Executive Committee. Warren has extensive experience investigating cases involving the illegal use of computer and networks and received the High Tech Crime Investigation Association's (HTCIA) "2001 Case of the Year" award. He is an IACIS Certified Forensic Computer Examiner (CFCE) and an (ISC)² Certified Information Systems Security Professional (CISSP). He lectures on computer forensics for Computer Security Institute (CSI) and has taught computer forensics at the SANS Institute and MIS Training Institute. He is the lead instructor of the hands-on intro and advanced Computer Forensics Bootcamps for Computer Forensic Services, LLC. Warren is a partner at Computer Forensic Services, LLC (www.computer-forensic.com).

To my wife, best friend, and source of unyielding support, Stacey.

—Michael G. Solomon

To my dad, Gerald, who has always encouraged me to be my own person.

—Diane Barrett

To my mother, thank you for always believing in me.

—Neil Broom

Acknowledgments

Anything worth doing is worth doing well, and doing anything well generally requires a lot of help. My family has helped me immensely throughout this project. Stacey, Noah, and Isaac are all great fun to be around and often serve as sounding boards. The one focal point of this book, however, is Kim Lindros at LANWrights/iLearning. She kept the project on track and worked things out regardless of what curve balls I may have sent her way. Kim deserves a huge ovation for her work to get this book into your hands. I truly appreciate the efforts of all the people at LANWrights/iLearning and Sybex to make this project a reality.

—*Michael G. Solomon*

Thanks to everyone at Sybex for making this book possible, especially Maureen Adams the acquisitions editor and Lori Newman the production editor. Thank you to the wonderful team at LANWrights/iLearning, especially Kim Lindros, who worked so hard behind the scenes to be sure that our work was accurate and completed in a timely fashion. To co-authors Michael Solomon and Neil Broom, thank you for the part each of you played in making this project successful. Thanks to Warren G. Kruse II, our technical reviewer, for making certain our writing was technically and procedurally sound. Finally, special thanks to my husband, Bill, for keeping a sense of humor during the hours I spent writing.

—*Diane Barrett*

Kim Lindros, you rock! Thank you for all the support and gentle nudging you provided to keep me writing. I also wish to say thank you to the cat and kitten rescue group that I work with, www.FurKids.org. Now that the book is finished, I can return to helping save the lives of our furry little friends.

—*Neil Broom*

Contents

Chapter 5   **Capturing the Data Image**   **95**

Chapter 6   **Extracting Information from Data**   **117**

Introduction

Want to know what computer forensics examiners really do? This book is intended to cover the essential basics of computer forensics, and it is especially designed for those new to the field. Many new stories and television shows highlight the role of forensics investigators in solving cases. It all seems so exciting, doesn't it? Computer forensics is really not that different from what we see on TV. It's quite a bit less glamorous, but similar in nature. To be honest, all forensics examiners lead lives that are a little less glamorous than what TV tells us.

After a crime or incident has occurred that involves a computer, a specialist trained in computer forensics can examine the computer to find clues as to what happened. That is the role of the computer forensics examiner. The specialist could work with law enforcement (LE) or with a corporate incident response team. Although the rules governing each activity can be dramatically different, the approach to the investigation is roughly the same.

This book covers the field of computer forensics, including the basic elements, concepts, tools, and common activities that will prepare you with a solid understanding of the field. You will be able to participate in investigations and understand the process of finding, collecting, and analyzing evidence. Although this book is not a definitive training guide for specific forensic tools, you will learn how to perform the most common tasks that you will encounter in an investigation.

The world's heightened awareness of security since the attacks of September 11, 2001, has also provided more nontechnical people with a view of security issues that were previously discussed only in security specialist circles. Computers play a central role in all activities, both legal and illegal. The material in this book can be applied to both criminal investigations and incident response activities. You don't have to be a member of law enforcement to benefit from the material presented here. Nontechnical people can also benefit from this book in that it covers the basic approach computer examiners take in an investigation.

If you like the comprehensive introduction to computer forensics we present in this book, you can pursue the topic further in several ways. Most major forensic tools vendors offer their own training on their products and their use in investigations. See Chapter 8, "Common Forensics Tools," and Appendix D, "Forensics Tools," for more information. Appendix B, "Forensics Resources," contains many references to where you can get more information. If you decide to pursue computer forensic certification, Appendix C, "Forensics Certifications," provides a list of common certifications and contact information for each. If your job involves computer investigations, this book can help you expand your knowledge and abilities. Keep it handy as a resource as you acquire more experience and knowledge. And good luck with your pursuit!

Who Should Read This Book

Anyone fulfilling, or aspiring to fulfill, the responsibilities of a computer examiner can benefit from this book. Also, if you just want to know more about what computer examiners do, this book will fill you in. The material is organized to provide a high-level view of the process and methods used in an investigation. Both LE personnel and non-LE will benefit from the topics presented.

Because you are reading this introduction, you must have some interest in computer forensics. Why are you interested? Are you just curious, do you want to start working in computer forensics, or have you just been given the responsibility of conducting or managing an investigation? This book addresses readers in all of these categories.

Although we recommend that you read the book from start to finish for a complete overview of the topics, you can jump right to an area of interest. If you bought this book for a concise list of forensics tools, go right to Chapter 8. But don't forget the other chapters! You'll find a wealth of information in all chapters that will help expand your understanding of computer forensics.

What This Book Covers

Chapter 1   This chapter lays the foundation for the rest of the book. It discusses the need for computer forensics and how the examiners' activities meet the need.

Chapter 2   This chapter addresses the necessary knowledge you must have before you start. When you finish this chapter, you will know how to prepare for an investigation.

Chapter 3   This chapter discusses computer evidence and focuses on identifying, collecting, preserving, and analyzing evidence.

Chapter 4   Most investigations include similar common tasks. This chapter outlines those tasks you are likely to see over and over. It sets the stage for the action items you will use in your activities.

Chapter 5   This chapter covers the first functional step in many investigations. You will learn the reason for and the process of creating media images for analysis.

Chapter 6   After you have an exact media image, you can start analyzing it for evidence. This chapter covers the basics of data analysis. You will learn what to look for and how to find it.

Chapter 7   Sooner or later, you will run into password-protected resources and encrypted files. This chapter covers basic encryption and password issues and discusses how to deal with them.

Chapter 8   Every computer examiner needs a tool box. This chapter covers many popular hardware and software forensic tools.

Chapter 9   When the analysis is done, you need to present the results. This chapter covers the elements and flow of an investigation report.

Chapter 10   If your evidence ends up in court, you need to know how to effectively present it. This chapter covers many ins and outs of being an expert witness and presenting evidence in court.

Appendix A   Provides the answers to the Review Questions

Appendix B   A list of forensics resources you can use for further research

Appendix C   A list of computer forensics certifications and contact information

Appendix D   A summary list of forensic tools, several of which are discussed in the text, with contact information

Glossary   A list of terms used throughout the book

Making the Most of This Book

At the beginning of each chapter you'll find a list of topics that the chapter covers. You'll find new terms (specific terminology) defined in the margins of the pages to help you quickly get up to speed on computer forensics. In addition, several special elements highlight important information:

Notes provide extra information and references to related information.

NOTE

Tips are insights that help you perform tasks more easily and effectively.

TIP

Warnings let you know about things you should do—or shouldn't do—as you perform computer investigations.

WARNING

You'll find Review Questions at the end of each chapter to test your knowledge of the material covered. The answers to the Review Questions can be found in Appendix A. You'll also find a list of Terms to Know at the end of each chapter that will help you review the key terms introduced in the chapter. These terms are compiled in the Glossary at the end of the book.

You'll also find special sidebars in each chapter titled "Tales from the Trenches," written by Neil Broom. These are war stories Neil has encountered throughout his career as a computer forensics examiner. They are written in first person, so you'll really get a sense of what it's like to go "on scene" and get your hands dirty.

Chapter 1

The Need for Computer Forensics

Computer forensics is a fascinating field. As enterprises become more complex and exchange more information online, high-tech crimes are increasing at a rapid rate. The industry has taken off in recent years, and it's no surprise that a profession once regarded as a vague counterpart of network security has grown into a science all its own. In addition, numerous companies and professionals now offer computer forensic services. A computer forensic technician is a combination of a private eye and a computer scientist. Although the ideal background for this field includes legal, technical, and law enforcement experience, a myriad of industries use professionals with investigative intelligence and technology proficiency. A computer forensic professional can fill a variety of roles such as private investigator, corporate compliance professional, or law enforcement official.

This chapter introduces you to the concept of computer forensics, while addressing computer forensic needs from both sides—corporate policy and law enforcement. It will present some real-life examples of computer crime. It will help you assess your organization's needs and discuss various training methods used for practitioners and end users.

Defining Computer Forensics

computer forensics
Computer investigation and analysis techniques that involve the identification, preservation, extraction, documentation, and interpretation of computer data to determine potential legal evidence.

The digital age has produced many new professions, but one of the most unusual is computer forensics. Computer forensics deals with the application of law to a science. The New Shorter Oxford English Dictionary defines *computer forensics* as "the application of forensic science techniques to computer-based material." In other words, forensic computing is the process of identifying, preserving, analyzing, and presenting digital evidence in a manner that is acceptable in a legal proceeding. At times, it is more science than art; other times, it is more art than science.

Although it is similar to other forms of legal forensics, the computer forensics process requires a vast knowledge of computer hardware and software in order to avoid the accidental invalidation or destruction of evidence and to preserve the evidence for later analysis. Computer forensic review involves the application of investigative and analytical techniques to acquire and protect potential legal evidence; therefore, a professional within this field needs to have a detailed understanding of the local, regional, national, and sometimes even international laws affecting the process of evidence collection and retention. This is especially true in cases involving attacks that may be waged from widely distributed systems located in many separate regions.

electronic discovery
The process whereby electronic documents are collected, prepared, reviewed, and distributed in association with legal and government proceedings.

Computer forensics can also be described as the critical analysis of a computer hard disk drive after an intrusion or crime. This is mainly because specialized software tools and procedures are required to analyze the various areas where computer data is stored, after the fact. Often this involves retrieving deleted data from hard drives and servers that have been subpoenaed in court or seized by law enforcement. During the course of forensic work, you will run into a practice that is called *electronic discovery*. Electronic discovery produces electronic documents for litigation. Items included in electronic discovery include data that is created or stored on a computer, computer network, or other storage media. Examples of such are e-mail, word-processing documents, plaintext files, database files, spreadsheets, digital art or photos, and presentations. Electronic discovery using computer forensics techniques requires in-depth computer knowledge and the ability to logically dissect a computer system or network to locate the desired evidence. It may also require expert witness testimony to explain to the court the exact method or methods by which the evidence was obtained.

Computer forensics has become a popular topic in computer security circles and in the legal community. Even though it is a fascinating field, due to the nature of computers, far more information is available than there is time to analyze, and a key skill is to know when to stop looking. This is a skill that comes with time and experience. For now, let's look at the major concepts behind computer forensics. The main emphasis is on recovery of data. To do that you must:

◆ Identify the evidence

◆ Determine how to preserve the evidence

◆ Extract, process, and interpret the evidence

◆ Ensure that the evidence is acceptable in a court of law

All of these concepts are discussed in great detail throughout this book. Because computer-based information is fragile and can be easily planted, rarely is the simple presence of incriminating material the evidence of guilt. So as you can see, electronic information is easy to create and store, yet computer forensics is a science that requires specialized training, experience, and equipment.

Real World Scenario

Tales from the Trenches: Why Computer Forensics Is Important

A computer forensics examiner might be called upon to perform any of a number of different types of computer forensics investigations.

We have all heard of or read about the use of computer forensics by law enforcement agencies to help catch criminals. The criminal might be a thief who was found with evidence of his crime when his home or office computer was searched, or a state employee who was found to have stolen funds from public accounts by manipulating accounting software to hide funds transfers.

Most of us know that computer forensics is used every day in the corporate business world to help protect the assets and reputation of large companies. Forensics examiners are called upon to monitor the activities of employees; assist in locating evidence of industrial espionage; and provide support in defending allegations of misconduct by senior management.

Government agencies hire computer forensics specialists to help protect the data the agencies maintain. Sometimes, it's as simple as making sure IRS employees don't misuse the access they have been granted to view your tax information by periodically reviewing their activities. Many times, it's as serious as helping to defend the United States by protecting the most vital top secret information by working within a counter intelligence group.

Every day, divorce attorneys ask examiners to assist in the examination of personal computers belonging to spouses involved in divorce proceedings. The focus of such investigations usually is to find information about assets that the spouse may be hiding and to which the other spouse is entitled.

Continues

More recently, defense attorneys have asked forensic examiners to reexamine computers belonging to criminal defendants. Computer forensics experts have even been asked to reexamine evidence used in a capital murder case that resulted in the defendant receiving a death sentence. Such reexaminations are conducted to refute the findings of the law enforcement investigations.

Although each of these areas seems entirely unique, the computer forensics examiner who learns the basics, obtains appropriate equipment, follows proper procedures, and continues to educate himself or herself will be able to handle each of these investigations and many other types not yet discussed. The need for proper computer forensics investigations is growing every day as new methods, technologies, and reasons for investigations are discovered.

Real-Life Examples of Computer Crime

An endless number of computer crime cases are available for you to read. Most of the ones in the following sections come from the Department of Justice website, which is at http://www.cybercrime.gov. In these cases, we'll look at several types of computer crime and how computer forensic techniques were used to capture the criminal. The five cases presented here illustrate some of the techniques that you will become familiar with as you advance through this book. As a forensic investigator, you never know what you may come across when you begin an investigation. As the cases in this section show, sometimes you find more than you could have ever imagined.

Hacker Pleads Guilty to Illegally Accessing New York Times Computer Network

Adrian Lamo, 22, was charged in a Manhattan federal court with hacking into the internal computer network of the New York Times. Lamo illegally accessed a database containing confidential information such as home telephone numbers and Social Security numbers for over 3,000 contributors. The records he accessed included entries for former President Jimmy Carter, Democratic campaigner James Carville, former secretary of state James Baker, actor Robert Redford, columnist William F. Buckley, Jr., and radio personality Rush Limbaugh among others.

Investigators found that the hacker had added an entry for Adrian Lamo, listing personal information such as a cellular telephone number, (415) 505-HACK, and a description of Lamo's areas of expertise including computer hacking, national security, and communications intelligence. Lamo also created five fictitious user accounts with a fee-based, online subscription service that provides news and legal and other information to customers. Over the course of three months, those five accounts were used to conduct upwards of 3,000 searches, incurring charges of approximately $300,000.

Source: Security Focus, September 5, 2003, http://www.securityfocus.com/news/6888; U.S. Department of Justice, Computer Crime and Intellectual Property Section (CCIPS), http://www.cybercrime.gov/lamoPlea.htm.

NOTE

In addition, Lamo admitted responsibility for a series of other computer intrusions on networks at Cingular, Excite@Home, MCI WorldCom, Microsoft, SBC Ameritech, and Yahoo!. If convicted, Lamo faces a maximum sentence of 15 years in prison and a $500,000 fine.

By using computer forensic techniques, his trail could be traced through proxy server logs, the accounts he created while on the internal network, and unauthorized LexisNexis searches for such information as his name, other individuals with the last name "Lamo," searches using his parents' Northern California home address, and searches for some of his known associates.

Stealing and selling proprietary information has become big business. The next two cases are examples of just that. When proprietary information is stolen, a computer forensic investigator may work in tandem with corporate human resources and compliance professionals to help not only examine how the theft occurred but also provide evidence for prosecution.

Man Pleads Guilty to Hacking Intrusion and Theft of Data Costing Company $5.8 Million

Daniel Jeremy Baas, age 25, of Milford, Ohio, pled guilty to exceeding authorized access to a protected computer and obtaining information. Baas was charged with illegally accessing a protected computer and stealing customer databases from Acxiom, a Little Rock, Arkansas-based company that maintains customer information for automotive manufacturers, banks, credit card issuers, and retailers, among others. The intrusion and theft of data cost Acxiom more than $5.8 million, which, in addition to the value of the stolen information, included employee time and travel expenses, and the cost of security audits and encryption software.

Baas worked as a computer systems administrator for a Cincinnati-based company that did business with Acxiom, which made files available for download for Baas' employer. With that access, Baas ran a password-cracking program on Acxiom computers, illegally obtaining about 300 passwords, including one with administrator-level privileges. That user account allowed him to download files belonging to other Acxiom customers, which contained confidential identification information.

Baas faced a maximum prison sentence of five years, a fine of $250,000 or twice the amount of gain or loss, and three years of supervised release.

Source: U.S. Department of Justice, Computer Crime and Intellectual Property Section (CCIPS), http://www.cybercrime.gov/baasPlea.htm.

NOTE

In this case, the forensic examiner might have found the program used to crack the password. If the program was deleted, parts of all of it could have been recovered as well as the password file. Other evidence might include the actual downloaded files or fragments of them. The download program itself might have a log file that would have recorded who accessed the program and what was downloaded. The forensic examiner has a wide variety of tools available to extract data and deleted information.

Three Men Indicted for Hacking into Lowe's Companies' Computers with Intent to Steal Credit Card Information

Brian A. Salcedo, Adam W. Botbyl, and Paul G. Timmins were indicted on November 19, 2003, by a federal grand jury on sixteen counts of unauthorized computer access, attempted possession of unauthorized access devices computer fraud, conspiracy, intentional transmission of computer code, and wire fraud.

Salcedo, Botbyl, and Timmins first accessed the wireless network at a Lowe's retail store in Southfield, Michigan. They subsequently hacked into the central computer network at Lowe's Companies, Inc. in North Carolina and then into computer systems in Lowe's retail stores across the United States. The men installed a program on computers in several of the retail locations that captured customers' credit card account numbers. If convicted on all counts, Salcedo, Botbyl, and Timmins face maximum sentences of 170 years in prison.

NOTE

Source: U.S. Department of Justice, Computer Crime and Intellectual Property Section (CCIPS), `http://www.cybercrime.gov/salcedoIndict.htm`.

The previous case spanned several states. Several federal agencies and various state and local agencies had to work together to track the illicit computer accesses. By compromising the system and then capturing credit card information, the three suspects unwittingly left a trail of forensic evidence. Some of the evidence possibly included the actual credit card information or remnants of this information, in addition to the program or parts of the program used to capture the information and log file records that indicated access to various locations on the corporate network.

The next case is one of employee revenge and destruction. This type of criminal activity has become common as more employees who are computer savvy try to find ways to get back at employers.

Former Chief Computer Network Program Designer Arraigned for Alleged $10 Million Computer Software Bomb

Timothy Allen Lloyd, of Wilmington, Delaware, was sentenced to 41 months in prison for launching a programming bomb on Omega Engineering Corp.'s network that resulted in approximately $10 million in damages. Lloyd, a computer network program designer for New Jersey-based Omega for 11 years, was terminated from his position on July 10, 1996. Twenty days later, a *logic bomb* was activated that permanently deleted all of the company's design and production software for measurement and control instruments used by the U.S. Navy and NASA.

In addition to the monetary loss in sales and contracts, the attack led to 80 layoffs within Omega. The case is apparently one of the most expensive computer sabotage cases in U.S. Secret Service history.

Source: U.S. Department of Justice, Computer Crime and Intellectual Property Section (CCIPS), http://www.cybercrime.gov/lloydSent.htm.

logic bomb
A virus or other program that is created to execute when a certain event occurs or a period of time passes. For example, a programmer might create a logic bomb to delete all his code from the server on a future date, most likely after he has left the company.

NOTE

In this case, computer forensic evidence may include the actual program or logic bomb, the date and time the file was created, and the username of the file creator. Time and date stamps are an important part of the computer forensic process. You will learn about these and other forensic techniques later in the book.

The following graphic is from the website of the Computer Crime and Intellectual Property Section of the Criminal Division of the U.S. Department of Justice. Here you can find a lot of useful information and additional cases. The last case concerns a computer crime committed by a child.

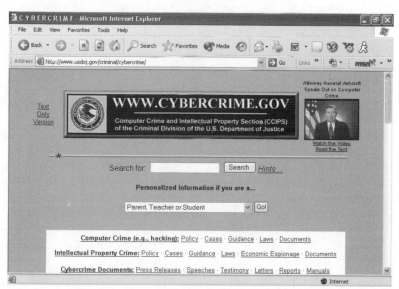

Juvenile Computer Hacker Sentenced to Six Months in Detention Facility

A juvenile, who goes by the name "c0mrade" on the Internet, accepted responsibility in a U.S. District Court in Miami for illegally accessing a military computer used by the Defense Threat Reduction Agency (DTRA), stealing usernames and passwords, and capturing e-mail messages exchanged between DTRA staff. DTRA, a Department of Defense agency, is responsible for reducing the threat from nuclear, biological, chemical, conventional, and special weapons to the United States and its allies.

backdoor
A software program that allows access to a system without using security checks.

Over a two-month period beginning in August 1999, the juvenile accessed the DTRA network by secretly installing a *backdoor* on a server in Virginia. In addition to capturing over 3,300 e-mail messages, he acquired at least 19 usernames and passwords of DTRA staff, 10 of which were on military computers.

The juvenile also admitted to illegally accessing 13 computers located at NASA's Marshall Space Flight Center on June 29 and 30, 1999, and downloading proprietary software worth approximately $1.7 million. The intrusions and data theft forced NASA to shut down the computer systems for 21 days in July, resulting in approximately $41,000 in contractor labor and computer equipment replacement costs.

——————— *NOTE* ———————

Source: U.S. Department of Justice, Computer Crime and Intellectual Property Section (CCIPS), `http://www.cybercrime.gov/comrade.htm`.

This case marks the first time a juvenile hacker was sentenced to serve time. In addition to his six-month sentence in a detention facility, c0mrade was required to write letters of apology to the Department of Defense and NASA and allowed public disclosure of information about the case.

disaster recovery
The ability of a company to recover from an occurrence inflicting widespread destruction and distress.

What kind of information was found that led to his arrest and conviction? A forensic investigator might have been able to recover a significant number of the captured e-mails if they were deleted. They might have been hidden in a directory or on a hard disk partition. In addition, a forensic investigator probably was able to trace the downloaded software, possibly to the suspect's computer.

best practices
A set of recommended guidelines that outline a set of good controls.

These cases illustrate that computer forensic investigators have no idea where their cases will end up. As a computer sleuth, you may be required to work across state lines and with various agencies. You may end up working with several companies in various countries. You may up at a dead end because it takes too long to get the information you need or the employer decides not to prosecute. At any rate, the computer forensics world is full of surprises.

Corporate versus Law Enforcement Concerns

The needs of the corporate world and those of law enforcement differ on several levels. Law enforcement officials work under more restrictive rules than corporate agents or employees. If a law enforcement agent asks you to do something, you can be bound by the same restrictions that they encounter. Face it: there is a big difference between a company deciding to log router traffic and a local or federal law enforcement officer asking the company to log the traffic.

Both law enforcement and corporate practitioners are guided by a set of *best practices* set forth by various agencies. In the law enforcement arena, a set of best practices exists for electronic discovery and how to properly retrieve data. The corporate world has established best practices for security and best practices for determining what comprises an *incident*. These best practices iterate *incident response* procedures regarding how to react to an incident. Because disasters are usually of a larger magnitude, best practices for *disaster recovery* may affect both. The focus of this book is to provide information that can be used in either discipline and not geared specifically toward law enforcement.

incident
A threatening computer security breach that can be recovered from in a relatively short period of time.

incident response
The action taken to respond to a situation that can be recovered from relatively quickly.

Corporate Concerns Focus on Detection and Prevention

Every day new articles are written about network security and vulnerabilities in software and hardware. This visibility has caused security to become a priority in most companies. Corporate efforts to make sure a network is secure generally are focused on how to implement hardware and software solutions, such as *intrusion detection*, web filtering, spam elimination, and patch installation. For example, an article from Silicon.com reported that during the first quarter of 2003, the number of security events detected by companies jumped 84 percent over the preceding three months. The SQL Slammer *worm* infected 200,000 computers running Microsoft's SQL Server. Ninety percent of all vulnerable servers were infected in the first 10 minutes the worm had been released on the Internet. Dealing with the threat of network damage through an intrusion or *virus* is a part of everyday life for corporate IT professionals, whereas forensic experts focus on the examination, analysis, and evaluation of computer data to provide relevant and valid information to a court of law.

Corporate focus is on minimizing the potential damage that may result from unauthorized access attempts through the prevention, detection, and identification of an unauthorized intrusion. This is done mainly by having *security policies* in place that dictate the level of security for various areas and computers. Along with these policies, incident response and disaster recovery plans set forth the procedures for investigations, including the when, who, and how in regard to contacting law enforcement.

intrusion detection
Software and hardware agents that monitor network traffic for patterns that may indicate an attempt at intrusion.

security policies
Specifications for a secure environment, including such items as physical security requirements, network security planning details, a detailed list of approved software, and human resources policies on employee hiring and dismissal.

virus
A program or piece of code that is loaded onto your computer without your knowledge and is designed to attach itself to other code and replicate. It replicates when an infected file is executed or launched.

worm
Similar in function and behavior to a virus, with the exception that worms do not need user intervention. A worm takes advantage of a security hole in an existing application or operating system and then finds other systems running the same software and automatically replicates itself to the new hosts.

Companies can access websites to find out about new vulnerabilities or security best practices. It is in the best interest of any company to assign someone to check this information on a regular basis to ensure that the network is protected.

You'll find in many corporate environments that incidents are not reported, often times due to the issue of legal liability. The "Let's just quietly fix it" approach to security incidents is common in the corporate world. Some laws now hold the management responsible for data breaches. A company is potentially liable for damages caused by a hacker using one of its computers, and a company might have to prove to a court that it took reasonable measures to defend itself from hackers. The following federal laws address security and privacy and affect nearly every organization in the United States.

The Health Insurance Portability and Accountability Act (HIPAA) of 1996 was enacted on August 21, 1996, to ensure the portability, privacy, and security of medical information. HIPAA was enacted to ensure that only patients and their healthcare providers have access to the patients' medical information. HIPAA requires that Patient Health Information (PHI) be kept private and secure. It imposes stiff fines and jail time both for healthcare institutions and individuals who disclose confidential health information.

The Gramm-Leach-Bliley (GLB) Act requires financial institutions to ensure the security and confidentiality of the personal information that they collect. This includes information such as names, addresses, phone numbers, income, and Social Security numbers. Basically, financial institutions are required to secure customer records and information regardless of size. Among other institutions, it includes check-cashing businesses, mortgage brokers, real estate appraisers, professional tax prepares, courier services, and retailers that issue credit cards to consumers.

The Sarbanes-Oxley Act, named for the two Congressmen who sponsored it, was passed to restore the public's confidence in corporate governance by making chief executives of publicly traded companies personally validate financial statements and other information. Congress passed the law to avoid future accounting scandals such as those committed by Enron and WorldCom. The law was signed on July 30, 2002. Large corporations must be in compliance by June 15, 2004, and smaller companies have to comply by April 15, 2005. The executives who have to sign off on the internal controls can face criminal penalties if a breach is detected. In other words, if someone can easily get into a secure or private part of your system because you use a three-character password such as "dog," it will be viewed as a sign of noncompliance.

Often, the victim company does not know which law enforcement entity to call. Company management might feel that the local or state police will not be able to understand the crime and the Federal Bureau of Investigation (FBI) and Secret Service are not needed. In addition, management might be afraid that the intrusion will become public knowledge, harming investor confidence and chasing away current and potential customers. They might also fear the effect of having critical data and computers seized by law enforcement. An investigation can seriously jeopardize the normal operations of a company, not only for the customers but for the employees as well. The interruption to the workplace causes confusion and disrupts employee schedules. Furthermore, cases are often hard to pursue if the suspect is a juvenile or the intruder is from another country, and in many states the amount of damage inflicted by the intruder is too small to justify prosecution. Lastly, pursuing such matters can take a long time and be costly.

Many businesses perceive that there is little upside to reporting network intrusions. ———— *NOTE* ————

Law Enforcement Focuses on Prosecution

Whereas the corporate world focuses on prevention and detection, the law enforcement realm focuses on investigation and prosecution. Each state has its own set of laws that govern how cases can be prosecuted. For cases to be prosecuted, evidence must be properly collected, processed, and preserved. In later chapters, we'll go through these processes. Technology has dramatically increased the universe of discoverable electronic material, thereby making the job of law enforcement much more complicated. Electronic evidence can include any and all electronically stored information that is in digital, optical, or analog form. Not only does evidence include electronic data, it also includes electronic devices such as computers, CD-ROMs, floppy disks, cellular telephones, pagers, and digital cameras.

Law enforcement must deal with incredible amounts of data. When the Internet is involved, crimes can be committed from other states and countries, thereby involving the laws and jurisdiction of those locales. The following high-profile case about hackers from Russia is a perfect example of this situation.

Russian Computer Hacker Indicted in California for Breaking into Computer Systems and Extorting Victim Companies

On June 20, 2001, a federal grand jury indicted a computer hacker on several federal charges for allegedly accessing computer systems owned by several companies, stealing credit card information, and requesting payments for computer security services from the companies. Alexey V. Ivanov, of Chelyabinsk, Russia, was charged with four counts of unauthorized computer intrusions, eight counts of wire fraud, two counts of extortion, and one count of possessing usernames and passwords for an online bank. Ivanov allegedly used one of the stolen credit card numbers to open an account with CTS Network Services, an Internet service provider in San Diego. He then hacked into CTS computers and used them to launch attacks against other e-commerce companies.

To obtain evidence for the case, the FBI set up a sting operation in which it advertised a job offer for a fictitious company named Invita Security, Inc., which drew Ivanov and his partner, 25-year-old Vasili Gorchkov, to the United States.

During the sting operation, the two men were invited to log on to their computer in Russia from the Invita offices. FBI agents captured the keystroke information, which they used to access the Russian's computer over the Internet and download its data. However, the FBI agents did not contact Russian law enforcement officials, thus violating Russian Criminal Code Article 272 that punishes "unlawful access to computer information" with up to two years in prison. The U.S. federal judge presiding over the case ruled that the downloaded evidence was admissible in court, finding that the FBI wasn't subject to Russian law. Gorchkov was subsequently convicted of 20 counts of wire fraud.

NOTE

Source: U.S. Department of Justice, Computer Crime and Intellectual Property Section (CCIPS), http://www.usdoj.gov/criminal/cybercrime/ivanovIndict2.htm.

For a case to stand up in court, most evidence must be attested to by a witness. In the case of electronic evidence, who's the witness of a computer making a log entry? How can a law enforcement officer show that the other 15 accounts logged in at the time didn't commit the deed? Despite the relative infancy of the law, electronic data is finding its way into the courtroom and is having profound impact in many cases. Courts are generally not persuaded by the authenticity, best evidence rule, chain of custody, and other challenges to the introduction of electronic data at trial. This type of issue has been brought up in court several times. A good example is *United States v. Tank*. The court addressed the question of the authentication of Internet chat room logs that were maintained by one of the co-defendants. The defendant claimed that the government did not have a sufficient foundation for the admission of the logs. The government provided evidence linking the screen name used by the defendant to the defendant. The government evidence also included testimony from one of the co-defendants about the method he used to create the logs and his recollection that the logs appeared to be an accurate representation of the conversations among the members. The court ruled in favor of the government, declaring that the government made a satisfactory showing of the relevance and the authenticity of the chat room log printouts.

With the increase of cybercrime, keeping up with caseloads has become nearly impossible. Department of Public Safety (DPS) crime lab personnel barely have time to answer the phone. How does law enforcement determine the priority of the complaints that they investigate and prosecute? Generally speaking, the following factors help determine which cases get priority:

The Amount of Harm Inflicted   Crimes against children or ones that are violent usually get high priority along with crimes that result in large monetary loss.

Crime Jurisdiction   Crimes that affect the locale are usually chosen especially when resources are taken into consideration.

Success of Investigation   The difficulty of investigation and success of the outcome weigh heavily in determining which cases to investigate.

Availability and Training of Personnel   Often crimes that don't require a large amount of manpower or very specific training may take precedence.

Frequency   Isolated instances take a lower priority than those that occur with regular frequency.

In addition, some associations offer help and guidance not only to law enforcement but the corporate world as well. The High Technology Crime Investigation Association (HTCIA) is one such organization. The national website is located at `http://htcia.org`. The website includes links to chapters throughout the world, which include information on local laws associated with computer crimes.

Training

To effectively fight cybercrime, everyone who deals with it must be educated. This includes the criminal justice and the IT communities, as well as the everyday user. Imagine what would happen to evidence if a law enforcement officer wasn't properly trained and, as a result of his actions, a good portion of evidence was destroyed. Many times, the judge or jury does not understand the topics discussed or lack the technical expertise to interpret the law. What would happen in a complex case if the jury, prosecutor, and the judge had little experience with computers? More likely than not, the defendant would end up getting away with the crime. We are faced with many scenarios where this is true, but probably none more so than that of child pornography. Child pornography issues present circumstances in which the prosecution might have to prove that a photograph is one of a real child due to rulings on virtual pornography. However, not all cases go to court, and the role of a forensic investigator can vary.

Before deciding what type of specific training you need, evaluate the role that you want to fill so that you get the most benefit. Here are some common roles that could involve the process of computer forensics:

- Law enforcement officials
- Legal professionals
- Corporate human resources professionals
- Compliance professionals
- Security consultants providing incident response services
- System administrators performing incident response
- Private investigators

The next sections discuss the types of employers for both the corporate and law enforcement worlds and the type of training available for them.

Practitioners

Civil litigators can utilize personal and business computer records in cases involving fraud, divorce, and harassment. Insurance companies might be able to reduce costs by using computer evidence of possible fraud in accident, arson, and workman's compensation cases. Corporations hire computer forensics specialists to obtain evidence relating to embezzlement, theft, and misappropriation of trade secrets. Individuals sometimes hire computer forensic specialists in support of claims for wrongful termination, sexual harassment, and age discrimination.

Law enforcement officials sometimes require assistance in pre-search warrant preparations and post-seizure handling of the computer equipment. Criminal and civil proceedings often use evidence revealed by computer forensics specialists. Criminal prosecutors use computer evidence in cases such as financial fraud, drug and embezzlement record-keeping, and child pornography.

All these various types of industries rely on properly trained computer forensics investigators. The following sections describe some of the training available to both the corporate and law enforcement worlds. The role that you will play as a computer forensic investigator will ultimately decide which type of training is right for you.

Law Enforcement

The position an individual holds in the criminal justice community dictates the type of training required. In other words, legislators need to understand the laws that are proposed and that they are passing, whereas prosecuting attorneys should have training on electronic discovery and digital data, and how to properly present computer evidence in a court of law. Detectives should have hands-on training in working with data discovery of all types and on various operating systems. They should know how to recover data, read log files, and decrypt data. When law enforcement professionals are originally trained at the academy, they should receive some type of basic training on computer crime and how to investigate such crimes. Ideally, all criminal justice professionals would receive training in computer crimes, investigations, computer network technologies, and forensic investigations. Here are some ideas on getting the training needed to pursue a career in computer forensics:

- ◆ Intense School's CCE Applied Computer Forensics Boot Camp: http://www.intenseschool.com/bootcamps/default.asp
- ◆ NTI's computer forensics and security training: http://www.forensics-intl.com/training.html
- ◆ WorldWide Learn's Computer Forensic Training Center Online: http://www.worldwidelearn.com/keycomputer/forensic-training.htm
- ◆ Mares and Company, LLC's basic and advanced computer forensic training: http://www.dmares.com/maresware/training.htm
- ◆ AccessData's computer forensic courses: http://www.accessdata.com/training/viewclasses.php
- ◆ DIBS computer forensic training courses: http://www.dibsusa.com/training/training.html

Many local community colleges offer classes in computer forensics. Law enforcement professionals can take advantage of them without having to pay the high cost of classes offered by private firms. An excellent resource for law enforcement is the International Association for Computer Investigative Specialists (IACIS), which is online at http://www.cops.org/.

New Technologies Inc. (NTI) also makes training films concerning computer evidence processing and computer security topics available to government agencies, law enforcement agencies, and businesses. The selection of training films is listed on NTI's Computer Forensics Information and Reference Page.

Corporate

Frequently, security and disaster recovery projects aren't funded because they don't produce revenue. An Ernst & Young annual security survey of 1,400 organizations states that only 13 percent think that spending money on IT training is a priority. This shows that training is needed not only for IT professionals but for management as well. In the corporate world, just as in the criminal justice world, the position an individual holds in an organization dictates the type of training they need. In order for end users to buy into security, management must buy in first. Managers have a legal responsibility to police what is happening within their own computer systems, as demonstrated by the Sarbanes-Oxley Act. Management training is usually geared more toward compliance issues and the cost of putting preventative measures in place. IT professionals, on the other hand, need training that is geared more toward return on investment (ROI) in order to obtain funding for security projects and computer crime awareness, which includes new vulnerabilities. They should be trained on how laws are made, how crimes are investigated, and how crimes are prosecuted. This training could help eliminate the reluctance that organizations have about contacting law enforcement when security breaches occur or when crimes are committed.

Education for every level of practitioner can be found on the SANS (SysAdmin, Audit, Network, Security) website at http://www.sans.org. The SANS Institute was established in 1989 as a cooperative research and education organization. Its programs are designed to educate security professionals, auditors, system administrators, network administrators, chief information security officers, and chief information officers. The graphic on the following page shows the SANS Information and Computer Security Resources webpage.

End Users

Legislation such as Sarbanes-Oxley will not change behaviors simply because it is law. This is similar to speeding. Laws against driving over a certain speed do not stop

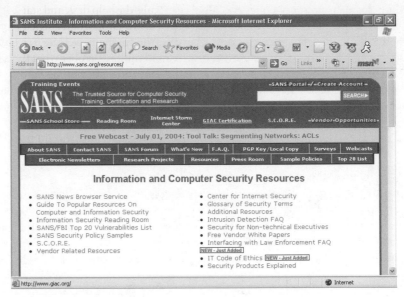

some people from speeding. In fact, many speeders are repeat offenders. Why? It's because certain behaviors are difficult to change. A person's behavior is based on their principles and values. People adopt new patterns of behavior only when their old ones are no longer effective. The goal of training is to change behavior. An effective training program helps the workforce adopt the organization's principles and values. As mentioned previously, management must be trained and become an integral part of the education and training process in order for the users to buy into it.

WARNING

The hardest environment to control is that of the end user. Training and education are vital parts of any organization that has computer users or Internet access.

Security Awareness

malware

Another name for malicious code. This includes viruses, logic bombs, and worms.

A network is only as strong as its weakest link. We hear this phrase time and time again. Humans are considered to be the weakest link. No matter how secure the hardware and software are, the network can be jeopardized in one phone call or click of a button if users aren't taught the dangers of social engineering, e-mail scams, and *malware*.

Social engineering plays on human nature to carry out an attack. Which is easier, getting an employee to give you a password or running password-cracking software? Obviously, getting an employee to give you the password would eliminate a lot of effort on your part. Social engineering is hard to detect because you have very little influence over lack of common sense or ignorance on the part of employees, but education should help eliminate ignorance. Most business environments are fast paced and service oriented. Human nature is trusting and often naïve.

Take this scenario for example. A vice president calls the help desk and states that he's in real trouble. He's trying to present a slideshow to an important client and has forgotten his password; therefore, he can't log onto the company website to run the presentation. He changed the password yesterday and can't remember what the new one is. He needs it right away because a room full of people are waiting, and he's starting to look incompetent. The client is extremely important and could bring millions of dollars in revenue to the company. However, if the help desk staff member supplies the password as requested, he could be giving it to an intruder.

When creating a security-awareness program, organizations should have these goals in mind:

- Evaluate compelling issues.
- Know laws and policies for protecting data.
- Look at values and organizational culture.
- Set baseline knowledge requirements.
- Define best practices.
- Make lasting cultural and behavioral changes.
- Create positive approaches and methods.

If you need help putting together these policies, the National Institute of Standards and Technology (NIST) has some great information in its Computer Security Resource Center (CSRC), as shown in the following graphic.

social engineering
A method of obtaining sensitive information about a company through exploitation of human nature.

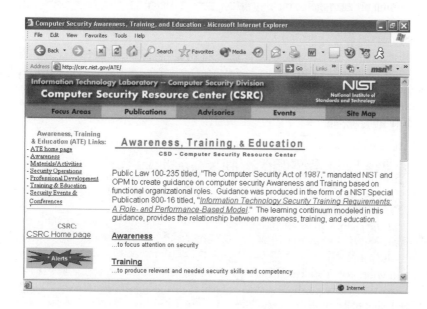

If you can't educate your employees yourself, make sure you set up training for them either in-house or with outside vendors. Not having the time to train them yourself is no excuse for not training employees at all.

How Much Is Actually Monitored?

Security experts have the capability to monitor vast amounts of data. They can track Internet access, read employee e-mail messages, record phone calls, and monitor network access. All this monitoring creates a large amount of data. How much you should monitor depends on how much information you want to store. Keep in mind that your monitoring plan should be clear-cut and built around specific goals and policies. Without proper planning and policies, you can quickly fill your log files and hard drives with useless or unused information. The following are some items to consider when you are ready to implement a monitoring policy:

◆ Identify potential resources at risk within your environment (for example, sensitive files, financial applications, and personnel files).

◆ After the resources are identified, set up the policy. If the policy requires auditing large amounts of data, make sure that the hardware has the additional space needed, as well as processing power and memory.

◆ Make time to view the logs. The information in the log files won't help protect against a system compromise if you don't read it for six months.

NOTE You can monitor as much or as little as you want, but if you don't read the logs, they are not serving their purpose.

Monitoring can be as simple or complex as you want to make it. Be consistent regardless of the plan you create. Many organizations monitor an extensive amount of information, while others, especially small ones, may monitor little or nothing. Just remember that it will be quite difficult to catch an intruder if you don't monitor anything.

What Are Your Organization's Needs?

Each organization has different needs. As a professional, it is your job to assess your organization's specific needs.

Law enforcement professionals may determine that their caseloads are too extensive for the manpower they have. Maybe the equipment they are using is outdated. Perhaps they have issues with a particular type of software.

Corporate organizations may want to make sure they formulate security policies by assessing risk, threats, and their exposure factor to determine how best to keep their networking environment safe. Corporations can also have outdated equipment or applications, making their networks more vulnerable.

Because every organization is different, with different policies and requirements, there are no "one size fits all" rules to ensure all security bases are covered. Training and education will make a good start, but you must constantly update your knowledge of new hardware, software, and threats. You should recognize how they affect your work and your organization so that you can continuously reassess your vulnerabilities. Remember, a computer forensic technician is a combination of a private eye and a computer scientist.

Terms to Know

backdoor	intrusion detection
best practices	logic bomb
computer forensics	malware
disaster recovery	security policies
electronic discovery	social engineering
incident	virus
incident response	worm

Review Questions

1. What is electronic discovery?

2. Name some examples of electronic discovery items.

3. The recovery of data focuses on what four factors?

4. Who works under more restrictive rules, law enforcement officials or corporate employees?

5. What is incident response?

6. What is the difference between a virus and a worm?

7. Why aren't incidents in many corporate environments reported?

8. What law was passed to avoid future accounting scandals such as those involving Enron and WorldCom?

9. Name some factors that will determine which criminal cases get priority.

10. Name a good resource for computer forensics training for law enforcement.

Chapter 2

Preparation—What to Do Before You Start

In This Chapter

- Knowing different types of hardware
- Checking for unauthorized hardware
- Keeping up-to-date with new trends in hardware devices
- Knowing various operating systems
- Knowing different types of filesystems
- Identifying maintenance tools
- Knowing legal rights and limits
- Forming an incident response team

Be prepared! This motto is especially true in the computer forensics field. In order to do a thorough job, a computer forensic investigator should know how the network under investigation is laid out, what devices are in use, what types of operating systems are installed, and what types of filesystems are being used. Most organizations have incident response teams that can help provide this information for forensic situations. As an investigator, you need to know your legal limits and be familiar with the laws of the locality where the crime was committed, as well as the laws where the perpetrator is located to be sure that any case you build will stand up in a court of law.

Most of the groundwork needed to build a case can be done ahead of time so that when the need arises, the task can be done more efficiently. This chapter guides you through these processes.

Know Your Hardware

Information can be retrieved from many hardware devices, even those not normally associated with a storage function (such as hard drives, CD-ROMs, and floppy disks). Information stored on these devices remains constant or intact. By comparison, devices such as keyboards, monitors, and printers do not permanently store data. These devices are used to send data to and receive data from the computer. After the computer is turned off, these devices do not store information. However, a trained computer forensic investigator using specialized techniques can find data or evidence on these devices even after they have been turned off.

Because technology is constantly changing, keeping up-to-date on new types of devices and methods of communication is important. You also need to determine which of these technologies and devices are permitted in the organization being investigated, because employees frequently add their own devices as a matter of convenience and intruders will use them as a method of gathering information.

What I/O Devices Are Used?

input/output (I/O)
Data transfer that occurs between the thinking part of the computer or CPU and an external device or peripheral. For example, when you type on your keyboard, the keyboard sends input to the computer which, in turn, outputs what you type on the screen.

Many of the terms used for computers actually describe the capability, use, or size of the computer. Even though the word "computer" can apply to just about any device that has a microprocessor in it, most of us think of a computer as a device that processes what we input using a keyboard or a mouse and then displays the result on our screen.

One of the first items on your planning agenda should be to list all of the types of *input/output (I/O)* devices used in the organization. This list will provide information on what tools will be needed to analyze information. It will also give you a good idea of what areas may be susceptible to intrusion and need more monitoring.

Servers

server
A computer that has the capacity to provide services to other computers over a network. Servers can have multiple processors, a large amount of memory, and many hard drives.

In the early days of computing, mainframes were the main method of storing and processing data. They were huge computers that could fill an entire room. Although the power of computers has increased, the size of computers has decreased. Many mainframes have been replaced by enterprise servers—although you'll still find mainframes in use, particularly in large companies.

———— **NOTE** ————

Servers can play various roles. By identifying the role that each server plays, you can more easily determine which tools you'll need.

Common server roles include application, file, web hosting, print, e-mail, and FTP. You should also determine where the server is situated. Is it accessed from the internal network only, from the external world, or both? This helps identify its vulnerabilities, as well as protective measures that should be in place on the server. This is important because, due to the anonymity of networks and the Internet, attacks on all types of servers are increasing. The reasons for such attacks can be attributed to anything from simple curiosity to malicious intent.

Workstations

The term *workstation* used to refer to extremely powerful *desktop* computers most often used by research and development teams. Because technology has advanced so rapidly and a lot of processing power can be packed into a small machine, *workstation* is often used interchangeably with *personal computer (PC)* or *desktop*.

Although they can also be used as stand-alone systems, such as in a home environment, workstations or PCs are typically linked together to form a local area network (LAN). The following illustration shows the relationship between a server and the workstations on a LAN.

workstation
A desktop computer that has enhanced processing power, memory, and capabilities for performing a special function, such as software or game development.

desktop
A PC designed to be set up in a permanent location because the components are too large to easily transport.

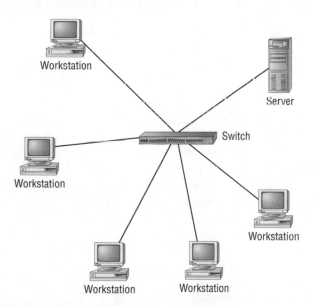

You should have an inventory of the workstations in the building, and you should also know who is using workstations from home to connect to the network.

———— *WARNING* ————

PC
A personal computer intended for generic use by an individual. PCs were originally known as microcomputers because they were built on a smaller scale than the large systems most businesses used.

In today's mobile society, telecommuting has become a way of life. Telecommuting saves overhead and energy costs. Many organizations hire contractors without providing workspaces for them in their offices. This is an important factor to keep in mind. Everyone has heard horror stories about people hacking into corporate networks through home computers.

> **John Deutch**
>
> A very notable case is that of ex-CIA director John Deutch. He had over 17,000 pages of classified documents on unsecured Macintosh computers in two of his homes. National security secrets were stored where almost anyone could access them. The computers, designated for unclassified use only, were connected to modems and regularly used to access the Internet and the Department of Defense (DoD). Family members were also allowed to use the computers. Additionally, unsecured classified magnetic media were found in Deutch's residences. A team of data recovery experts retrieved the data from Deutch's unclassified computers and magnetic media. The results of the inquiry were submitted to CIA senior management.
>
> Deutch pled guilty to keeping government secrets on unsecured home computers in exchange for receiving no prison time. Deutch was pardoned by President Bill Clinton hours before his presidency ended.

Workstation security is often overlooked. Yet this is one of the areas that can easily attract intruders because it is often the path of least resistance to deploying an attack.

Personal Digital Assistants (PDAs)

personal digital assistant (PDA)
A tightly integrated handheld device that combines computing, Internet, and networking components. A PDA can use flash memory instead of a hard drive for storage.

Personal digital assistants (PDAs) can also be referred to as palmtops, pocket computers, or handhelds. The two major categories they fall into are handheld and palm-sized. The differences between the two are size, display, and method of data entry. Handheld computers tend to be larger, with larger liquid crystal displays (LCDs), and might use a miniature keyboard in combination with touch-screen technology for data entry. Palm-sized computers are smaller and lighter with smaller LCDs and stylus/touch-screen technology or handwriting recognition programs for data entry. They can also have voice recognition technologies. A typical PDA can function as a cellular phone, fax, web browser, and personal organizer. The following illustration shows two typical PDAs.

Handheld
Computer

Palmtop

PDAs are designed to work in conjunction with your desktop or laptop. The communication between the PDA and PC is typically done through a serial or USB port on the PDA. Some PDAs can rest in a stand while they are hooked up to the

PC. Besides being able to communicate through a cable, PDAs can use an infrared (IR) port, wireless methods, or telephone modem accessories to transfer data.

PDAs, Palm Pilots, and pocket PCs are all mobile devices. They are very susceptible to theft because they are small, valuable, and frequently contain important information about a company. Many of them use wireless or infrared technology so that any data they transfer can be intercepted if it is not protected.

PDAs are the one of the fastest selling consumer devices in history. You should know if they are used on the network because malicious individuals can use them to transfer sensitive information for later use.

Other Devices

Many other devices can be used to transport or transmit data. They mainly consist of removable media. When you think of removable media, you probably think of floppy disks or CDs and DVDs, which are used in *floppy drives* and *CD/DVD-ROM/RW drives*, respectively. However, you should be aware of other devices and determine if any of them are being used.

Zip disks are slightly larger than conventional floppy disks, and they are about twice as thick. Jaz or Zip disks can be carried in your shirt or blouse pocket and can hold much more data than floppies.

Zip drives and disks come in three sizes: 100MB (which holds the equivalent of 70 floppy disks), 250MB, and 750MB. Zip drives can be used for exchanging large files with someone, putting a system on another computer (such as a laptop computer), and keeping certain files separate from files on a hard disk (for example, hacking utilities). The following illustration shows a Zip drive.

A Jaz drive cartridge holds the equivalent of more than 700 floppies. In addition, the Iomega Zip drive comes with a software utility that allows you to copy the entire contents of a hard disk to one or more Zip disks.

Iomega's *Jaz drives* back up more data and are more sophisticated than Zip drives, but they can be used for the same purposes. The Jaz 2GB drive uses 2GB cartridges, but it also accepts the 1GB cartridge used by the original Jaz. The backup program has a security feature that limits access to the cartridge by using a password. The password is stored on the Jaz media, and the method used to encrypt the password is very weak. To obtain the encryption password, you simply need to issue od-c at a command prompt on the backup file. The password is the first nonzero block past the description (and a 001) and usually resides around offset 0470 (octal). You will learn about passwords, encryption, and decryption in Chapter 7, "Passwords and Encryption."

 Real World Scenario

Tales from the Trenches: Preparation War Story

The computer forensics expert must always follow the Scout motto, "Be prepared!"

While working with a group of computer forensics specialists who were preparing for a trip to a "far off land" to recover information of "interest to the nation," we organized a list of every item that might possibly be needed during their extended stay. The team was assembled based on each member's unique talents and skills. We brainstormed for days, running through every possible scenario we could imagine to determine how best to prepare for the upcoming mission.

The team developed a list incorporating all the normal items you would expect such a trip to require, including strong, secure shipping containers, appropriate commercial forensics recovery tools, a collection of various-sized hard drives, commercial hard drive duplication hardware, and adapters to read an assortment of different forms of media. We collected a copy of each operating system that we anticipated seeing in the field as well as an assortment of application CDs and a variety of other software.

We conducted an intensive "ramp up" training program to bring all team members "up to speed" and "on the same page" with the policies and procedures required for this mission. Each team member was instructed on the legal limits and requirements for conducting searches and seizing evidence in this foreign location. Everyone was reminded that any evidence located might be used in court proceedings at a later date. Everyone was ready to go. We had planned for every possible contingency.

With all the preparation completed and the equipment safely packed away, the team departed for their new assignment, confident they had the training, equipment, and resources necessary to accomplish their mission. The team arrived on site and began to set up their lab equipment in a safe and secure location to protect their equipment and to preserve the integrity of any evidence they processed. Members of the team were assigned to test the equipment and ensure everything was working properly. Other team members were dispatched to locate potential evidence to bring back to the lab for analysis.

Continues

Within a few days the team had begun to locate items of interest and began conducting forensics analysis of computers and hard drives. Each case was fully documented and each investigation appeared to be running smoothly. All the prior planning appeared to be paying off and every part of the operation was running successfully. And then, right on time, Mr. Murphy made his much anticipated appearance!

With every well-conceived plan, something always seems to go wrong. Usually it is something very small—something that typically would cost only a minor amount of time and money to fix, had we considered it before the team left home. It is usually something so superficial no one has anticipated it could occur. And, as usual, it was something so important that the team was stopped dead in their tracks until the problem was solved.

After all the planning, all of the training, and all of the preparation, we had forgotten one very important piece of equipment required to complete the mission. We forgot something so old and so outdated that most team members had never even seen one, let alone used one. We had forgotten that in this part of the world not every piece of computer equipment gets updated every 18 months. We had made the cardinal mistake of not fully understanding the environment in which the investigation would be taking place. We had not shipped all the equipment that the team would need. We had forgotten a very simple item.

In this part of the world, the old 5 1/4-inch floppy disks can still be found in use; and the team had located a large collection of these disks that very possibly contained evidence linked to the investigation. The team had no blank 5 1/4-inch media on which to copy the evidence and, of course, no 5 1/4-inch disk drives were in any of the computers in the lab. Even the training had not covered this issue and the younger members of the team had to be instructed in the proper technique for write-protecting these disks to safeguard evidence. New 5 1/4-inch media had to be flown in from another country along with properly working new 5 1/4-inch disk drives. While this issue did not stop the team from ultimately accomplishing their mission, it did cause a minor delay in processing very time-critical information.

What can be learned from this? No matter how much planning and preparation you do for a case, something usually pops up for which you are not equipped. It certainly is nice when you can run down to your local computer superstore and buy whatever you need; but sometimes you will just have to make due until proper supplies arrive. Planning is important, but so is another skill that the Scouts might just want to add to their list—the ability to improvise.

As a rule, these drives are external in that they sit next to your computer and are attached to it by a cable. However, some computers come equipped with an internal Zip or Jaz drive.

Networked printers, webcams, networked fax machines, and networked copiers also have vulnerabilities that can lead to data exposure or denial of service. They can be used as gateways for attacks on other systems. These types of I/O devices are often taken for granted, and their security is rarely questioned. Sometimes organizations use the same printers to print sensitive documents that they use to print public documents, such as announcements for company parties. Don't forget about these types of devices when you inventory the environment.

Check Computers for Unauthorized Hardware

Frequently, employees just assume that it's okay to install a device on the network or their PC. Such unauthorized installations present security issues to an organization. Once you have inventoried the approved devices in use in the organization you're investigating, it's time to look for installed hardware that has not been approved. You might be surprised at what you will find.

Modems

Modems are used via the phone line to dial into a server or computer. Wireless modems convert digital data into radio signals and convert radio signals back into digital signals. Modems are gradually being replaced by high-speed cable and digital subscriber line (DSL) solutions, which are faster than dial-up access.

However, plenty of modems and modem pools or banks can still be found in corporations and small office/home office environments. Most companies use modems for employees to dial into the network and work from home. These modems are usually configured to be available for incoming calls. War dialing attacks take advantage of these situations and target connected modems that are set to receive calls without any authentication.

modem
A shortened version of the words modulator-demodulator. A modem is used to send digital data over a phone line. The sending modem converts data into a signal that is compatible with the phone line, and the receiving modem then converts the signal back into digital data.

war dialing
Uses an automated software application that attempts to dial numbers within a given range of phone numbers to determine if any of those numbers are actually used by modems accepting dial-in requests.

NOTE

War dialing was extremely popular years ago. However, because newer technologies have replaced connected modems that are set to receive calls without any authentication, this may be an unlikely threat for a LAN. It just depends on how advanced an organization's technology is.

Cable and DSL modems are more popular these days. These devices are not prone to dial attacks, but they present a danger because they maintain an always-on connection to the Internet. Cable modems enable Internet access through shared cable medium, which means everything that travels to and from a connected machine can be intercepted by other cable users in the area.

Key Loggers

Key loggers record and retrieve everything typed, including e-mail messages, instant messages, and website addresses. To install the hardware key logger, you unplug the keyboard cable from the back of the PC, plug it into one end of the key logger, and then plug the other end back into the PC. See the following graphic for a visual of Allen Concepts' KEYKatcher-mini product.

key logger
Device that intercepts, records, and stores everything that the user types on the keyboard into a file. This includes all keystrokes, even passwords.

Real World Scenario

Former Employee of Local Internet Service Provider Sentenced to Prison for Computer Attack

On June 16, 2004, Peter Borghard, a former network administrator at Netline Services, Inc., a Manhattan-based Internet service provider, was sentenced in Manhattan federal court to five months in prison and five months of home confinement. He was ordered to pay $118,030 in restitution, stemming from his electronic attack on Netline's computer system in January 2003.

Borghard was Netline's computer systems administrator between June and the end of October 2002. He left the company abruptly and without explanation at the end of October 2002. Shortly after quitting, he demanded back salary he claimed that Netline owed him. Netline refused to pay and, in December 2002, Borghard sued Netline to collect approximately $2,000. On two separate dates in January 2003, Netline experienced computer intrusion attacks on its network. The first attack took place on January 15, 2003, and it temporarily crippled the system. Netline's system was down, and its customers were denied e-mail service for approximately 15 hours. On January 25, 2003, Netline was hit with another electronic intrusion and attack.

In the course of the investigation, computer forensics analyses conducted by the FBI revealed that, although Netline's attacker had attempted to erase all electronic traces of his identity, the attacks on Netline's system could be linked by certain computer records to other computers outside Netline that were in use or otherwise controlled by Borghard. Among those outside computers was a computer that was unnoticed but nevertheless being operated by Borghard. It was in Borghard's former cubicle at a company where Borghard had worked prior to joining Netline.

On February 10, 2004, Borghard pled guilty to a felony charge of computer intrusion, admitting that he had committed the attacks on Netline.

As you can see from this case, knowing who has access to what machines is important. The fact that Borghard still had control of a computer at a former place of employment is astounding, yet it happened. Cases have been documented where former employees have accessed networks well after a year past their termination.

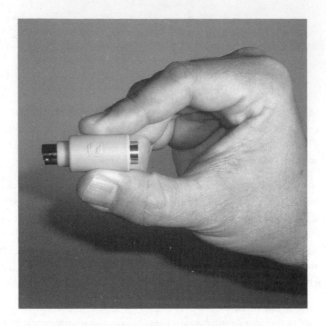

(Photograph Courtesy of Allen Concepts, Inc. 2004, www.keykatcher.com)

Key loggers are used by organizations for the following reasons:

◆ As a tool for computer fraud investigations

◆ As a monitoring device for detecting unauthorized access

◆ To prevent unacceptable use of company resources

◆ As a backup tool

So why are they on the list of unauthorized hardware? Simply put, anything can be used for bad intent, and unauthorized individuals can use them to capture logins and passwords. Unless an organization has a policy for using them, they should not be on a network.

NOTE   **Key logging is not restricted to hardware alone. A variety of key logging software programs are readily available on the Internet.**

Software key loggers are easier to detect as time goes on because the log files grow. You'll eventually be able to tell when one is being used because available hard-drive space will decrease.

Real World Scenario

Key Logging Scam Targets Bank Users

On March 7, 2003, Ko Hakata, 35, a former computer software developer, and Goro Nakahashi, 27, a businessman, were accused of theft and illegally accessing information on the Internet. The Metropolitan Police Department arrested the two men on suspicion of stealing 16 million yen through an online banking scheme that might involve hundreds of victims.

The scheme started when the two secretly installed *key catcher* software onto computers at Internet cafes. They visited the cafes every couple of weeks to acquire the PIN numbers and passwords of Internet users who had visited the cafes and typed their information into the computers. On September 18, Hakata allegedly used a computer and Internet connection at a cafe in Tokyo's Shibuya Ward to access the accounts at a foreign bank of five self-employed people. Using stolen passwords, Hakata allegedly withdrew about 16.5 million yen from the five accounts and deposited the money in an account created under a fictitious name. Nakahashi then withdrew the money from the account. Police indicated that this case could be the tip of an iceberg.

Police refused to say when the two men, who haven't been charged, were detained. They also would not comment on what happened to the money that was not withdrawn by Nakahashi. If charged with theft, they could face up to 10 years in prison.

Police said Hakata has admitted to paying Nakahashi 1 million yen for his help and spent the remainder on such things as betting on horse races. He also reportedly told police that he recorded so much personal information that it became difficult to keep count of it all. The suspects had installed the software in about 100 computers at 13 Internet cafes since 2001. Police seized 719 ID numbers and passwords from the homes of the two suspects. According to police, Hakata had 720 debit and credit card numbers and the profiles of 195 female users, who had accessed a dating site, in a file he had stored on the Internet, when the police arrested him. They suspect Hakata of being involved in additional crimes.

I/O Devices

Besides key loggers and modems, you could find a myriad of unapproved and potentially dangerous devices on an organization's network. The technologies behind many of them will be discussed in the next section. Here is a list of some of the devices:

- A Syquest SyJet drive has similar capabilities as the Jaz drive; however, it has a 3.5-inch removable cartridge that holds 1.5GB of data.

◆ A Lexar Media JumpDrive allows you to plug into a USB port and save up to 512MB of data. Sizes vary, but the drives are typically affordable and no software is required. They are easily portable.

◆ A Pockey drive holds 20GB of data and fits in the palm of your hand.

◆ A microdrive is a tiny hard drive built into small cards that can hold anywhere from 340MB to 30GB of data. It is about the size of a matchbox.

◆ A portable laptop drive can be only 1-inch thick and weigh less than 12 ounces, yet it can store 60GB.

The common factor in all of these devices is that they are small, hold a lot of data, and are easy to transport. Knowing if they are being used on a network can be almost impossible because they are easy to conceal, and their data transfer rates are quite fast. Corporate policy should address the use of these devices.

Keep Up to Date with New I/O Trends

As new technologies emerge, so do ways for intruders to infiltrate networks. Because technology is always changing, you have to evaluate new technologies before the devices appear on networks. You should spend some time reading about these new technologies as they are developed.

USB Devices

Universal Serial Bus (USB)
A connectivity standard that allows for the connection of multiple devices without the need for software or hardware.

In the early days of computing, each computer came with a limited number of ports to which you could attach devices. Printers connected to parallel printer ports, and most computers had only one port. Modems used the serial port, but so did Palm Pilots and digital cameras. Most computers had two serial ports. New technology was needed to allow for all of the I/O devices people wanted to attach to their computers. All computers now come with one or more *Universal Serial Bus (USB)* connectors on the back. USB connectors let you attach devices to your computer quickly and easily. Compared to other ways of connecting devices to your computer, USB devices are quite simple. Some of the USB devices that can be attached to your computer are printers, scanners, mice, modems, and storage devices.

You might need to attach more devices to a computer than you have USB ports to attach them. Purchasing an inexpensive USB hub will allow you to connect your additional USB devices to your computer. The following illustration depicts a USB hub.

The USB standard supports up to 127 devices, and USB hubs are a part of the standard. A hub typically has four ports, but it can have many more. Just plug the hub into your computer's USB port, and then plug your devices into the hub.

You can add dozens of available USB ports on a single computer by chaining hubs together using USB cables.

USB standard version 2, which was released in April 2000, can support data rates up to 480Mbps.

NOTE

USB devices are also *hot pluggable*. This means they can be attached to and ejected from the computer without turning off the system. No special settings are necessary. Many of the USB devices that hold data are quite small. For example, JMTek offers a USBDrive that is small enough to fit on a key ring. You just plug it into your USB port. The operating system recognizes it immediately, allowing you to transfer files at your convenience. When you're done, simply eject the drive, plug it into another system, and transfer the files from the USB drive to the system. The following is a photo of the drive.

(Photograph Courtesy of JMTek Corporation©2004)

FireWire

FireWire was originally developed by Apple and now has become the official IEEE 1394 industry standard with more than 60 vendors belonging to the 1394 Trade Association. FireWire has a bandwidth nearly 30 times greater than USB 1, making it the ideal interface for transferring extremely large data files. It supports up to 63 devices on a single bus with speeds of up to 400Mbps for IEEE 1394a and 800Mbps for IEEE 1394b. Connecting to a device is similar to using USB.

TIP Just like USB, FireWire is plug-and-play compliant and hot swappable, meaning you can connect and disconnect devices without shutting down your computer.

Because this technology is ideal for high-quality digital, video, and audio, using it is an ideal way to store pornography or proprietary company designs. It can also be used as an additional computer storage peripheral, allowing large amounts of data to be copied and then removed. The EZQuest Cobra+ Slim FireWire/USB is a good example of a FireWire hot-pluggable drive. It is only 1/2-inch thick and weighs 0.7 pounds, yet it offers up to 100GB of storage space. It can copy a 170MB multilevel file directory in 25 seconds.

In order to use the drive, you simply connect one of its two IEEE 1394 interfaces to the port on your notebook. Just as with many of the USB devices, FireWire hard disk drives hold large amounts of data in a small amount of space.

Standard cables and connectors replace the variety of I/O connectors used by consumer electronics equipment and PCs. FireWire cable is similar to 10BaseT Ethernet cable, which is used to connect computers; however, it is much more flexible. It can accommodate different data types and topologies in alternative networking systems.

Bluetooth

Bluetooth was named after Harald Bluetooth, the king of Denmark in the late 900s. It doesn't require any special equipment to work. The devices simply find one another and begin communicating.

NOTE Bluetooth operates on a frequency of 2.45GHz, which is the same radio frequency band as baby monitors, garage door openers, and newer cordless phones.

The design process makes sure that Bluetooth and other devices don't interfere with one another. Bluetooth uses a technique called "spread-spectrum frequency hopping." This means a device will use randomly chosen frequencies within a designated range and hop or change from one range to another on a regular basis. Bluetooth transmitters change frequencies 1,600 times every second.

Other Technologies

In addition to the new technologies we have already discussed, a few others are worth mentioning, especially wireless. The world of wireless is rapidly expanding, and you may find yourself investigating issues that involve capturing data through wireless devices. Here are brief descriptions of some of those technologies:

- 802.1*x* is a standard developed for wireless local area networks (WLANs). It utilizes port-based network access control. Current standards range from 802.11a to 802.11j.

- Infrared (IR) transmissions use an invisible light spectrum range for device communication so the devices have to be in direct line of sight with each other.

- I-Mode is NTT DoCoMo's mobile Internet acccess system that originated in Japan.

- BlackBerry is an end-to-end wireless solution developed by Research In Motion Limited.

These technologies make our lives easier, yet they can pose a great threat to a network environment. A wireless device advertises that it is out there, making it easy for an intruder to pick up and monitor.

Know Your Operating System

Once you have a good inventory of the I/O devices on the network and have identified what kind of unapproved devices you might encounter, you need to look at what operating systems are in use throughout the organization. It used to be that you would find only one type of operating system on a network. With the advent of mobile computing, Internet business, and corporate mergers, networks have become more complex. Typical computer examinations must adhere to the fast-changing and diverse world in which computer forensic science examiners are required to work. Before you can begin your forensic investigation, you have to be familiar with the various operating systems you might encounter.

Different Operating Systems

Not only do different *operating systems* exist, but each operating system has different versions, such as server and workstation, and new releases. How you handle and extract information from a computer running Linux will be very different from how you handle and extract information from a Windows computer.

operating system
Acts as a director and interpreter between the user and all the software and hardware on the computer.

Windows

Although you probably won't find it in use anymore, Microsoft's first attempt at a graphical operating system was Microsoft Windows 1. The versions that followed, Windows 3.1, Windows 3.11, and Windows for Workgroups 3.11, were used in the early 1990s, prior to the creation of Windows 95. In 1993, Windows NT was released. The "NT" stands for "New Technology." Windows NT was specifically designed for the corporate environment and intended for use on high-powered servers and workstations. In 1995, Microsoft introduced Windows 95, which was a significant improvement over Windows 3.x and was Microsoft's first truly consumer-oriented graphical operating system for PCs. NT came into its own with Windows NT 4, which was released in 1996 and became quite popular in the late 1990s. Then came Windows 98, followed by Windows 2000 and Windows Me (Millennium Edition). Microsoft's latest release for workstations is Windows XP and Windows Server 2003 for servers. The most common Microsoft systems you will encounter are Windows 98, Windows 2000, and Windows XP.

Unix/Linux

The Unix operating system was originally created at AT&T's Bell Laboratories and licensed freely to most universities and research facilities. Unix was designed to allow a number of programmers to simultaneously access a single computer and share its resources. The operating system coordinates the use of the computer's resources, and it controls all of the commands from all of the keyboards and all of the data being generated. It permits each user to work as if he or she were the only person working on the computer.

Bell Labs distributed the operating system in its source language form. By the end of the1970s, dozens of different versions of Unix had been developed. The success of the Unix operating system has led to many of the technologies which today are part of the IT environment. Although Unix is usually installed on mainframes, versions of Unix have found their way into the PC world. Some of the different versions available are BSD, HP-UX, SCO, IBX AIX, Sun Solaris, and Digital.

Linux is a Unix-like operating system that was written by Linus Torvalds in 1991. Originally named Freax, it was hosted on the Minix operating system. Linux is an *open source* operating system, meaning that the code is readily available. This availability has allowed thousands of people to contribute patches, fixes, and improvements. Installing Linux has become easier as the versions and products have evolved. The earlier versions were all text-based and, frequently, hardware support had to be compiled into the kernel. Newer versions have graphical-based installations, making the process much less complicated. Various versions of Linux are available. Some of the more popular ones are Mandrake, SuSE, Caldera, MkLinux, Debian, Slackware, and Red Hat. You will probably encounter Red Hat most often.

Macintosh

Apple introduced the Macintosh line of personal computers in 1984. The first Macintosh, or Mac for short, had 128KB of memory and a unique design. The monitor and floppy disk drive were built into the same cabinet that housed its main circuitry. In 1994, Apple introduced the PowerMac. In 1998, the third generation of Macs was born with the release of the iMac. Early versions of the operating system were called System x.x, where x.x was the version number. With the release of Mac OS 8, however, Apple dropped the word "System." Now the versions are simply known as Mac OS with the version number. The most current version is OS X, which is based on the Unix BSD operating system. Macs are mostly used for high-end users and graphic or drawing applications, such as CAD. You might encounter Mac OS 8, 9, and X.

Other Operating Systems

The first operating system used on the earliest IBM PCs was called the Disk Operating System (DOS). Microsoft's version of DOS is the most common one and is called MS-DOS. Those of you who have been around the computing environment for a while might remember that IBM Corporation also produced a DOS product called PC-DOS. If you run into a DOS machine, you probably won't find a mouse and you certainly won't find a colorful screen. To run a DOS operating system, you issue commands at a prompt on the screen.

Linspire, formerly Lindows, is a full-featured operating system like Microsoft Windows XP or Apple Mac. It will run Windows applications on top of Linux so they appear as they would on Windows 98, NT, and XP.

In the early 1990s, IBM and Microsoft joined forces to create OS/2. Microsoft and IBM created OS/2 with high hopes that it would revolutionize the PC desktop by replacing DOS. OS/2 took longer to develop than originally planned, and Microsoft left IBM. IBM continues developing OS/2 to make improvements to its functionality and performance.

BeOS takes up less space than other modern operating systems, such as Mac OS and Windows, but it has a user-friendly graphical user interface (GUI). It is made by a company called Be, Inc. It's very fast, and extremely stable. On most computers, it boots in less than 15 seconds.

The operating systems used by PDAs are not as complex as those used by PCs. PDAs typically have one of two types of operating systems: 3Com's Palm OS or Microsoft Windows CE, which is now called PocketPC. PocketPC is a Microsoft product that supports color displays, graphics, Word, Excel, and built-in MP3 players or MPEG movie players. Palm OS 5 has been available to customers for almost two years. Palm OS Garnet, an enhanced version of Palm OS 5, supports a broad range of screen resolutions, a dynamic input area, improved network communication, and Bluetooth.

Know What Filesystems Are in Use

filesystem
The operating system's method of organizing, managing, and accessing files through logical structuring on the hard drive.

Filesystems interact with the operating system so that the operating system can find files requested from the hard disk. The filesystem keeps a table of contents of the files on the disk. When a file is requested, the table of contents is searched to locate and access the file.

To understand this better, let's take a quick look at hard disks. The hard disk on which an operating system is installed is broken into large pieces called *clusters* or *allocation units*. Each cluster contains a number of sectors. A disk partition contains the sectors. Without additional support, each partition would be one large unit of data. Operating systems add a directory structure to assign names to each file and manage the free space available to create new files. The directory structure and method for organizing a partition is called a filesystem. Different filesystems reflect different operating system requirements. Some work better on small machines; others work better on large servers. The same hard disk can have partitions with filesystems belonging to DOS, NT, or Linux. When more than one filesystem type is installed on a hard drive, this is called a *multiboot* or *dual-boot configuration*.

FAT/NTFS

File Allocation Table (FAT)
A simple filesystem used by DOS, but supported by later operating systems. The FAT resides at the beginning of a disk partition and acts as a table of contents for the stored data.

The filesystem keeps a table of contents of the files on the drive. When a file is requested, the table of contents is searched to locate and access the file. One of the most common filesystems is *File Allocation Table (FAT)*. Each cluster has an entry in the FAT that describes how it is used. The operating system uses the FAT entries to chain together clusters that form files. In the 1970s, PC filesystems were designed to support floppy disks. Hard disk support came a little later. DOS uses the FAT filesystem, which is also supported by all other DOS- and Windows-based operating systems. Early versions of DOS used FAT12. The FAT system for later versions of DOS and older versions of Windows 95 is called FAT16. It is simple, reliable, and uses little storage. The FAT is stored at the beginning of the partition to act as the table of contents. To protect the partition, two copies of the FAT are kept in the event that one becomes damaged. The FAT structure doesn't have a lot of organization; files are given the first open location on the disk.

Virtual FAT (VFAT)
Also called FAT32, an enhanced version of the FAT filesystem that allows for names longer than the 8.3 convention and uses smaller allocation units on the disk.

Virtual FAT (VFAT) is an enhanced version of the FAT filesystem. This filesystem is also called FAT32, and it is available in Windows 95 and early versions of Windows NT. It allows files to have longer names than the 8.3 convention adopted by DOS. FAT32 also accommodates the use of smaller allocation units on a disk.

New Technology File System (NTFS)
A file system supported by Windows NT and higher Windows operating systems.

New Technology File System (NTFS) was developed expressly for versions of Windows NT and Windows 2000. Windows NT supports NTFS 4 and Windows 2000 and higher support NTFS 5. Only Windows NT and higher Windows operating systems can use data on an NTFS volume. NTFS organizes files into directories, which are then sorted. It also keeps track of transactions against the filesystem, making it a recoverable filesystem. The following graphic shows a copy of the file structure on a Windows XP computer.

Notice the lines on the left side of the screen. Those lines indicate how many directories deep you are.

Various Unix/Linux Filesystems

Unix has been around for decades, making it the oldest of all filesystems used on PC hardware. Unix filesystems are also probably the most different from the other filesystems used on PCs. The Unix filesystem is organized as a hierarchy of directories starting from a single directory called root, which is represented by a slash (/). Unix looks at all disks and storage devices as part of one filesystem. All of the Linux files are in one tree; there is no concept of drives such as A, C, and D. Storage devices are linked to the directory structure. In other words, a floppy disk may be accessed at /mnt/floppy and a CD-ROM on /cdrom. Any subdirectories that are created use the storage space assigned to their parent directory—unless they are assigned their own storage space. Filenames are case sensitive. TEST and test are two different files.

High-Performance File System (HPFS) was designed for the OS/2 operating system to allow greater access to larger hard drives. HPFS maintains the directory organization of FAT, but it adds automatic sorting of the directory based on filenames. HPFS also includes two unique special data objects called *super block* and *spare block*. The super block contains a pointer to the root directory, and the spare block is used for hot fixing bad sectors.

High-Performance File System (HPFS)
A filesystem designed for the OS/2 operating system. HPFS automatically sorts the directory based on the filename, and it includes the super block and spare block.

———————— *WARNING* ————————

If the super block is lost or corrupted due to a bad sector, the contents of the partition are also lost, even if the rest of the drive is fine.

The Linux operating system supports multiple different filesystems. To enable the upper levels of the core of the operating system to deal with these filesystems, Linux defines an intermediary layer, known as the Virtual Filesystem (VFS). Just as in Unix, there are no drive letters in Linux. Instead, Linux creates a virtual filesystem, which makes all the files on all the devices appear to exist on one device. In Linux, just as in Unix, there is one root directory, and every file you can access is located under it.

Second/Third Extended Filesystems (ext2/ext3)

State-based filesystems used by the Linux operating system.

Second/Third Extended Filesystems (ext2/ext3) are state-based filesystems. This means the filesystem maintains the state of all open files in memory. All open files have entries in data structures in memory. Beginning with the release of Red Hat Linux 7.2, the default filesystem changed from the ext2 format to the journaling ext3 filesystem. The ext3 filesystem is an enhanced version of the ext2 filesystem. It keeps logs and checkpoints for all the transactions so that a filesystem check is no longer necessary after an unclean system shutdown. This way, if a system crashes, it can restore the filesystem using the logs.

Network File System (NFS)

Provides remote access to shared file systems across networks. The primary function of NFS is to mount directories to other computers. These directories can then be accessed as though they were local.

Network File System (NFS) was originally developed by Sun Microsystems in the 1980s as a way to create a filesystem on diskless clients. NFS provides remote access to shared filesystems across networks. The primary function of NFS is to mount directories to other computers. These directories can then be accessed as though they were local. This works the same way that mapped drives work in Microsoft networking.

BeOS File System (BFS)

Designed for the BeOS, BFS has the built-in capability to work with FAT 12, FAT 16, VFAT, and HPFS partitions.

The BeOS operating system is designed to use its own filesystem, called the *BeOS File System (BFS,* or sometimes BeFS). Its primary strength is that it has the built-in capability to access other filesystems such as FAT12, FAT16, VFAT, and HPFS partitions. Support for FAT32 and NTFS partitions has been added with the appropriate drivers.

Maintain Tools and Procedures for Each Operating System and Filesystem

The challenge to computer forensic scientists is to develop methods and techniques that provide valid and reliable results while preserving evidence and preventing harm to information. You need to have procedures and tools in place so that you can more easily collect the evidence you need.

What happens if a system is set up to log every event imaginable? The system's hard drive space will fill up, and someone will have to weed through all the collected information to figure out which events really can help an investigation. Having good procedures in place and conducting proper maintenance of your tools will help make the forensic process run more smoothly.

Preinstalled Tools Make Forensics Easier

For computer forensic science to be effective, it must be driven by information discovered during an investigation. Many systems currently have 60GB or higher capacity hard disks. From a practical standpoint, it could be impossible to examine every file stored on a seized computer system. It could be equally difficult for law enforcement personnel to sort through, read, and comprehend the amount of information contained within files on today's huge systems. So, we will take a look at some tools that can help you with this enormous task.

Eventually, you will work with a forensic toolkit. For now, let's look at the tools that are already installed on most operating systems. These are tools that you can readily take advantage of and use. All operating systems come with the ability to log events. Because Windows XP is a popular operating system these days, we'll look at how it logs events.

Event Viewer allows you to audit certain events. Event Viewer maintains three log files: one for system processes, one for security information, and one for applications. The following graphic was captured on a Windows XP computer. In Windows 2000 Server and Windows Server 2003, you will also find directory services, DNS server, and file replication logs.

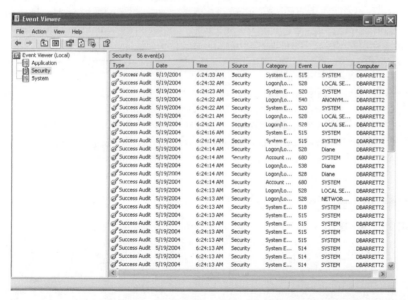

Auditing is the process of tracking users and their actions on a network. You should audit access use and rights changes to prevent unauthorized or unintentional access by a guest or restricted user account. This will prevent access to sensitive or protected resources. How much you should audit depends on how much information you want to store. Keep in mind that auditing should be a clear-cut plan built around goals and policies.

auditing
The process of keeping track of who is logging in and accessing what files.

When deciding what to audit, first identify potential resources at risk within your networking environment. These resources might typically include sensitive files, financial applications, and personnel files. After the resources are identified, set up the audit policy through the operating system tools. It can be useful to monitor successful as well as failed access attempts. Failure events allow you to identify unauthorized access attempts; successful events can reveal an accidental or intentional escalation of access rights.

Each operating system will have its own method for tracking and logging access. Auditing is resource intensive and can easily add an additional 25 percent load on a server. Make time to view the logs. Log files won't help protect against a system compromise if an intrusion is recorded in your logs and you don't read the logs for the next six months. Most operating systems produce log files in text file format. Viewing data graphically is much easier than interpreting text. If possible, import the log files into some type of database.

TIP Auditing can be as simple or as complex as you want to make it. Regardless of the plan you devise, be consistent.

Most operating systems also have built-in utilities for tracking the address of a computer and tracing the route it takes to get to a destination on the Internet. This type of information can be of significant importance when internal users are causing malicious activity. With the advent of business-to-business activities, using tracking utilities is also a good way to know when employees are accessing the sites of business partners.

This section discussed tools that are already in place to track information traveling across a network. After you obtain this information, how can you use it? Can you accuse an employee of hacking based on the information that you have gathered? This type of question falls under the scope of knowing your legal limits, so let's move on and see what you can and cannot do with this information.

Know Your Limits

When an intrusion is detected, you must know to what lengths you can go to minimize the damage and also whether or not you can seize property. For example, let's say that you have determined that an employee has installed hacking tools on your network and he has hacked into a business partner's network. He proceeded to hack into their network and steal passwords. Can you search his computer for evidence without a warrant? What about that JumpDrive he is carrying around his neck? Is it a work-related item or a personal item? These are the types of questions you'll need to answer before you act.

Legal Organizational Rights and Limits

Employers can be either public or private. The distinction is important because government employers are bound by the Fourth Amendment, which is discussed in the next section. Despite laws, not everything that passes through the confines of a business door can be considered part of the workplace. For example, the contents of an employee's purse or briefcase maintain their private character even though the employee has brought them to work. Although circumstances might permit a supervisor to search in an employee's desk for a work-related file, a supervisor usually will have to stop at the employee's purse or briefcase.

When confronted with this issue, courts have analogized electronic storage devices to closed containers, and they have reasoned that accessing the information stored within an electronic storage device is akin to opening a closed container. Because individuals generally retain a reasonable expectation of privacy in the contents of closed containers, they also generally retain a reasonable expectation of privacy in data held within electronic storage devices. The following are some cases that can be used as references:

- United States v. Ross, 456 U.S. 798, 822-23 (1982)
- United States v. Barth, 26 F. Supp. 2d 929, 936-37 (W.D. Tex. 1998)
- United States v. Reyes, 922 F. Supp. 818, 832-33 (S.D.N.Y. 1996) United States v. Lynch, 908 F. Supp. 284, 287 (D.V.I. 1995)
- United States v. Chan, 830 F. Supp. 531, 535 (N.D. Cal. 1993)
- United States v. Blas, 1990 WL 265179, at *21 (E.D. Wis. Dec. 4, 1990)

This analysis has interesting implications for items such as JumpDrives or floppy disks, which can be either work-related or private, depending on the circumstances. It is probably reasonable for employers to assume that floppy disks found at an office are part of the workplace, but a court could treat a floppy disk or JumpDrive as if it were a private, personal item.

Generally speaking, an employer may consent to a search of an employee's computer and peripherals if the employer has common authority over them. There are currently no cases specifically addressing an employer's consent to search and seize an employee's computer and related items. However, cases exist that discuss searches of an employee's designated work area or desk.

In an electronic environment, employees do not know when a network administrator, supervisor, or anyone else accesses their data. As a practical matter, system administrators can, and sometimes do, look at data. But when they do, they leave no physical clues that would tell a user they have opened one of his files. Some users who are unfamiliar with computer technology may believe that their data is completely private. If an organization has published clear policies about privacy on the network, this effort would support the position that the user has implied consent to a search by working there under said policy. However, if an organization or administration has not addressed these issues with the users and the situation is ambiguous, the safest course would be to get a warrant.

Search and Seizure Guidelines

The Fourth Amendment limits the ability of government agents to search for evidence without a warrant. It states "The right of the people to be secure in their persons, houses, papers, and effects, against unreasonable searches and seizures, shall not be violated, and no Warrants shall issue, but upon probable cause, supported by Oath or affirmation, and particularly describing the place to be searched, and the persons or things to be seized."

A warrantless search does not violate the Fourth Amendment if one of two conditions is met. Accordingly, investigators must consider two issues when asking whether a government search of a computer requires a warrant. First, does the search violate a reasonable expectation of privacy? And if so, is the search nonetheless reasonable because it falls within an exception to the warrant requirement?

The most basic Fourth Amendment question in computer cases asks whether an individual enjoys a reasonable expectation of privacy in electronic information stored within computers or other electronic storage devices under the individual's control. For example, do individuals have a reasonable expectation of privacy in the contents of their laptop computers, floppy disks, or pagers? If the answer is Yes, the government ordinarily must obtain a warrant before it accesses the information stored inside. A search is constitutional if it does not violate a person's "reasonable" or "legitimate" expectation of privacy [Katz v. United States, 389 U.S. 347, 362 (1967) (Harlan, J., concurring)]. In most cases, a defendant's subjective expectation of privacy focuses on whether the individual's expectation of privacy was reasonable.

Recognizing that government agencies could not function properly if supervisors had to establish probable cause and obtain a warrant every time they needed to look for a file in an employee's office, the Supreme Court held that two kinds of searches are exempt. Specifically, both (1) a noninvestigatory, work-related intrusion and (2) an investigatory search for evidence of suspected work-related employee misfeasance are permissible without a warrant and should be judged by the standard of reasonableness (ID at 725-6). These exemptions are stated under the Federal Guidelines for Searching and Seizing Computers. You can find the entire document at `http://www.knock-knock.com/federal_guidelines.htm`.

Agents must evaluate whether a public employee retains a reasonable expectation of privacy in the workplace on a case-by-case basis, but written employment policies can simplify the task dramatically. See O'Connor, 480 U.S. at 717 (plurality). Courts have uniformly deferred to public employers' official policies that expressly authorize access to the employee's workspace, and they have relied on such policies when ruling that an employee cannot retain a reasonable expectation of privacy in the workplace. See the following cases:

- American Postal Workers Union, Columbus Area Local AFL-CIO v. United States Postal Serv., 871 F.2d 556, 59-61 (6th Cir. 1989)
- United States v. Bunkers, 521 F.2d 1217, 1219-1221 (9th Cir. 1975)

When planning to search a government computer in a government workplace, agents should look for official employment policies or "banners" that can eliminate a reasonable expectation of privacy in the computer.

Will This End Up in Court?

In the event that an incident is of enormous proportion and the organizational policy is to prosecute, an investigation could end up in court. Courts are requiring that information instead of equipment be seized and that ample, unaltered information is presented in each case. Court compliance could require cooperative efforts between law enforcement officers and the computer forensic examiner to make certain that the technical resources are sufficient to address both the scope and complexity of a search.

Computer forensic examiners can help prosecute a case with advice about how to present computer-related evidence in court. They can help prepare the case and anticipate and rebut defense claims. In addition, forensic examiners can assist prosecutors in complying with federal rules pertaining to expert witnesses. Under these rules, the government must provide, upon request, a written summary of expert testimony that it intends to use during its case. There is a reciprocal requirement for a summary of defense expert witness testimony, as long as the defense has requested a summary from the government, and the government has complied.

Should the situation arise, make sure the evidence was processed properly. Good laboratory practices ensure the quality and integrity of evidence by dictating how examinations are planned, performed, monitored, recorded, and reported. Unless you are law enforcement, you probably don't have a lab to process evidence; however, most organizations do have a specially trained team to identify and collect evidence of any incidents that arise. Often incidents happen that aren't actually crimes and require only internal investigations. This specially trained team conducts those investigations and is also aware of what constitutes a crime that would require law enforcement involvement. Let's take a closer look at how such a team is organized and how it works.

Develop Your Incident Response Team

Organizational policies and practices are structural guidance that applies to forensic examinations. They are designed to ensure quality and efficiency in the workplace. In an effort to properly preserve evidence, you must have an *incident response team (IRT)* ready, and the team needs to know how to handle situations.

incident response team (IRT)
A team of individuals trained and prepared to recognize and immediately respond appropriately to any security incident.

Organize the Team

incident response plan
The actions an organization takes when it detects an attack, whether ongoing or after the fact.

Incident response plans are needed so that you can intelligently react to an intrusion. More importantly, there is the issue of legal liability. You are potentially liable for damages caused by a hacker using your machine, and you will want to preserve the evidence. You must be able to prove to a court that you took reasonable measures to defend yourself from hackers and present any evidence as clearly and concisely as possible. If a plan is not in place and duties are not clearly assigned, your organization could end up in a state of panic. The components of an incident response plan should include preparation, roles, rules, and procedures. Once your plan is in place, the incident response team members should be appointed. Realize that this team is not a full-time assignment; it is simply a group of people who have obligations to act in a responsible manner in case of an incident.

NOTE

Do not overlook the effect an incident will have on employees. The interruption to the workplace not only causes confusion, but also disrupts their schedules.

The incident response team is responsible for containing the damage and getting the systems back up and running properly. These steps include determination of the incident, formal notification to the appropriate departments, and recovering essential network resources. With this in mind, the team should be comprised of the following personnel:

- Security and IT personnel
- Someone to handle communication with management and employees
- Someone to handle communication with vendors, business partners, and the press
- Developers of in-house applications and interfaces
- Database managers

The entire team is responsible for the success of the incident handling, and the entire team should remain assembled until the incident is completely handled.

State Clear Processes

The basic premise of incident handling and response is that a company needs to have a clear action plan on what procedures should be in place when an incident happens. These procedures should include:

- Identifying the initial infected resources by obtaining preliminary information about what kind of attack you are dealing with and what potential damage exists.

- ◆ Notifying key personnel, such as the security department and the response team.

- ◆ Assembling the response team for duty assignment and deciding who will be the lead for the incident.

- ◆ Diagnosing the problem, identifying potential solutions, and setting priorities. The security response team has to be clear about what to do, especially if the potential damage is high.

- ◆ Escalating the problem to additional teams if necessary. The key is to understand what actually happened and how severe the attack was.

- ◆ Gathering all of the information learned about the incident up to this moment and storing it in a secure location on secure media, in case it will be needed for potential legal action.

- ◆ Communicating the incident. This may include reporting it to law enforcement, IT security companies, and possibly customers.

If an event is newsworthy, expect to be contacted by the media. Make sure someone is authorized to speak to the media.

NOTE

The team should prepare an incident report to determine and document the incident cause and its ultimate solution. This report should be an internal document that puts everything, from the minute the incident was noticed until the minute service is restored, into perspective.

Coordinate with Local Law Enforcement

Local law enforcement relies on network administrators to report when their systems are hacked. Intrusion victims are often reluctant to call law enforcement. This reluctance has been reflected in the surveys conducted jointly by the Computer Security Institute and the FBI. Only 25 percent of the respondents who experienced computer intrusions reported the incidents to law enforcement.

If organizations do not report incidents, law enforcement cannot provide an appropriate or effective response. Networks are going to get more complex and more vulnerable to intrusions. Law enforcement agencies are familiar with computer crime investigations, view intrusions as important, and will respond appropriately. They are able to promptly refer reports to the proper agencies if they are not equipped to handle more complex cases.

Publicity is frequently an issue for victims of computer crime. Law enforcement has been trained to be sensitive to victims' concerns arising from the publicity and seizure of data from corporate networks. Many investigations also require information from the victim's incident response team.

Terms to Know

auditing	key logger
BeOS File System (BFS)	modem
Bluetooth	Network File System (NFS)
CD/DVD-ROM/RW drives	New Technology File System (NTFS)
desktop	operating system
file allocation table (FAT)	personal computer (PC)
filesystem	personal digital assistant (PDA)
FireWire	Second/Third Extended Filesystems (ext2/ext3)
floppy drive	server
High-Performance File System (HPFS)	Universal Serial Bus (USB)
incident response plan	Virtual FAT (VFAT)
incident response team (IRT)	war dialing
input/output (I/O)	workstation
Jaz drive	Zip drive

Review Questions

1. What is the difference between a server and a PC?

2. How many devices can USB support?

3. Which has a faster transfer rate, FireWire or USB 1?

4. How does Bluetooth communicate?

5. What types of filesystems will you find in the Windows environment?

6. What is the difference between NTFS and NFS?

7. What does an incident response team do?

8. Approximately what percentage of organizations report intrusions?

9. Can an employer search an employee's designated work area or desk?

10. Search and seizure laws are guided by which amendment?

Chapter 3

Computer Evidence

In this chapter, you'll learn about computer evidence—what it is and what makes it different from regular evidence. You'll also learn how to identify, collect, handle, and present evidence in and out of court.

Simply put, *evidence* is something that provides proof. You'll need evidence to prove that someone attacked your system. Without evidence, you only have a hunch. With evidence, you might have a case. Good, solid evidence can answer several of the five Ws and an H of security violations: who, what, when, where, why, and how. You'll use the evidence you collect to further the discovery of the facts in an investigation. That same evidence might provide the proof necessary to result in a legal finding in your favor. Understanding computer evidence is the first step in successfully investigating a security violation.

What Is Computer Evidence?

The main purpose of computer forensics is the proper identification and collection of computer evidence. It is both an art and a science. Computer evidence has common characteristics and differences with regular evidence. Forensic examiners need to understand the specifics of computer evidence so that they can properly collect it for later use.

Incidents and Computer Evidence

Computers can generally be involved in security violations in one of two ways. First, a computer can be used in the commission of crimes or violations of policy. Second, a computer can be the target of an attack. In the first case, one or more computers are used to perform an inappropriate action. Such actions might be illegal (for example, fraud or identity theft) or simply disallowed under an organization's security policy (for example, participating in online auctions on company time).

Regardless of whether an action is a crime, any violation of security policy is called a *security incident*. Actually, any intended violation of a security policy is an incident as well. A company's security policy should outline the appropriate response for each type of incident. As discussed in Chapter 2, "Preparation—What to Do Before You Start," most incidents that do not constitute crimes generally require only internal investigations. Internal investigations are normally carried out by an organization's incident response team (IRT). The incident response team is specially trained to identify and collect evidence of the incident. The team is also aware of what incidents are crimes and require law enforcement involvement.

In general, the incident response team deals with incidents in which the computer is the target of an attack. Criminal investigations are frequently conducted to investigate the first incident type in which a computer is used as a tool in committing a crime. In both cases, the process of computer forensics produces evidence of the activity carried out during the incident.

computer evidence
Any computer hardware, software, or data that can be used to prove one or more of the five Ws and an H of a security incident (i.e., who, what, when, where, why, and how).

To properly investigate an incident and possibly take action against the perpetrator, you'll need evidence that provides proof of the identity and actions of an attacker. *Computer evidence* consists of files and their contents that are left behind after an incident. The existence of some files, such as pictures or executable files, can provide evidence of an incident. In other cases, the contents of files, such as log files, provide the necessary proof. Recognizing and identifying hardware, software, and data you can use is the first step in the evidence collection process.

Types of Evidence

Four basic types of evidence can be used in a court of law:

- Real evidence
- Documentary evidence

- Testimonial evidence
- Demonstrative evidence

Computer evidence generally falls into the first two categories of evidence. Before you start looking for evidence, understand that most successful cases are based on several types of evidence. As you conduct an investigation, be aware of the different types of evidence you can gather. Although computer forensics tends to focus on one or two evidence types, a complete investigation should address all types of available evidence. In the following sections, we'll look more closely at each of the four types of evidence.

Real Evidence

The type of evidence most people are familiar with is *real evidence*. Real evidence is anything you can carry into a courtroom and place on a table in front of a jury. In effect, real evidence speaks for itself. It includes physical objects that relate to the case. In a murder trial, the case's real evidence might include the murder weapon. In the context of computer forensics, the actual computer could be introduced as real evidence. If the suspect's fingerprints are found on the computer's keyboard, such real evidence could be offered as proof that the suspect did use the computer. Sometimes real evidence that can conclusively relate to a suspect is called *hard evidence*.

Other types of real evidence in a computer forensics investigation could be the hard drive from a suspect's computer or a personal digital assistant (PDA). Real evidence is the most tangible and easiest to understand type of evidence. When presenting a case to a jury, real evidence can make the case seem more concrete. You may be asked to present real evidence, even when the most compelling evidence is not physical evidence at all. Remember that not all courtroom participants are technically savvy. A physical piece of pertinent evidence can often help your case. Without real evidence, a case can sometimes be perceived as weak and circumstantial.

Never overlook potential evidence when conducting an investigation. Other types of evidence may involve or refer to real evidence. It is very common to use log file contents when arguing a case. The process of establishing the credibility and authenticity of such data is often easier when you start with the physical disk drive and/or computer from which you extracted the log file. In this example, the real evidence supports your log file data.

Assume you have been asked to investigate an e-mail spammer. Due to the nature and volume of e-mails being sent, local law enforcement has been called in to investigate and they have called you. You arrive on the scene to begin your investigation.

Before you touch anything, look around the scene and take pictures of everything. Digital pictures are inexpensive, but they can be valuable later. As you progress through the investigation, you'll want to be able to refer back to images

real evidence
Any physical objects that you can bring into court. Real evidence can be touched, held, or otherwise observed directly.

hard evidence
Real evidence that is conclusively associated with a suspect or activity.

Hot Java, Cold Jury

The case of Cool Beans, Hot Java versus James T. Kirkpatrick is a fictitious case we'll use to illustrate the importance of real evidence. Kirkpatrick was charged with launching spam campaigns from a public terminal in the Cool Beans, Hot Java coffee shop. The Cool Beans network administrator provided ample proof that Kirkpatrick was in the shop during the alleged spam activity. Cool Beans provided security camera images of Kirkpatrick and accompanying computer access logs showing activity consistent with spam floods. Any technical person had to agree this case was a slam dunk. However, the jury acquitted Kirkpatrick due to a lack of compelling evidence. When questioned, the jurors said that they found it difficult to convict a man based on little more than computer printed reports and pictures showing him in the shop. They wanted more concrete evidence. Perhaps the actual computer Kirkpatrick used would have helped to convince the jury, or a network diagram showing how IP addresses are assigned, would have helped the jury make the jump from the virtual to the physical world.

---

of the way you found everything. It's not uncommon to find additional evidence in the original pictures after extracting digital evidence from a suspect's machine.

After you take pictures of everything, start identifying all of the real evidence you think is pertinent and that you have permission to search or seize. Notice the suspect's computer. It has a scanner and a PDA cradle plugged into it. That tells you to look for the PDA and scanner source or target data. PDAs can be a valuable source of documentary evidence (which we discuss in the next section). Most people who use PDAs store a lot of personal data on them. Find the PDA and make sure it has power. When a PDA's battery runs down, the PDA loses all of its data. If you are authorized to seize the PDA, make sure you take the power supply as well.

After looking for the PDA, look for any source documents (for example, printed hard copies) the suspect might have scanned. Also look for CD/DVD-ROMs the suspect might have used to store scanned images. Next, examine the physical computer and surrounding area for other clues of evidence. You should look for additional clues such as:

- Handwritten notes. Even technically savvy people use notes. In fact, because handwritten notes are not stored on a computer, many people consider them to be more "secure."
- Any peripheral device that is, or can be, connected to the computer. This could include:
  - Storage devices
  - Communication devices
  - Input/output devices

- ◆ All removable media, such as:
  - ◆ CD/DVD-ROMs (CD/DVD-Rs and CD/DVD-RWs as well)
  - ◆ Zip disks
  - ◆ Floppy disks
  - ◆ Tapes and other magnetic media

This is not an exhaustive list. It is simply a teaser to get you thinking about real evidence. After you have all the real evidence you can collect, it's time to consider other types of evidence.

Documentary Evidence

Much of the evidence you are likely to use in proving a case will be written documentation. Such evidence includes log files, database files, and incident-specific files and reports that provide information indicating what occurred. All evidence in written form, including computer-based file data, is called *documentary evidence*. All documentary evidence must be authenticated. Because anyone can create an arbitrary data file with desired contents, you must prove that the evidence was collected appropriately and the data it contains proves a fact.

Documentary evidence authentication can be quite complex when you're trying to convince nontechnical jurors (or judges) that the contents of a file conclusively prove an attacker performed a specific action. Opposing attorneys will likely attack the method of authenticating documentary evidence as well as the evidence itself. We have all heard of hard evidence that was thrown out of court because it was collected illegally. Computer evidence can be even more difficult to collect properly. We will cover evidence admissibility in the section titled "Evidence Admissibility in a Court of Law" later in this chapter.

documentary evidence
Written evidence, such as printed reports or data in log files. Such evidence cannot stand on its own and must be authenticated.

Best Evidence Rule

In addition to the basic rules that affect all computer evidence, you must consider an additional rule. Anytime you introduce documentary evidence, you must introduce the original document, not a copy. This rule is called the *best evidence rule*. The purpose of this rule is to protect evidence from tampering. If the original document is required, there is less opportunity for a modification to occur during a copy operation. Of course, you'll have to convince the judge and jury that what you bring into court is actually the original document.

As you progress through an investigation, you will use utilities and tools to explore the contents of the computer and storage media. All files and file contents that support your case will be considered documentary evidence. This is where you'll find the bulk of your evidence for many investigations.

Keep in mind that most of your documentary evidence will come directly from items on the real evidence list. Some documentary evidence will be supplied by third parties, such as access logs from an Internet Service Provider (ISP), but most will come from your own investigation activities.

best evidence rule
When a document is presented as evidence, you must introduce the original document. You cannot introduce a copy.

You'll constantly be reminded to document every step of your investigation. Always document. There will be a test. Rest assured, if you testify in court, you'll be asked to justify your investigation and the actions you took to extract evidence.

Looking for physical evidence is easy. Use your eyes and your brain. Really look at the scene and think about how any physical device or object might provide the evidence you need to prove your case, whether the evidence you find will be presented in a court of law or just appear in an incident report. After you have a handle on the physical evidence, you can start looking at the physical media's content for digital evidence. How do you look for digital evidence? You will use a collection of forensic tools to search for documentary evidence. Some of these tools are as simple as file listings or viewers, while others are developed specifically for forensic investigations. Chapter 8, "Common Forensic Tools," covers common forensic tools and their use in an investigation. Until Chapter 8, we'll just refer to tools designed to examine file system contents as *forensic tools*.

So, what are you looking for? Use forensic tools to look for any file or file contents that show what the suspect did while using the computer. This could include many types of log files and other activity files. For example, WS_FTP is a common File Transfer Protocol (FTP) client. When you use it to transfer files, the program keeps a list of activity in a file named `wsftp.log`. Look for instances of this file. You'll be surprised how often people leave such audit trails lying around. Here's a list of some of the steps you'll want to take while looking for documentary evidence:

- Catalog all programs installed on the target system.

- Harvest all audit and activity log files you can find that use default filenames. (To do this, you might have to research some web pages from each identified program.)

- Examine operating system and application configuration files for noted uses of nonstandard audit and activity log filenames.

- Search for any files that are created as a result of using any identified program.

As with real evidence, your experience will guide you in identifying and extracting the documentary evidence you'll need. Be creative and persistent.

Testimonial Evidence

testimonial evidence
Evidence consisting of witness testimony, either verbal or in written form. Testimonial evidence can be presented in person by the witness in a court or through a recorded deposition.

The testimony of a witness, either in verbal or written form, is called *testimonial evidence*. The most common form of testimonial evidence to the general public is through direct witness testimony in a court. The witness is first sworn in, and then he or she presents testimony that directly relates the witness's knowledge of the incident. Testimonial evidence does not include any opinion, just the direct recollection of the witness.

The second common form of testimonial evidence is testimony delivered during a deposition. As with live testimony, the witness delivers testimony under oath. The testimony, as it is delivered, is recorded by a court reporter. The record of the deposition can be entered into evidence just as the testimony of a live witness in court. Each type of testimony has its advantages, but a deposition can often be taken much sooner when the events are fresher in the witness's mind.

You'll often need to use testimonial evidence to support and augment other types of evidence. For example, you may have the system administrator testify that your server keeps logs of all user accesses and has done so for the last two years. This testimony would help validate the documentary evidence of access log contents taken from the server's hard disk drive (physical evidence).

When you first looked at the e-mail spammer scene, you contacted every possible witness, right? You'll want to talk with every person who has physical access to the suspect's computer, as well as has substantive contact with the suspect. Interviewing witnesses is a task better left to law enforcement when dealing with a criminal investigation, but you should include their testimony in your investigation. Quite often, witness testimony can give you extra information that will lead you to more documentary or physical evidence.

A witness could give you clues to the hiding place of key storage media or computer usage habits of the suspect. If you have reason to believe the suspect carried out illegal activities during lunch, you can limit the initial amount of data you must examine. Work with whoever is interviewing witnesses to have your questions presented. The answers could save you a lot of work.

Demonstrative Evidence

Many types of computer evidence may make sense to technical people but seem completely foreign to others. In order for judges and juries to understand the finer points of your case, it is often necessary to use visual aids or other illustrations to help explain some of the more technical details of the evidence. Such evidence that helps to explain, illustrate, or re-create other evidence is called *demonstrative evidence*. Demonstrative evidence does not stand on its own like other types of evidence. It exists to augment other evidence.

demonstrative evidence
Evidence that illustrates, helps explain, or demonstrates other evidence. Many times, demonstrative evidence consists of some type of visual aid.

Let's assume you want to use a web server's log file to show how an attacker exploited a new vulnerability. The attack resulted in crashing the server and causing substantial loss of business while the system was down. The task of explaining how web servers work can be made easier by using charts, flowcharts, and other visual aids. Demonstrative evidence is often the necessary component to successful use of other types of evidence.

Often, you'll be called on to explain highly technical concepts to nontechnical people. For example, in our e-mail spammer case, you'll have to explain how a spammer works. Although most people have heard of spam, not many understand how it originates or spreads. Further, you'll have to explain why it is difficult to catch the originator of the messages and why spam causes problems in the first place. It would be a good idea to start with the basics. Show how normal e-mail works and how a spammer can cause problems by using excessive network bandwidth. Several illustrations would likely help get the message across.

For example, you might want to start at the beginning. Building a complex technical argument from the ground up requires a little basic education. The following is an illustration you could use to show how e-mail works.

Where does your e-mail originate?

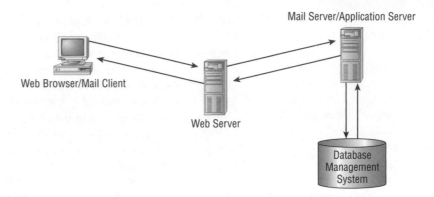

Developing the right visual aids normally comes after the bulk of other evidence has already been collected. Remember, demonstrative evidence is used to explain or demonstrate other evidence. Use it to make your point clear to the judge and jury.

Now that we have looked at the different types of evidence, let's see how we can legally obtain evidence.

Search and Seizure

You probably won't have unobstructed access to all evidence. Before you collect evidence, you must make sure you have the right to either search or seize the evidence in question. This section briefly discusses the options and restrictions of searching and seizing evidence.

Voluntary Surrender

voluntary surrender
Permission granted by a computer equipment owner to search and/or seize the equipment for investigative purposes.

The easiest method of acquiring the legal right to search or seize computer equipment is through *voluntary surrender*. This type of consent occurs most often in cases where the primary owner is different from the suspect. In many cases, the equipment owner cooperates with the investigators by providing access to evidence. Be aware that the evidence you want might reside on a business-critical system. Although the equipment owner may be cooperative, you must be sensitive to the impact your requests for evidence may have on the equipment owner's business. Although you might want to seize all the computers in the Human Resources department to analyze payroll activity, you can't put the whole department out of operation for long. If your activities will alter the business functions of an organization, you may need to change your plans. For example, you could make arrangements to create images of each drive from the Human Resources department computers during off-business hours. If you can image each drive overnight, you could get what you need without impacting the normal flow of operations.

You would also have voluntary consent in cases in which an employee signed search and seizure consent as a condition of employment. Such prior consent relieves you from having to get additional permission to access evidence. As in any investigation, the value of evidence often diminishes over time. The sooner you collect evidence, the higher the likelihood that evidence will be useful. If no such consent exists, you are going to have to get a court involved.

Never assume you have consent to search or seize computer equipment. Always ensure you are in compliance with all policies and laws when conducting an investigation. Few things are more frustrating than having to throw out good evidence because it was acquired without proper consent.

Subpoena

In the cases where you do not have voluntary consent to search or seize evidence, you'll have to ask for permission from a court. The first option using a court order is a *subpoena*. A subpoena compels the individual or organization that owns the computer equipment to surrender it.

subpoena
A court order that compels an individual or organization to surrender evidence.

A subpoena is appropriate when it is unlikely that notifying the computer equipment owner will result in evidence being destroyed. A subpoena provides the equipment owner ample time to take malicious action and remove sensitive information. Make sure you are confident a subpoena will not allow a suspect to destroy evidence. A common use of a subpoena is when the nonsuspect equipment owner is unwilling to surrender evidence. An owner could have many reasons for being unwilling to release evidence. The evidence could contain sensitive information and company policy could require a court order to release such information. Many times, the court order is required by policy or regulation to document that sufficient authority exists to release information. In any case, where cooperation is based on proper authority, a subpoena may provide the access to evidence you need.

Search Warrant

When you need to search or seize computer equipment that belongs to a suspect in the investigation, the possibility exists that evidence may be damaged or rendered useless. You need to have the court grant law enforcement officers permission to search and/or seize the identified computer equipment without giving the owner any prior notice. A *search warrant* allows law enforcement officers to acquire evidence

search warrant
A court order that allows law enforcement to search and/or seize computer equipment without providing advance warning to the equipment owner.

from a suspect's machine without allowing the suspect to taint the evidence. You should resort to a search warrant only when a subpoena puts evidence at risk. If you are working as an independent investigator, you do not have the option to execute a search warrant. This option is available only to law enforcement officials.

Because a search warrant is an extreme step, courts are reluctant to issue such a ruling without compelling reasons to do so. Make sure you are prepared to justify your request. If you are operating on a "hunch," you are likely to be refused. Before asking for a search warrant, gather some preliminary evidence that points to the suspect and his or her machine as a crucial part of the evidence chain.

Chain of Custody

After you understand how to identify computer evidence and you know what equipment you can access, you are ready to begin collecting it. The steps you take in the collection process determine whether the evidence will be useful to you once the investigation is complete. You must ensure your evidence was acquired properly and is pristine. This section discusses several concepts necessary to ensure that collected evidence will be valid for later use.

Definition

chain of custody
Documentation of all the steps that evidence has taken from the time it is located at the crime scene to the time it's introduced in the courtroom. All steps include collection, transportation, analysis, and storage processes. All accesses of the evidence must be documented as well.

All evidence presented in a court of law must exist in the same condition as it did when it was collected. Simply put, evidence cannot change at all once you collect it; the evidence must be in pristine condition. You'll be required to prove to the court that the evidence did not change during the investigation. Yes, you'll have to provide your own evidence that all collected evidence exists, without changes, as it did when it was collected. The documentation that chronicles every move and access of evidence is called the *chain of custody*. The chain starts when you collect any piece of evidence.

The chain of custody is so named because evidence has the potential to change each time it is accessed. You can think of the path evidence takes to the courtroom as a chain in which each access is a link in the chain. If any one link breaks, (i.e., breaks the integrity of the evidence), the whole chain breaks at that point.

The court expects the chain of custody to be complete and without gaps. You demonstrate a complete chain of custody by providing the evidence log that shows every access to evidence, from collection to appearance in court. A complete chain of custody log also includes procedures that describe each step. For example, an entry might read "checked out hard disk drive serial number BR549 to create a primary analysis image." You should also include a description of what "creating a primary analysis image" means. The defense will examine the chain of custody documents, looking for any gaps or inconsistencies. Any issue with the chain of custody has the real potential of causing the court to throw out the evidence in question. Once that happens, the evidence you have collected becomes useless and your credibility will probably be questioned.

Controls

Each step in the chain of custody must have specific controls in place to maintain the integrity of the evidence. The first control could be to take pictures of the evidence's original state. This, of course, is only applicable for real evidence. Once you photograph and/or document the initial state of the entire scene, you can begin to collect evidence.

From the very first step, you must list all procedures you use in the collection process and be ready to justify all your actions. For example, when you collect a disk drive for analysis, you must carefully follow standard practices regarding disk identification, removal, handling, storage, and analysis. Each step in the evidence collection and handling process must have at least one associated control that preserves the state of the evidence.

Continuing our disk drive evidence example, you must use proper handling techniques when handling disk drives, and you must also document each step in the process. Before you start, you want to take precautions against disk drive damage. Such precautions might include:

◆ Grounding to prevent static discharge

◆ Securing and padding the work surface to prevent physical shock

◆ Noting power requirements to protect against inadvertent power-related damage

You'll also need to implement and document all controls that prevent accidental changes to the evidence. These precautions might include:

◆ Implementing a write blocker to prevent accidental writes to the media

◆ Generating a snapshot of the media using a hash or checksum before any analysis

◆ Using analysis tools that have been verified to run using read-only access

Needless to say, you need to plan each step of the way. At each step, make sure at least one control is in place to ensure your evidence stays pristine and unaltered. The upcoming section titled "Leave No Trace" will cover some specific controls; however, the preceding list gives you an idea of the level of detail that is required to satisfy a court of law that the evidence has not changed since it was collected.

The following steps are an example of how to handle a disk drive you suspect contains evidence:

1. After you have determined that you need to analyze a hard disk drive, the first step is to seize the drive. You must fully document the entire process, including:

   ◆ Seizure authority

   ◆ Seizure process

- ◆ Safety precautions
- ◆ Source location, time, and person who performed seizure actions
- ◆ Packing and transportation method
- ◆ Destination location, time, and person who transferred the item to secure storage
- ◆ Description of storage facilities, including procedures to ensure evidence security

2. After seizing the drive, mount it in read-only mode and make a copy of the drive for analysis. Make sure you:

- ◆ Document the process of mounting the device
- ◆ Describe the precautions taken to prevent changes to the media
- ◆ List all of the steps in the copy process

3. Compare your copy of the drive to the original to ensure you have an exact copy. Make sure you:

- ◆ Describe the process and tools used to compare drive images

4. After you have a clean copy of the original drive, you can begin your analysis.

The previous steps are illustrated in the following graphic.

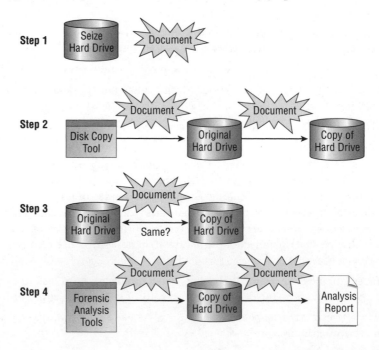

Real World Scenario

Tales from the Trenches: Computer Evidence

The computer forensics expert is often called on to save the day, even when that "day" occurred over a year and a half ago.

The statute of limitations for sexual harassment can range from as few as 30 days for federal employees to as long as three years in certain states. After being contacted by the senior management of a small publicly traded company located in a state that extends the statute of limitations, I boarded a flight to see if I could help locate evidence that was over 18 months old.

A senior manager for the company was being sued for sexual harassment by an employee who had left the company 18 months earlier. The employee had not made any allegations when leaving the company and had only recently filed a lawsuit. After speaking with the senior manager named in the suit, the company officials were hoping I might be able to locate proof that the romance was mutual and consensual and was not sexual harassment.

As is the norm in a majority of businesses, when the complaining employee left the company, the employee's desktop computer hard disk had been reformatted, reloaded, and the computer had been assigned to another employee. The company CIO was able to track down the computer and presented it to me to see what I could locate. By this time, the computer had been in use by another employee for almost 15 months. The senior manager's laptop computer was lost six months earlier. In addition, the company recently implemented a new installation of Microsoft Exchange and had no backup tapes of the old e-mail server.

I imaged the hard drive using the Image MASSter Solo 2 Forensics Portable Evidence Seizure Tool from Intelligent Computer Solutions and created a new case file using AccessData's Forensic Toolkit (FTK). I added the acquired image of the hard disk as evidence in the case file in FTK and then indexed the case. After this prep work, things happened quickly.

One of the strengths of FTK is its ability to quickly locate e-mails. I swiftly sorted all the e-mails by date and began reading a string of "love letters" sent from the employee to the manager and from the manager to the employee. It was obvious from the tone of the letters that the relationship was indeed mutual. Additionally, I was able to locate calendar entries from the employee's Outlook .pst file that listed planned meeting times and locations for the couple. I found one particularly humorous and potentially case-defeating file on the computer in an e-mail attachment sent from the employee to the manager. It was a self-photographed nude picture of the employee taken using a mirror.

I located more than enough information to show the relationship was mutual. When presented with all the evidence, the employee dropped the lawsuit. This case illustrates that potential evidence can be found on computers even after long periods of time have elapsed, if the investigator takes the time and knows how to look for it.

Documentation

The first item in your hands when you enter a crime scene is a camera, and the second item should be a pencil. The key to providing a chain of custody that a court will accept is meticulous documentation. You must enter notes into an evidence log, listing all information pertinent to the access of the evidence. Each and every time evidence is accessed (including initial collection) the evidence log should contain at least the following information:

- Date and time of action
- Action type
  - Initial evidence collection
  - Evidence location change
  - Remove evidence for analysis
  - Return evidence to storage
- Personnel collecting/accessing evidence
- Computer descriptive information
  - Computer make and model
  - Serial number(s)
  - Location
  - Additional ID information
  - BIOS settings specific to disk drives
- Disk drive descriptive information
  - Disk drive manufacturer and model number
  - Drive parameters (heads, cylinders, sectors per track)
  - Jumper settings
  - Computer connection information (adapter, master/slave)
- Handling procedure
  - Preparation (static grounding, physical shock, etc.)
  - Contamination precautions taken
  - Step-by-step events within action
  - Inventory of supporting items created/acquired (i.e., hash or checksum of drive/files)
- Complete description of action
  - Procedure used
  - Tools used
  - Description of each analysis step and its results

◆ Reason for action

◆ Notes

    ◆ Comments that are not specifically requested anywhere else in the log

    ◆ Notes section can provide additional details as the investigation unfolds

This log provides the court with a chain that can be traced back to the point at which the evidence was collected. It provides the beginning of the assurance that the evidence has not changed from its original state. The next step in the process is to justify that each step in the chain was carried out according to industry best practices and standards. Once you establish that you have handled evidence in an appropriate manner and maintained the integrity of the evidence, you are ready to take it to court.

The following graphic illustrates a minimal log format. This type of log usually needs supporting documents for each line item. The minimal log format gives a brief overview of evidence handling history, and the detailed description for each line item would provide the additional details mentioned previously.

Chain of Custody Log

Line	Item	Date	Time	Who	Description
1	Hard disk drive, ser #123456	7/15/04	10:15 AM	M. SOLOMON	Seized hard drive from scene, permission provided by business owner
2	Hard disk drive, ser #123456	7/15/04	10:45 AM	M. SOLOMON	Transported HDD to evidence locker in main office
3	Hard disk drive, ser #123456	7/16/04	7:30 AM	M. SOLOMON	Removed HDD to create analysis copy
4	Hard disk drive, ser #123456	7/16/04	9:15 AM	M. SOLOMON	Returned HDD to evidence locker
5					

Before you take evidence to court, you need to ensure it will be acceptable. In the next section, we cover the rules that govern what evidence is admissible in a court of law.

Evidence Admissibility in a Court of Law

All evidence is not appropriate for admission into a court. The court applies specific rules to the evidence submitted. It would be a waste of time to carefully analyze evidence that the court refuses to consider. Some evidence never has a chance of making it to court, and good evidence can be tainted by an investigator on its way to court, making it unacceptable.

Know what separates valid evidence from invalid evidence. It will save you substantial amounts of time, and it could make the difference between a successful and unsuccessful case.

Relevance and Admissibility

relevant evidence
Evidence that serves to prove or disprove facts in a case.

The courts apply two basic standards to all evidence. Any evidence you want to use in a court case must be relevant and admissible. *Relevant evidence* is any evidence that proves or disproves the facts in a case. If evidence does not serve to prove or disprove the facts in a case, it can be deemed irrelevant and, therefore, not allowed.

admissible evidence
Evidence that meets all regulatory and statute requirements, and has been properly obtained and handled.

In addition to evidence being judged relevant, the evidence must also be admissible. *Admissible evidence* is evidence that conforms to all regulations and statues in nature and the manner in which the evidence was obtained and collected. Certain evidence may be relevant, but not admissible.

There are many reasons evidence could be inadmissible. Unfortunately, investigators can contribute to the inadmissibility of evidence. The two quickest ways to render good evidence inadmissible are

1. Illegally collect the evidence.

2. Modify the evidence after it is in your possession.

It is extremely important that investigators be diligent in all activities to preserve all evidence in an admissible state. Inadmissible evidence weakens your case, and the effort you put into obtaining evidence that is deemed inadmissible is often wasted time.

Make every effort to maintain the admissibility of evidence, starting from the beginning of your investigation. All too often, investigations start as internal incident response efforts that do not include law enforcement. During an investigation, you might determine that an incident involved criminal activity. At that point, it is time to involve law enforcement. This is why it is important to preserve evidence before criminal activity is discovered. IRT procedures should be consistent with court requirements for collecting and handling evidence. If not, valuable evidence might become inadmissible before the criminal investigation gets underway.

Techniques to Ensure Admissibility

Your main goal in an investigation is to ensure the admissibility of evidence. The IRT is responsible for ensuring that the damage from an incident has been contained and the organization's primary business functions can continue. As an investigator, you must operate with different goals. In smaller organizations, separating these two responsibilities can be difficult.

You must remember the importance of evidence preservation. Make sure you collect and handle evidence properly at each step. The success of your court appearance may depend on the quality of your part of the investigation.

Know the Rules

Before you ever participate in an investigation, you should know the rules surrounding evidence collection and handling. Each state imposes slightly different rules, so know your local laws and policies. There are also very different rules for different types of evidence. For example, analyzing a database that contains confidential personal medical information will have more stringent requirements than a database containing a parts inventory. Ask questions before engaging in evidence collection. In this case, forgiveness is far more difficult to obtain than permission.

The best place to start is by developing a relationship with your local law enforcement agents. Call your local agency and ask for the computer forensics unit. Meet with them and take the time to learn how they approach investigations. Most of the time, law enforcement officers will gladly provide guidance to you and help you comply with their investigative requirements. Learning from them will save both of you substantial time and effort when an event occurs that requires law enforcement involvement.

Also spend some time with your own organization's legal folks. They can provide valuable input that will guide your investigative efforts as well. The goal is to ensure your processes comply with any statutes, regulations, and policies before an investigation starts.

Protect the Chain of Custody

Once you find yourself in the midst of an investigation, take every effort to protect the chain of custody. The best process is worthless if it is not followed and enforced. If your process requires that the evidence locker is physically locked at all times, never leave it unlocked while you "run a quick check." Even small deviations from the published policy can render evidence inadmissible.

Be doggedly diligent in protecting evidence. You should allow only trained personnel near evidence. Make sure they are trained in the importance of evidence handling. The cost of training is far less than the cost of losing valuable evidence due to a single careless event. Defense attorneys will look for such mistakes. Take care to ensure you do not make any.

Treat Each Incident as a Criminal Act

The single most important practice to keep in mind is that of treating every incident as a criminal act. Always assume that the evidence you collect will be used in a court case. You'll go a long way to ensure all collected evidence is admissible. It is a lot easier to loosen up the evidence collection standards, once you decide there will be no need for law enforcement involvement, than it is to fix a sloppy collection effort later in the investigation.

Always assuming evidence will be used in court will also tend to make you more diligent in evidence handling procedures. The knowledge that evidence is only for internal use can foster a more casual atmosphere that may lead to more mistakes. Take the high road and treat all evidence as though a judge will see it. It will increase the overall quality of your investigative work.

If you assume you will end up presenting your evidence in court, you have to ensure it is pristine. In the next section, we'll look at issues related to keeping evidence pure and unspoiled.

Leave No Trace

The Boy Scouts embrace a philosophy that protects our environment from the effects of hiking, camping, and other outdoor activities. It is called "Leave No Trace," and it affects most outdoor endeavors. The basic idea is that after engaging in an outdoor activity, there should be no trace that you were ever there. The reality is that most outdoor venues allow a more relaxed version, possibly called "Leave Almost No Trace."

In computer forensics, though, you must adhere to a strict "Leave No Trace" policy. You must prove that none of your analysis efforts left any trace on the evidence media. In fact, you'll have to prove that you never modified the evidence in any way. Decide which approach you'll take before the investigation starts (or at least before the analysis of a particular piece of evidence starts).

Read-Only Image

One method to ensure no changes occur to media is through the use of read-only images. There are multiple ways to access media in read-only mode. One method is to mount the evidence volume in read-only mode. Although this is a safe option when performed properly, it is exceedingly difficult to convince a court that you used the correct options when *mounting*, or accessing, a volume.

Further, it is very easy to accidentally mount the volume using the wrong options and inadvertently write to the volume. This is a huge risk when working with the primary copy because writing anything to the primary copy makes the volume inadmissible.

If you decide to mount a suspect's volume in read-only mode, only mount the volume to make a full copy of the volume (or selected files). Be diligent in documenting and verifying the options you used. However, if another option exists (i.e., write-blocking devices), use it instead. You'll have an easier time convincing the court of the volume's integrity.

Software Write Blocker

One method of ensuring that no writes impact the mounted volume is through the use of a *software write blocker*. A software write blocker is a layer of software that lives between the operating system and the actual device driver for the disk. All disk access requests that use standard operating system calls are prevented from writing to the disk.

software write blocker
Software that lives between the operating system and disk driver and blocks any write requests.

Although this approach is generally quite safe, some software write blockers allow direct disk access in some cases. Be sure you do your homework and verify that the tool you use is secure in all cases. You also need to ensure that your tool of choice is updated to the latest version and keep track of the version you use for each investigation. If any vulnerability is detected in a version of the software you are using for an investigation, document its effect on your analysis.

Most vendors that produce computer forensics software and tools provide a software write blocker. Take a look at several tools and the utility they provide. Make sure their capabilities match your needs.

The last step in any media analysis is to run a checksum on the volume and compare it to the checksum run on the same volume prior to analysis. If the two do not match, the volume has changed. If this ever happens, there is clearly a problem with the software write blocker. (Checksums and hashes are discussed in Chapter 4, "Common Tasks.")

Hardware Write Blocker

Another method of preventing writes to media is through the use of a *hardware write blocker*. Some courts view hardware write blockers as more secure than software write blockers because a physical connection blocks any other paths to the disk. The concept behind the hardware write blocker is the same as the software write blocker. Normal access to the device is supported, except all write requests are blocked.

hardware write blocker
A hardware device that is plugged in between the disk controller and the physical disk, and blocks any write requests.

Several vendors sell hardware write blockers, from inline cable devices to full subsystems that support multiple interfaces. As with software write blockers, do your homework to ensure the manufacturer's claims are validated. Any court will likely require that you provide independent proof that the device you chose to use performs as advertised.

> **Software and Hardware Write Blockers**
>
> The following are a few products that block disk writes. Take a look at all of them and evaluate their features to decide which one is right for your use.
>
> **Write Block Software Tools**
>
> - PDBLOCK, by Digital Intelligence, Inc. (www.digitalintel.com)
>
> - EnCase, by Guidance Software (www.guidancesoftware.com)
>
> **Write Block Hardware Devices**
>
> - ACARD Write Block Kit, by ACARD Technology (www.acard.com)
>
> - DriveLock and FastBloc, by Intelligent Computer Solutions (www.ics-iq.com)
>
> - NoWrite, MyKey Technology, Inc. (www.mykeytech.com)
>
> - UltraKit and UltraBlock, by Digital Intelligence, Inc. (www.digitalintel.com)
>
> - FastBloc, Guidance Software (www.guidancesoftware.com)
>
> Also look at the Computer Forensics Tool Testing (CFTT) Project website for further analysis of the tools listed previously (and more). You can visit the CFTT website at www.cftt.nist.gov.

Terms to Know

admissible evidence	real evidence
best evidence rule	relevant evidence
chain of custody	search warrant
computer evidence	software write blocker
demonstrative evidence	subpoena
documentary evidence	testimonial evidence
hard evidence	voluntary surrender
hardware write blocker	

Review Questions

1. What are two general ways in which computers are involved in security violations?

2. What is computer evidence?

3. What is an incident response team?

4. What is real evidence?

5. What is documentary evidence?

6. What is demonstrative evidence?

7. What is a subpoena?

8. What is a search warrant?

9. What is the chain of custody?

10. What is admissible evidence?

Chapter 4

Common Tasks

The goal of computer forensics is to get to the truth. You get to the truth by identifying and acquiring sufficient evidence to prove the identity or the activities of a computer user. Items of interest to investigators and examiners are either the result of prohibited activity or those that support other prohibited activity. The previous chapter discussed computer evidence and the process of collecting and handling it. This chapter looks at the entire forensic process from a common flow approach.

You will learn the basic tasks present in nearly all forensic investigations. When you first approach a crime scene, you must identify any and all pertinent evidence. After you have identified the evidence, you will collect it and handle it in a manner that preserves its state. Remember from the previous chapter that you always want to treat evidence, at least initially, as though it will be admitted into a court of law. After you have custody of the evidence, you can analyze it and present your findings.

This chapter addresses common tasks that are common to computer investigations.

Evidence Identification

Your initial task in an investigation is to identify the evidence you need for your case. Remember, without evidence you don't really have much more than an opinion. Every case is different, so you will likely need different types of evidence for each case. Knowing what evidence you will need is an integral part of a successful investigation. The rule of thumb is to take everything. Unfortunately, there are substantial legal and logistical issues involved with this approach. More realistically, you should take anything and everything that could be remotely related to your case. Religiously adhere to the chain of custody guidelines and label everything as it is removed.

Who Will Use the Evidence You Collect?

You should treat every computer forensics investigation as if the case you build will end up in court. The case in question does not need to involve criminal activity to warrant such care. You may be surprised how even simple investigations can end up as prime evidence for lawsuits in the future. Don't take chances. Protect your organization's assets by providing evidence that can be admitted into a court of law, if needed.

---

distributed denial of service (DDoS) attack

An attack that uses one or more systems to flood another system with so much traffic that the targeted system is unable to respond to legitimate requests.

The facts surrounding the target of the investigation will determine the methods you employ. An investigation into how a server was used in a *distributed denial of service attack (DDoS)* is different from gathering evidence of illegal images on a laptop. Always understand the purpose of your investigation before you start.

Suppose you were called to investigate possible stolen credit cards. The law enforcement officers who are working on this case expect to find incriminating evidence on the suspect's home computer. They have interviewed some of the suspect's coworkers and have found that he talked about a "database of valuable information at home." When you arrive at the suspect's home, where should you start? What type of evidence should you look for? Try to answer these questions by looking at some common guidelines of investigations.

site survey

Notes, photographs, drawings, and any other documentation that describes the state and condition of a scene.

When you enter a crime scene, carefully look around. Always document the scene by taking photographs, drawing sketches, and writing descriptions of what you see. The notes you take and photographs or drawings together form the initial *site survey*. As you progress in your investigation, you may find that looking back at the site survey gives you more context clues that show where to look next.

TIP

Don't get too caught up in finding specific evidence. Rather, treat an investigation like a large puzzle. Avoid fixating on the picture (on the puzzle's box); instead, look at the shapes and how the pieces fit together. When you focus on the end product too much, you can miss important evidence that may lead you in a different direction. Try to avoid looking only for evidence you expect to exist. Be on the lookout for any evidence that would be of interest to your case.

Physical Hardware

You would expect that the primary focus of a computer forensics investigation is computer hardware; however, that's not always true. Often, much more evidence than just physical hardware can be found. Although not the only type of evidence, hardware is a crucial type of evidence you must consider.

Take a look around your own office. How many types of computer hardware do you see? Chapter 2, "Preparation," covered different types of hardware and encouraged you to know what you use in your organization. You probably use several different types of hardware on a daily basis. Physical hardware is a great place to get fingerprints. If part of your case depends on proving that a certain person used specific hardware, fingerprints may provide the evidence you need. Think about the hardware you tend to touch on a routine basis:

- ◆ Keyboard
- ◆ Mouse
- ◆ Touchpad
- ◆ CD-ROM/DVD drive
- ◆ Laptop case
- ◆ Scanner lids
- ◆ Personal digital assistant (PDA) cradle (especially the Hotsync button)
- ◆ Keyboard-video-monitor (KVM) switches (if your office has more computers than monitors)
- ◆ Game controller
- ◆ Media storage units (CD/DVDs, tape, floppy cases, and drawers)

And the list goes on. Your investigation may not require you to establish that a user touched specific hardware, but be prepared do so when necessary. Beyond the appeal of fingerprints, physical hardware is important because it holds the more common target of an investigation—data. Because all data resides on some type of hardware, you need access to the hardware to get at the data. Ensure that you have the proper authority to either seize or search the hardware before you continue.

What Else Can Hardware Tell You?

Pay attention to all clues that hardware provides. If you find an expensive, high-speed scanner attached to a suspect's computer, you should probably find a repository of scanned documents on the computer or server. If you are investigating possible confidential information disclosure and you do not find many scanned documents on the computer in question, find out where the documents are. Few people invest in an expensive scanner unless they plan to use it. Look in not-so-obvious places for the scanned documents.

After you have the proper authorization, you will need to start cataloging the physical evidence. Different people choose different starting points. Some examiners start with the most prominent computer, normally the one in the center of the workspace. Others choose a point of reference, such as the entry door, as a starting point. Regardless of where you start, you should move through the scene carefully and document your actions as you proceed. Start where you are most comfortable. The goal is to consider all physical evidence. Choosing a starting point and moving through the scene in a methodical manner makes it more unlikely that you will miss important evidence.

Follow all communications links. If a computer you are examining is connected to a network, follow the cable or scan for the *wireless access point (WAP)*. Know how this computer is connected to other computers. Your investigation might need to expand to other computers connected to the investigation target. Be careful to avoid unnecessarily expanding the scope of your investigation, though. You might not need to examine all of the computers to which the target is connected, but you do need to know about any network connections.

wireless access point (WAP)
Network device that contains a radio transmitter/receiver and that is connected to another network. A WAP provides wireless devices access to a regular wired network.

The crown jewel of most computer investigations is the hard disk drive. By and large, most evidence lives on a hard drive somewhere. Issues surrounding hard disk drives will be discussed later in this chapter. Remember that the hard disk drive is only one type of hardware. Take the time to consider all types of hardware as you identify evidence for later analysis.

Let's apply our discussion to the real world. Suppose you arrive at the home of the suspected credit card thief. The local law enforcement officers have executed a search warrant and have asked you to help in the investigation. You cannot seize anything, but you can search the computer and associated hardware. You take pictures and start looking around. You notice the normal hardware that surrounds computers, but there is one little black block that catches your eye. Closer inspection reveals a small credit card swipe device with a Universal Serial Bus (USB) cable. You know this could be the device used to read stolen credit cards. Great! Juries love things they can touch and see. Now you need to find where the stolen numbers are stored.

Removable Storage

Removable storage is commonly used for several purposes. You'll find files of all kinds lying around if you look. Refer to Chapter 2, "Preparation—What to Do Before You Start," for more detailed information about different types of hardware. Removable media are also common repositories for evidence. Take the time to carefully inspect all removable media you find for possible value to your investigation. Think about how most people use removable media. It generally serves the following purposes:

◆ Data archival/backups

◆ Data transport

◆ Program installation

Real World Scenario ——————————————————————

Tales from the Trenches: The Missing Man

Computer forensics examiners are sometimes called upon to locate missing individuals. One day I was contacted by the Chief Executive Officer of an Internet startup company and asked if I could come to his office to discuss a matter of some importance. Because his office was located only a few miles from my lab, I told him I would be there within the hour.

As soon as I arrived, the CEO greeted me, took me into his office, and closed the door. (This is always the sign that I am about to hear a really good story.) The CEO explained that the Vice President of Sales for the company had not reported to work in over a week. This was to say the least, highly unusual. The CEO had contacted everyone he could think of, but he had been unable to locate the VP. He had even driven to the VP's apartment and had the landlord check to see if everything was okay at the apartment. When the landlord went inside, he located nothing, and I mean nothing. The entire apartment was empty. No clothing, no furniture, and of course no VP.

The CEO asked me to examine the VP's desktop computer to see if I could locate any information as to where the VP might have gone and why he might have left. At this point, I asked the CEO if he had contacted the police yet. He said he had, but because there was no evidence of foul play, they only took a report and "would get back to him." The VP was not married and had no family, so there was really no one else looking for the VP besides the CEO. He went on to explain the VP had handled all of the sales, marketing, and collections for the company and really handled a large portion of running the business. Now without him, the company was suffering.

The CEO escorted me to the VP's office and unlocked the door. I located the VP's desktop computer sitting on the desk and noted that it was powered off. I removed the hard drive from the computer so that I could take it back to my lab. Following normal procedures, I completed a chain of custody form and gave a receipt for the hard drive to the CEO. I let him know I would get back with him as soon as possible and inform him of what I found.

After creating a forensically sound image of the hard drive, I imported the image into a commercial forensics utility, the Forensics Toolkit from AccessData, and began looking for clues as to what the VP had been doing prior to his disappearance. I located many graphics images of tropical beaches and real estate properties in Grand Cayman. I also located evidence that the VP had visited many Internet sites researching the banking privacy laws in the Cayman Islands, in the days just prior to his disappearance. Of course, I was beginning to suspect that the VP might have traveled to the Cayman Islands. I located a copy of an online airline reservation for a one-way flight to the Island just over a week ago along with a hotel reservation for a two-week stay.

Continues

I had located the VP. Well, that was the good news. Now it was time to find out what the VP had been up to just prior to his departure and maybe figure out why he left. I reviewed a number of e-mail messages the VP had sent to and received from several of the company's clients. The messages referenced that the client should send their payments for services rendered by the company to the company's new address and to please make the checks out to "Service Tech." He explained that this was the new division within the company that would be handling their accounts. I found that 18 different customers had received similar e-mails and responded to the VP acknowledging the change. I compiled my findings and made an appointment to speak with the CEO immediately.

Before I informed the CEO of my findings, I had to ask him a few questions. I let him know I thought I knew exactly where the VP was and why he left so quickly. I told him about the e-mail messages and asked him about the "Service Tech" division and the address change for billing. As I had thought, the CEO had no idea what I was talking about. There was no "Service Tech" and the billing address had been the same since the company was founded.

At that point I informed the CEO that it would be best if we contacted the police again, and he did so. The investigation ultimately found that the VP had opened a bank account in Grand Cayman in the name of "Service Tech" and deposited over $900,000 in checks from the company's customers. Law enforcement agents were able to locate the now ex-VP based on the information provided by my investigation, and most of the money was eventually returned to the company.

This definitely isn't an example of a "normal day at the office," but it shows that the work we do can often times be very exciting and worthwhile.

The first two uses of removable storage are of the most interest to us. Although you may not be successful in finding the evidence you need on a hard disk drive, always look for backups or other secondary copies. Be especially persistent when looking for historical evidence. Removable storage devices come in many shapes and sizes. In years past, the only types of removable storage devices available to most users were floppy disks and magnetic tapes. Those days are long gone. You need to be on the lookout for many places to store evidence, including:

- Floppy disks
- Zip disks
- Magnetic tapes
- CDs and DVDs
- USB drives and storage devices
- Flash memory cards

Generally, you will find two types of files on removable media: intentionally archived and transient. Intentionally archived files are copied to removable media to keep as extra copies, or they are copied prior to deleting the originals.

If you find a system that looks like it has been cleansed of any suspicious files, start looking for backup copies. In fact, the presence of software that cleanses systems, such as Evidence Eliminator or Window Washer, generally means the user may be hiding something. It is a good bet that some evidence was copied to removable media before the last cleansing cycle.

Many organizations that process large volumes of data often clear log files frequently. For example, many ISPs do not keep activity logs longer than 30 days. You may find that the ISP archives old log files, but they may not. Don't depend on archived data. Removable storage is only one part of evidence collection.

NOTE

The other type of files you tend to find on removable media is transient. Transient files are files, or file remnants, that have been temporarily copied onto removable media. Such media is often used to transport data from one computer to another. Although files are commonly deleted from the removable media after they have served their purpose, you might find lingering files. In any case, you will probably find files you can at least partially recover. Few people take the time to securely cleanse removable media.

Removable media analysis is painstakingly slow. Most offices usually have a lot of CDs and floppies lying around, and the devices used to read them are typically far slower than most hard drives. Take your time and look at what is on each disk, tape, and device. Your persistence might pay off by producing evidence that cannot be found anywhere else.

TIP

The rule of thumb with respect to removable media is to take all that you can legally find and seize. Subsequent analysis will be slow, but it can yield evidence you will not find anywhere else.

Documents

The last type of common evidence is hard-copy documents. A hard-copy document is anything written that you can touch and hold. Evidence that consists of documents is called *documentary evidence*. Although this discussion is concerned with written evidence, recall from Chapter 3, "Computer Evidence," that data stored in computer files is also classified as documentary evidence. Printed reports, handwritten notes, cocktail napkins with drawings, and white boards are all examples of documentary evidence.

The most important characteristic of documentary evidence is that it cannot stand on its own. It must be authenticated. When you find suspicious files on a hard drive (or removable media), you must prove that they are authentic. You must prove that the evidence came from the suspect's computer and has not been altered since it was collected. Refer to Chapter 3 for a discussion of evidence handling.

NOTE

Take pictures of all white boards and other writings. Carefully examine the crime scene for any documents that might be admissible as evidence. Look around the computer for sticky notes. It is amazing how many people keep passwords on sticky notes attached to the side of their monitors. Also look around, behind, on top of, and under all hardware components. Another common place to hide notes is in, or under, desk drawers.

Back at the credit card investigation scene, you notice a white board on the wall during your site survey. It looks like it has been used a lot but it has been wiped clean. Fortunately for you, no one took the time to use cleaning fluid to clean the board. If you look closely, you can still read some of what was written and then erased. It looks like a list of filenames. You write them down for later use.

Most people keep some notes handy to jog their memories. Sit down at the subject's desk and carefully look around. Every scrap of paper could potentially be evidence. Look for any written notes that contain either information directly related to the investigation or information that gives you some insight into the subject's activities. You could be looking for any of these pieces of written information:

- ◆ Password
- ◆ Encryption key or pass code
- ◆ Uniform Resource Locator (URL)
- ◆ IP address
- ◆ E-mail address
- ◆ Telephone number
- ◆ Name
- ◆ Address
- ◆ Filename
- ◆ Upload/Download/Working directory

This list is just a sampling of information that could assist your investigation. Anything that helps point you toward or helps you access evidence is valuable information. Most people have to write some things down to remember them. Look for those notes. They can help direct you to more evidence in a fraction of the time it would take to perform an exhaustive search.

Evidence Preservation

Before you can prove that you have maintained the integrity of data you present as evidence, you must prove that you have maintained the integrity of the hardware that contains the data. From the beginning of your investigation, you must take precautions, and document those precautions, to protect the hardware.

The main goal of evidence preservation is to ensure that absolutely no changes have taken place since the evidence was collected. Your collection and handling procedures will be examined. Take all necessary precautions to protect collected evidence from damage that might change its state. Static electricity discharge is a significant concern. You must bring static protection devices with you on each investigation. Use them, and make notes that explain the steps you take to avoid inadvertent damage.

You will have to address several concerns throughout your investigation. Do not handle any evidence until you are absolutely sure you can legally acquire the evidence and that the collection and analysis process will not change the evidence. The following sections cover some of the general issues of evidence preservation.

Pull the Plug or Shut It Down?

One of the classic debates in computer forensics circles is the correct approach to handling a live system. If the computer system in question is operating when you approach it, should you turn it off? The question becomes more pronounced when you are brought in as part of an incident response team during an ongoing attack. Before you switch into investigator mode, you need to limit the extent of the damage. However, disconnecting the computer from the network or power supply can damage or destroy crucial evidence.

Let's assume you want to "freeze" the system as it is and immediately halt all processing. In that case, you may want to literally pull the power plug out of the wall (or pull it from the back of the computer). Removing power immediately stops all disk writes, but it destroys anything in memory. Such an abrupt crash could also corrupt files on the disk. You may find that the very evidence file you want was corrupted by the forced crash. One client once unknowingly tested their disaster recovery plan in a very real way. Early one morning, the Unix computer that hosted the company's central database had the power cord pulled from the back of the computer. When power was restored, the filesystem detected one file that was hopelessly corrupted and promptly deleted it. Unfortunately, the file was the core database file. The client lost the entire database. Fortunately, the backup process had completed only 15 minutes prior to the crash, and no data had been entered since. Although newer operating systems tend to behave, be aware that a sudden loss of power can have negative results.

On the other hand, you may want to perform a proper system shutdown. Although shutting the system down protects any files from accidental corruption, the shutdown process itself writes many entries to activity log files and changes the state of the evidence. Further, a suspect computer could run procedures that cleanse many log files on shutdown. A proper shutdown might wipe out crucial evidence.

A third option is to leave the system up and running. Several of the popular computer forensics software suites support live forensics. With a small footprint, these tools allow you to take a snapshot of the entire system, including memory and disks, while it is still running. The easiest way to do this is to install the small monitor program on the computer prior to any incidents. Of course, this approach only works if you have a manageable number of workstations and you have the authority to install such programs. This is possible in an environment where the organization owns the hardware and can dictate what software is loaded. If you are fortunate enough to deploy forensics software on all of the computers in your organization, the forensics process can be greatly simplified.

You can still run live forensics even if you have had no previous access to the computer. A common way to do this is to carry the required forensic software on a USB drive. You can run the forensics directly from the USB drive, and save any output to it as well. This option gives you the ability to take a snapshot of the live system without changing its state in the process. The availability of large-capacity USB drives that fit on a key ring makes it possible to carry your entire tool set with you inconspicuously wherever you go.

Returning to the credit card investigation scene, you need to look for the files that match the name found written on the white board. Because you carry your USB flash drive with Maresware forensic utilities preloaded, all you have to do is plug in the USB drive.

NOTE   We haven't talked about specific forensic tools at this point, but stay tuned. We cover many of the most common hardware and software tools used in computer forensics investigations in Chapter 8, "Common Forensics Tools."

You immediately have access to the utility you need to search for the files in question. Because you can only search the suspect's computer and not seize it, you'll need to search the drive without copying it first. That may sound like a strange restriction, but you'll probably run into many interesting situations as an investigator. So, search away!

Proving a Forensic Tool Is Safe

If your investigation ends up in a court of law, be prepared to provide evidence that the tools you used did their job without corrupting the evidence. That can be a tough sell if you try to prove it by yourself. An easier course would be to use commercially available forensic tools that have been accepted by courts. If in doubt, ask your local law enforcement contact which tools are accepted in local courts. If you use tools a judge has seen before, you are likely to avoid a lot of wasted time.

Supply Power As Needed

Some types of evidence require uninterrupted power to maintain the contents of memory. The most common type of hardware in this category is the personal digital assistant (PDA). PDAs are quite common and often contain valuable evidence.

They also come in a variety of shapes and sizes. You can find traditional PDAs, as well as PDAs that are integrated into wireless phones and even wristwatches. Regardless of their design, they share one common trait: when the power runs out, the data is lost.

Let's assume you find a gold mine of information on a suspect's PDA. You extract the information and analyze it to find just what you were looking for. After a job well done, and after the self congratulations, you lock up all the evidence in the evidence locker and await the assigned trial date. When your trial date arrives, you open the evidence locker and find that the PDA battery had run out of power. Your original evidence is gone. Well, your analysis report should still exist. You can proceed with documentation of your findings, but it would be a lot easier to show the PDA with data still on it. Although you know what was there, it no longer corresponds to the PDA from which it was originally taken.

If you seize devices that require power to maintain data, seize the charger as well. Make sure you either seize the charger or are prepared to buy a charger for the device. Also be prepared to explain your actions in court. Another interesting feature of PDAs is that their very operation changes the stored data. You may have to explain to a judge or jury how PDAs keep track of current time in order to notify the user of timed events. Be careful when asked if the data in the PDA has changed since it was seized; it has. You simply have to explain how the evidence did not change.

Provide Evidence of Initial State

So, you have the system you need to analyze. How do you poke around the data and convince a judge or jury that you didn't change anything in the process? If you're talking about a disk drive, the answer is really quite simple. Just take a snapshot of the drive before you touch anything, and then compare the snapshot to the drive after your analysis. If they are the same, you didn't change anything.

The most common method of taking a snapshot of a drive is to calculate a *hash* of the entire drive. Most forensic tool sets include a utility to calculate either a cyclic redundancy check (CRC) or Message Digest 5 (MD5) hash value. Although other valid methods exist to generate a single value for a file, or collection of files, the CRC and MD5 hash values are the most common. Both algorithms examine the input and generate a single value. Any changes to the input will result in a different value.

After you have ensured the physical integrity of the media (static electricity countermeasures, stable workspace, etc.) you can mount the media and access it in read-only mode. It is important that you explicitly separate the suspect media from other media during any access to the data. The only safe way to ensure that nothing changes the data on the drive is to use trusted tools to access the media only once. The only reason to directly access suspect media is to copy it for analysis.

hash
A mathematical function that creates a fixed-length string from a message of any length. The result of a hash function is the hash value, sometimes called a message digest. Hash functions are one-way functions. That is, you can create a hash value from a message, but you cannot create a message from a hash value.

Write Blockers

When available, use a write-blocking device to access suspect media. You can use software or hardware write blockers (see Chapter 3). Software write blockers prevent any operating system write operations from modifying the media. In essence, the software write blocker lives between the operating system and the device driver. Any requests for writes to the media are rejected.

Hardware write blockers are physical devices that sit between the drive itself and the controller card. The cable that transmits write instructions and data is physically altered to disallow any writes. Between the two options, the hardware write blocker is harder to bypass and is generally easier to explain in court.

If you have no access to either software or hardware write blockers, you can mount media in read-only mode. You will have to meticulously document the mount options you used to provide evidence to the judge or jury that you allowed no writes during analysis.

State Preservation Evidence

After you mount the suspect media, the first step you take is to create a hash. Use your own utility or a tool from your forensic tool set to create an MD5 hash of the entire media. This provides a reference to the initial state of the media you will use throughout your investigation. After the volume is mounted and you have calculated the hash, you can create a bit-by-bit copy of the suspect media. You will perform all further actions on the copy of the original media, not the original.

That's all you do with the original media. After the copy operation, discontinue any access to the original. It is important that you follow these steps with each media device you analyze:

1. Mount the suspect media in read-only mode (use a write blocker when possible).

2. Calculate an MD5 hash for the entire device.

3. Create a bit-by-bit copy of the media.

4. Unmount the media and return it to the evidence locker.

NOTE   Take extra precautions to protect the original media and the initial hash. You will need both at the time of trial so that you can ensure that evidence you find is admissible. Even if your investigation does not lead to court, being able to prove that your activities made no changes to a disk drive is extremely helpful. You'll need the initial hash to prove such a claim.

The next step in the investigative process is the most time-consuming. After you have copies of the original media, it is time to start the analysis.

Evidence Analysis

Before you begin your media examination, create a hash of the copy you made of the original media. Does it agree with the hash of the original? If so, you may proceed. If not, find out why. Perhaps you mounted the copy and allowed some writes to occur. Or perhaps the copy process was flawed. In any case, don't start the analysis until you have a clean copy.

Most computer forensics tool sets include utilities that create device copies and calculate checksums where appropriate. If you are using the Unix operating system, you can obtain and use the md5sum utility to calculate checksums. You can find a Linux version of the md5sum utility at http://www.gnu.org/software/coreutils/. If you would like a Windows version of the utility, go to http://www.etree.org/md5com.html.

NOTE

The next several sections discuss how to approach media analysis. The actual analysis process is part science and part art. You have to develop a sense of where to look first, and then possess the technical skills to extract the information. We'll focus on the high level here, as opposed to the specific actions you take with individual tools. Chapter 8 covers specific tools, so we'll save the details and recommendations until then.

Knowing Where to Look

There is no easy answer to the question "Where do I look for evidence?" As with any investigation, not all evidence is clear and easily available. Some evidence is subtle, and some has been deliberately hidden or damaged. The specific type of evidence you are searching for depends on the goal of your investigation. If you are looking for evidence for a music CD pirating case, you will likely be looking for stored sound files. If you are gathering evidence in an e-mail fraud case, you will likely look at activity logs and e-mail-related files.

Let's get back to the credit card investigation. Where would you look for credit card numbers? You know the information to use credit card numbers includes the number, expiration date, and possibly card owner information. That kind of information could be stored in a spreadsheet or database data. You searched the hard disk for files that looked similar to the filenames you found on the white board. Unfortunately, you didn't find anything in the filesystem, deleted files, or in slack space. Where do you look next? In this investigation, you chose to look for removable media. We'll rejoin the investigation a little later.

You need to be comfortable with the operating system running on the suspect computer. You might be using Unix-based forensic tools, but if the suspect media is an image of the primary drive from a computer running Windows, you'd better be comfortable with Windows as well. Default locations for files are dramatically different among various operating systems. In fact, the file location defaults can be different between releases of the same operating system family. Therefore, know the operating system with which you are working.

Activity logs and other standard files are commonly stored in default locations on many systems. Always look in the default locations for any logs and configuration files. This step alone can tell you about the suspect. If all logs and configuration files live in the default locations, you can be confident the suspect either does not know about security measures or is too busy to implement security. On the other hand, if you find several applications using nonstandard paths and file storage locations, your suspect may have hidden files well.

Use every means at your disposal to understand what the suspect was trying to do with the computer. Consider all of the supporting evidence you have uncovered so far. This is where the documentary evidence you collected at the scene might be helpful. As you are working through the different types of evidence, your forensic tool set can help by flagging unusual data on the suspect media.

Good forensic tools help you by providing access to areas of a computer that can be used to hide data. But, before you look for hidden data, look for the evidence that you can get to easily. Depending on what you are looking for, you might find it helpful to look at where the suspect has been surfing on the Web. Look at the history and cache files for each web browser on the system. Look at the cookies as well. Although web browsers allow you to look at some historical data, get a tool designed to explore web browser activity. Likewise, look into e-mail correspondence for each e-mail client installed on the computer.

NOTE | **Make absolutely sure you have the legal authority to examine a system. You may only be allowed to look for a certain type of files or activity. Do not exceed your authority.**

As mentioned previously, we'll discuss specific forensic tools in Chapter 8. For now, let's look at a few of the different types of tools you'll need in the computer forensics process.

Viewers

file viewer
A utility that provide thumbnail images of files. Such tools are useful for visually scanning a group of files.

File viewers provide small images of file contents. The programs scan a directory for files that match your criteria and show what is in the files. Viewers are great for finding pictures or movie files. Although most use a file's extension to identify graphics files, some of the more sophisticated tools can look at a file's header to identify it as a graphics file.

Some viewers also handle nongraphics file types, such as word processing document files. The advantage of a viewer tool is that it provides a visual representation of a file. This presentation can make scanning for inappropriate pictures far easier than looking at each one individually.

Extension Checkers

Another type of tool that is useful is an *extension checker*. This type of tool compares a file's extension with its actual data type. A favorite method of hiding data from casual users is to change the file extension. For example, if you want to hide the picture in the file named `blueangels.jpg`, you could rename the file to `blueangel.db`, or even something totally obscure, such as `br.549`. An extension checker utility looks at the extension and compares it to the file's actual header. Any discrepancies are reported as exceptions.

> **extension checker**
> A utility that compares a file's extension to its header. If the two do not match, the discrepancy is reported.

Unerase Tools

Most people are familiar with *unerase tools* that recover deleted files. They have been around the DOS and Windows worlds for years. On older versions of Windows, a simple unerase tool can recover files easily. Newer operating systems complicate the process. After you empty the Recycle Bin, you can recover files with the help of forensic utilities. File-recovery utilities, available for nearly all filesystems in use today, help in identifying and restructuring deleted files.

> **unerase tool**
> A utility that assists in recovering previously deleted files. In some cases, files can be completely recovered. At other times, only portions of the file can be recovered.

Searching Tools

Forensic examiners often need to search a large number of files for specific keywords or phrases. Several *searching tools* support such large-scale searches. Each investigation may have certain words or phrases that can help identify evidence. Searching for known IP addresses or e-mail addresses of people's names can often link pieces of evidence together.

> **searching tool**
> A tool that searches for patterns (mostly string patterns) in a large number of files.

Wading through the Sea of Data

The first thing you will notice when you start to use the types of tools discussed in the previous section is the enormous volume of results that are returned. No matter how narrowly you define the scope of your activities, you will end up with more data than is useful. Your job is to sift through all the data and extract the pertinent information.

Log files provide great audit trails of system activity. They can tell you nearly every event that occurred within a specific scope. For example, web server log files *can* keep track of every request from and response to web clients. However, most applications allow for minimal logging to avoid performance impact. Before you spend too much time looking through the log files, make sure you know the level of detail each application is generating.

One type of tool that helps make sense of large log files is a log file scanner. Log scanner utilities do little more than scan log files and extract events that match your requested event pattern. For text log files, a simple text search utility could provide a similar result in some cases. Most log file scanners make the process easier by allowing queries for specific times that involve certain events.

One type of intrusion detection system (IDS), log-based IDS, provides a convenient method to analyze multiple log files. When searching for activity that would be consistent with a network intrusion, let the IDS look at the log files and highlight any suspicious activity. This information is not helpful for every investigation, though. Sometimes, there are few tools that help lighten the load of looking at a lot of data.

In some cases, you may be able to use tools that help analyze the data. In other cases, you will have to physically look at all the data yourself. In either case, one of the more difficult aspects of computer forensics is in the process of extracting only the evidence that matters from everything else.

Sampling Data

Sometimes you will find that the volume of data is so large there is no feasible way to consider it all. Some log files can contain so much detail that it is nearly impossible to use it all. You might be able to process it, but the amount of useful evidence can be overwhelming.

Any time you have more data than is practical, consider taking samples of the data. You can use data sampling for either input or output data. For example, suppose you are analyzing a large drive with over 1 million pictures. Your job is to find out if there are any pictures of classified equipment. One way to approach the task is to use a viewer utility on an arbitrary collection of pictures. Determine whether patterns exist. If you find from looking at samples of 25 pictures that the files are organized by department, you have some additional information to help narrow your search.

On the other end of the spectrum, suppose your search yielded 5,000 pictures of classified equipment. You would not want to initially submit all 5,000 pictures as evidence. Too much evidence can be overwhelming if it is presented all at once. Instead of submitting all 5,000 pictures together, you may want to select a representative sample to submit, along with information describing the remaining group pictures. All 5,000 pictures would be entered as evidence, but only the sample would be presented. The same approach applies to log file entries. Whenever a large volume of data or large number of redundant data exists, use a sample to represent the whole data set.

Evidence Presentation

After the analysis is complete, it is time to present the results. The goal in any case is to persuade the audience using evidence. Your audience can be a judge, jury, or a group of managers meeting in a conference room. Your goal is to use the evidence you have collected to prove one or more facts. Even with great evidence, the success of a case often depends on the effectiveness of the presentation.

This section covers some of the basic ideas to remember when presenting evidence. The ideas are simple and common to many presentations. Although they are simple, they are important and bear repeating.

Know Your Audience

Before presenting any topic, you should get to know as much about your audience as possible. Know why they are willing to listen to you and what they expect to take from your presentation. A group of Information Services (IS) managers will have different expectations and motivations from a jury in a criminal trial. The more you know about them, the better you can prepare to deliver a convincing presentation.

Do Your Homework

When possible, find out who will be in your audience. If you are presenting evidence in a court of law, you will know who the judge and jury will be. You will also know quite a lot about the judge and the jurors. It may take more work to find out about your audience when presenting to other groups. Try to get as much basic demographic information about the audience participants as possible.

For example, if you find that you are presenting to a group of IS managers, your presentation will probably be different than if you were speaking to a group of auditors. Although the content will be the same, the tone and presentation style may be different. The more successful you are at knowing and understanding the needs of your audience, the better your presentation will be accepted.

Another common presentation venue is the trade show or convention. You may be asked to present the findings from an actual case you have worked on. In this type of setting, there is a better chance that the audience will be more IS literate and technically minded. Organize your presentation to interest your particular audience. Take the time to do your homework, and develop the ability to speak to the needs and interests of your audience

Read the Room

After you begin your presentation, pay attention to the response you receive from the audience. Sometimes you will see the rapt attention in their eyes as they hang on every word of your descriptions of the evidence. The other 98 percent of the time, though, the response is likely to be blank stares of mild interest. Seriously though, always watch for signs of boredom. When you do see the blank stares and fidgeting, change your pace, your tone, or even your approach. Remember that it is hard to bore someone into believing you.

Far too many presenters ignore their audience. They might have a canned presentation, and they deliver it the same way regardless of the audience. You can't do that and be successful as a computer forensics examiner. You may or may not be called upon to present the evidence you uncovered. You should be prepared nonetheless. Skilled presenters aren't necessarily less boring than anyone else—they simply know how to detect boredom early on and what to do about it. Many fine texts cover presentation techniques. Browse a few of them to get some ideas on getting the point across.

Presenting facts is quite simple. Follow these basic steps:

1. Tell what you did.

2. Tell why you did it.

3. Tell how you did it.

4. Tell what you found.

Think about what you would want to hear if you were in the audience. The facts remain the same, but the delivery approach can change to appeal to each audience. For example, technical audiences like facts and "how-to" types of information. Managers tend to like higher-level presentations. For a group of managers, skip the gory details and talk more about the big picture. Although you are focusing on big picture topics, be prepared to answer detailed questions if they arise.

Speaking and presentation books cover far more on reading an audience. Remember that boring someone does little more than bore them. A persuasive argument is rarely boring. Watch the audience and react to them. You will connect more and have a better chance of getting them to seriously consider the points you present.

Target the Points

When planning a presentation, write an outline of the points you want to make. Always start with an outline, no matter how rough. Use the evidence and the process to collect it to support or explain your points. A random list of evidence will likely leave the audience more confused than convinced.

Take the time to list each point you want to make and then expand the point with evidence. The core of your presentation is the evidence, so your evidence should dictate the flow of the presentation. Your points should specifically address each piece or type of evidence, and your evidence should support each point in the presentation. Although the relationship between presentation points and evidence seems circular, the actual points should be the target of your initial outline.

Add to your initial outline until you have a structure that brings out all of the evidence you choose to present. The next section discusses the organization of a presentation. But don't worry about organization until you are confident that you are able to address each of the important points in your presentation.

Your points can be either generic or specific to a particular case. A generic outline might look like this:

1. Initial site survey

2. Evidence collection

3. Evidence handling and storage

4. Initial site analysis

5. Data analysis

6. Findings

Your initial outline should reflect your own style and comfort level. The important point is to ensure that your presentation is clear and concise. Spend your audience's time wisely; don't waste it. Include all the information you need to and nothing more.

Start with a simple outline. You don't have to produce the final product in one sitting. You might be far more productive when you get something into an outline, and then go back over the material to edit it. Getting a memory dump into an outline makes sure you don't overlook crucial ideas while wrestling with the details.

TIP

Organization of Presentation

After you have an outline and a general flow, you need to consider how to organize the presentation. Although each presentation is different, you can use a few common rules of thumb. First, use a presentation method you are comfortable with. If you are most comfortable drawing pictures as you go, set up a white board and dispense with the PowerPoint presentation. If you do use PowerPoint, plan for about 30 slides each hour. This guideline works well for general presentations. If you feel you need to spend more time on one topic, consider creating multiple slides for that topic. If you spend too much time on a single slide, it can become stale, and you risk losing your audience's attention.

Use what works best for your personality. Remember that the main purpose for your presentation is to present evidence you believe proves one or more facts in a case. Take the audience on a tour through the evidence trail that leads them to a conclusion as to what happened that resulted in this case. Sometimes the presentation should take a chronological approach. At other times, a topical approach keeps consistency and cohesion.

Don't get locked in to a particular type of presentation organization. Think through what you want your audience to take away from your presentation. Use the flow and organization that makes sense to you and that leads the audience where you want them to go.

The outline approach works best for us. Whether we are writing a report or developing a presentation, we always work from an outline. As the outline grows and matures, we expand the content into the final format. For presentations, we frequently use PowerPoint. We generally move from an outline to PowerPoint only when we have each slide listed and the major points for each slide. Experiment and find a method that works well for your style.

TIP

Keep It Simple

KISS method
KISS stands for "Keep It Simple, Stupid" and is an acronym that reminds us to avoid making things overly complex.

Above all else, use the *KISS method* when presenting technical information to others (even other technical people). The KISS method stands for "Keep It Simple, Stupid." It's a silly reminder to us all that complexity breeds confusion. Part of the challenge in any presentation of evidence is to make the complex seem simple. Always use the simplest techniques you can think of to present evidence.

Whenever possible, use visual aids. The common saying, "a picture is worth a thousand words," is truer today than ever. Humans process visual images far more efficiently than written words. Whenever you can use a picture, drawing, or chart to convey a concept with just few words, use it. The audience will remember a picture far longer than any words you use to describe it. Use pictures of the crime scene. If your audience is nontechnical, use a picture of a disk drive to explain the process of searching for hidden files. Always look for opportunities to simplify the presentation.

Disk Sector

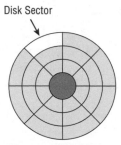

Files are stored in sectors.

Another decision you will need to make when planning a presentation is how much technology you should use. Multimedia presentations with video and sound can be impressive, but they can also be distracting. Use technical props when they simplify the presentation, not to impress the audience. Although some presenters use technology to add pizzazz to a presentation, it can come across as showy. In such cases, the added technical features do not add to the substance of the presentation. So, use technology when it adds to the audience's understanding. Don't use it when it just adds complexity. A simple presentation allows the audience to concentrate on the evidence. Always remember to consider your audience as you develop your presentation. Don't make it too complex. Keep it simple.

Terms to Know

checksum	searching tools
distributed denial of service attack (DDoS)	site survey
extension checker	unerase tools
file viewer	wireless access point (WAP)
KISS method	

Review Questions

1. What is the first common task when handling evidence?

2. Which type of hardware is never of interest to an investigation?

3. When attempting to prove that an individual used a computer, what clues might computer hardware provide?

4. In addition to hard disk drives, where else might data containing evidence reside?

5. Should handwritten notes be considered in a computer forensics investigation?

6. What is the primary concern in evidence collection and handling?

7. Can you analyze a system that is intact and running?

8. What happens when a PDA's battery runs down?

9. What device prohibits any changes to a hard disk drive?

10. How can you prove that you made no changes to a disk drive during analysis?

Chapter 5

Capturing the Data Image

Now that you have a background in what constitutes computer evidence, and you are familiar with the various the computer components and some of the common tasks a computer forensics investigator performs, it's time to look at what happens when an investigation begins. Just like any other items of evidence, computer system components and other electronic devices must be handled correctly. An examiner must follow certain procedures for documenting their receipt and handling. Each computer examination is unique, and the investigator must consider the total effects of the circumstances as the investigation proceeds.

A forensic investigator must also be familiar with the types of evidence that may be encountered on a machine and how to properly preserve each type. Properly processing computer evidence starts with capturing the data in proper order. When you encounter a particular situation, should you immediately turn the machine off or should you leave it running and examine it quickly? What happens to the evidence when the machine is shut down? This chapter will answer these questions and more as we look at how to extract the evidence once an investigation is needed.

Full Volume Images

Part of your role as an investigator is to ensure that a nearly perfect snapshot of the system can be taken. The only problem with this is that nearly anything you do to a system can change it. For example, unplugging the network cable will change the system—but leaving the network plugged in will change it too! Even if you decide to do nothing, the system will change because the time on the system constantly changes. So, you can see the dilemma a computer forensics investigator faces. The best you can do is to capture as accurate a representation of the system as possible, documenting what you did and why.

Evidence Collection Order

Request for Comments (RFC)
Started in 1969, RFCs are a series of notes about the Internet. An Internet document can be submitted to the Internet Engineering Task Force (IETF) by anyone, but the IETF decides if the document becomes an RFC. Each RFC is designated by an RFC number. Once published, an RFC never changes. Modifications to an original RFC are assigned a new RFC number.

Before we get into imaging, let's go over the order in which you process evidence. *Request for Comments (RFC)* 3227, entitled "Guidelines for Evidence Collection and Archiving," lists the following example order of volatility for a typical system proceeding from the volatile to the less volatile:

- Registers, cache
- Routing table, ARP cache, process table, kernel statistics
- Memory
- Temporary filesystems
- Disk
- Remote logging and monitoring data that is relevant to the system in question
- Physical configuration, network topology
- Archival media

This chapter focuses on collecting this type of information and covers the collection of some specific items later in the chapter. In the meantime, let's go over some procedures you want to avoid. An individual who uses the suspect system itself to search for evidence often jeopardizes their investigation. An example of this would be an investigator who used the built-in search capabilities of a Windows computer under analysis to search for and open files. By opening a file to review the file's properties, the access date changes, as illustrated in the first graphic on the next page.

Avoid doing forensics on the evidence copy or running programs, such as XCOPY, that modify the access time of all files on the system. The DOS XCOPY command copies the contents of one hard disk to another. See the second graphic and the one on the following page for a better explanation.

Notice the date and time of the 3com.zip file in the first of the two graphics— 12/23/02, 7:42p. Now, look at the next graphic, which shows the properties of the 3com.zip file, and carefully examine the created and accessed dates, which now differ after the XCOPY command was issued to copy the 3com.zip file. What do

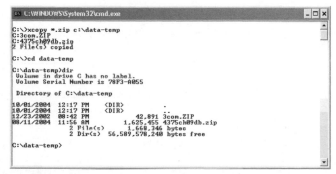

you think just happened to your evidence? These actions have the potential to destroy valuable data as well as prevent any uncovered evidence from being presented in court. It's easy to destroy evidence unintentionally.

Preparing Media and Tools

Use properly prepared media when making forensic copies to ensure that there is no commingling of data from different cases. Sanitize all media that is to be used in the examination process. If you cannot afford new media for each case, be sure that all previous media has been properly sanitized and that it doesn't contain any viruses or other such contaminants. To properly sanitize a drive, all data must be removed and overwritten. The sanitization process writes to active and inactive file space, bad sectors and tracks, the space between the end of a file and the end of a block or sector, file allocation tables, directories, and block maps.

The U.S. Department of Defense, in the clearing and sanitizing standard DoD 5220.22-M, recommends the approach to overwrite all addressable locations with a character, its complement, and then a random character and verify for clearing and sanitizing information on a writable media. Note that this method is not approved for media containing top secret information. To sanitize your media:according to this method, overwrite first with a certain byte value, such as **10101010 - 0x55**, and then with its complement, which is **01010101 - 0xAA**, and finally with random byte values.

During the sanitization process, document your steps. You can sanitize and document the process in several different ways. Software sanitizing programs (such as Maresware Declasfy, Ontrack DataEraser, and WinHex) are available for this purpose. All of them work by overwriting the entire disk, usually several times, in a way designed to destroy all traces of preexisting information.

Besides software programs, some companies have equipment designed specifically for this process. The device shown in the following graphic—the Image MASSter Wipe MASSter—can sanitize nine hard drives, conforms to U.S. Department of Defense Standard DoD 5220.22-M, and gives you a forensic audit printout after wiping each drive.

WinHex

A universal hexadecimal editor used in computer forensics, data recovery, low-level data processing, and IT security.

Next, check to make sure that all forensic software tools are properly licensed for use and that all lab equipment is in working order. Several companies offer forensic imaging tools. The second image shows a handheld software duplication device made for computer disk drive data seizure. Image capture operations can be performed from a suspect's drive to another hard drive.

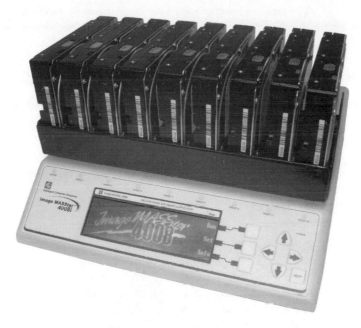

(Photograph Courtesy of Intelligent Computer Solutions, Inc. 2004)

(Photograph Courtesy of Intelligent Computer Solutions, Inc. 2004)

Forensic kits are also available. A kit includes additional tools that you may need for capturing data. The kit shown in the following graphic includes tools made for seizing data from computers that cannot be opened in the field. High-speed data transfers can be performed between any suspect hard drives through the computer's FireWire or Universal Serial Bus (USB) port. The kit includes a bootable CD to boot the suspect's computer and run the acquisition program.

(Photograph Courtesy of Intelligent Computer Solutions, Inc. 2004)

Collecting the Volatile Data

In some cases, evidence that is relevant to a case may only temporarily exist. Evidence can be lost when a computer is powered down. This is why the Guidelines for Evidence Collection start with the volatile data. By capturing the volatile data before unplugging the computer, you get a snapshot of the system at the time you arrived on the scene. The following information should be collected:

◆ System date and time
◆ Current network connections

- Current open ports and applications listening on those ports

- Applications currently running

To capture this information, you should conduct a *live response*. In a live response, the information is collected without impacting the data on the system. The two most practical ways to do this are to save the information to a remote forensic system or to save it to a removable USB drive. To do this, you can use a tool called Netcat, which is a free tool used to create a reliable TCP connection between the target system and the forensic workstation. Using Netcat allows you to get on and off the target system in a relatively short amount of time. You can then analyze the data you have collected at a later time. You can also use Cryptcat, which is an encrypted version of Netcat. With Cryptcat, the traffic is encrypted between the target system and the forensic workstation. By using this type of process, the risk of data contamination or compromise is nearly eliminated.

Let's look at how you can gather some pieces of information with individual tools starting with volatile components first. One of the first places to capture information is from the *Address Resolution Protocol (ARP)* cache. The ARP cache is a table that maintains a mapping of each physical address and its corresponding network address. This information tells you to which other computers the computer you are working with is connected. The ARP cache also indicates the network and hardware addresses. For example:

Address Resolution Protocol (ARP)
A protocol used on the Internet to map computer network addresses to hardware addresses.

You can see that the computer has maintained a listing of the addresses for two additional computers. This information can be especially useful for a forensic situation in which a company may have been attacked from the inside (internally). The information in the ARP cache is held for a maximum of 10 minutes, and then the entries are deleted.

Another useful piece of information is the output of the *traceroute* command. Originally developed for the Unix operating system, `traceroute` is used for many operating systems and most routers. (Windows uses the `tracert` command, which produces the same type of information as `traceroute`.) You use `traceroute` to track the path a packet takes to get to its destination. For example, if you need to request records from service providers in regard to a case, the information contained in the `traceroute` output tells you through which company's routers the data traveled.

traceroute
A command used to see where a network packet is being sent and received in addition to all the places it goes along the way to its destination.

Many firewalls do not issue error messages, so the `traceroute` client might time out. This means that it may stop at a certain point due to firewall restrictions or router rules.

WARNING

The following graphic shows an example of `tracert` command output.

```
D:\WINDOWS\system32\cmd.exe                                              _ □ ×
D:\Documents and Settings\Administrator>tracert lanw.com

Tracing route to lanw.com [206.224.65.194]
over a maximum of 30 hops:

  1    127 ms    124 ms    124 ms  nas24.tempe1.az.us.da.qwest.net [67.3.128.24]
  2    124 ms    124 ms    124 ms  67.3.128.190
  3    124 ms    124 ms    124 ms  tmp-core-02.inet.qwest.net [67.3.128.197]
  4    124 ms    124 ms    124 ms  tmp-core-01.inet.qwest.net [205.171.129.97]
  5    140 ms    140 ms    138 ms  bur-core-03.inet.qwest.net [205.171.8.1]
  6    138 ms    124 ms    139 ms  bur-core-01.inet.qwest.net [205.171.13.5]
  7    122 ms    842 ms    124 ms  bur-brdr-01.inet.qwest.net [205.171.13.10]
  8    137 ms    139 ms    139 ms  sl-bb22-ana-6-2.sprintlink.net [144.232.9.237]
  9    843 ms    140 ms    139 ms  sl-bb20-ana-15-0.sprintlink.net [144.232.1.178]

 10    140 ms    139 ms    124 ms  sl-gw22-ana-9-0.sprintlink.net [144.232.1.42]
 11    140 ms    137 ms    139 ms  sl-timewarner-11-0.sprintlink.net [144.228.173.2
2]
 12    137 ms    140 ms    139 ms  core-02-ge-0-3-0-0.lsag.twtelecom.net [168.215.5
4.101]
 13    171 ms    171 ms    171 ms  core-01-so-0-0-0-0.dlfw.twtelecom.net [66.192.25
5.90]
 14    171 ms    171 ms    171 ms  dist-01-so-0-0-0-0.ausu.twtelecom.net [168.215.5
3.94]
 15    171 ms    171 ms    171 ms  66-192-253-161.gen.twtelecom.net [66.192.253.161
]
 16    171 ms    171 ms    171 ms  64.132.190.46
 17    171 ms    170 ms    171 ms  iocom-pnet-fa1-0.iocomcorp.net [206.224.79.81]
 18    171 ms    171 ms    171 ms  www.lanw.com [206.224.65.194]

Trace complete.
```

You can see that the path a packet took from our computer to the final destination passed through the following companies:

◆ Qwest

◆ Sprint

◆ Time Warner Telecom

◆ IO.COM Corporation

Exercise caution when performing a `route trace`. The packet will go to the suspect's computer, and the suspect could be listening.

Next, an investigator might want to collect a list of the processes running. The following graphic shows the file output of a program called PsService, which we used to capture this data.

```
C:\WINDOWS\System32\cmd.exe                                             _ 日 ×

C:\>psservice !more

PsService v2.12 - local and remote services viewer/controller
Copyright (C) 2001-2004 Mark Russinovich
Sysinternals - www.sysinternals.com

SERVICE_NAME: Alerter
DISPLAY_NAME: Alerter
Notifies selected users and computers of administrative alerts. If the service i
s stopped, programs that use administrative alerts will not receive them. If thi
s service is disabled, any services that explicitly depend on it will fail to st
art.
        TYPE              : 20 WIN32_SHARE_PROCESS
        STATE             : 1  STOPPED
                             (NOT_STOPPABLE,NOT_PAUSABLE,IGNORES_SHUTDOWN)
        WIN32_EXIT_CODE   : 1077 (0x435)
        SERVICE_EXIT_CODE : 0  (0x0)
        CHECKPOINT        : 0x0
        WAIT_HINT         : 0x0

SERVICE_NAME: ALG
DISPLAY_NAME: Application Layer Gateway Service
Provides support for 3rd party protocol plug-ins for Internet Connection Sharing
 and the Internet Connection Firewall
        TYPE              : 10 WIN32_OWN_PROCESS
        STATE             : 4  RUNNING
                             (STOPPABLE,NOT_PAUSABLE,IGNORES_SHUTDOWN)
        WIN32_EXIT_CODE   : 0  (0x0)
        SERVICE_EXIT_CODE : 0  (0x0)
        CHECKPOINT        : 0x0
        WAIT_HINT         : 0x0

SERVICE_NAME: AppMgmt
DISPLAY_NAME: Application Management
Provides software installation services such as Assign, Publish, and Remove.
        TYPE              : 20 WIN32_SHARE_PROCESS
        STATE             : 1  STOPPED
                             (NOT_STOPPABLE,NOT_PAUSABLE,IGNORES_SHUTDOWN)
        WIN32_EXIT_CODE   : 1077 (0x435)
        SERVICE_EXIT_CODE : 0  (0x0)
        CHECKPOINT        : 0x0
        WAIT_HINT         : 0x0
```

Netstat displays the active computer connections. This information provides the investigator with a list of what protocols are running and what ports are open.

Netstat
A utility that displays the active port connections on which the computer is listening.

```
C:\WINDOWS\System32\cmd.exe                                        _ □ x

C:\>netstat -a

Active Connections

  Proto  Local Address          Foreign Address              State
  TCP    XP28GHZ:epmap          XP28GHZ:0                    LISTENING
  TCP    XP28GHZ:microsoft-ds   XP28GHZ:0                    LISTENING
  TCP    XP28GHZ:1025           XP28GHZ:0                    LISTENING
  TCP    XP28GHZ:1026           XP28GHZ:0                    LISTENING
  TCP    XP28GHZ:2869           XP28GHZ:0                    LISTENING
  TCP    XP28GHZ:3302           XP28GHZ:0                    LISTENING
  TCP    XP28GHZ:3308           XP28GHZ:0                    LISTENING
  TCP    XP28GHZ:3549           XP28GHZ:0                    LISTENING
  TCP    XP28GHZ:5000           XP28GHZ:0                    LISTENING
  TCP    XP28GHZ:3302           64.12.30.236:5190            ESTABLISHED
  TCP    XP28GHZ:3308           hal-d021a.blue.aol.com:5190  ESTABLISHED
  TCP    XP28GHZ:3549           skjalda.frisk-software.com:http  CLOSE_WAIT
  TCP    XP28GHZ:15961          XP28GHZ:0                    LISTENING
  TCP    XP28GHZ:3001           XP28GHZ:0                    LISTENING
  TCP    XP28GHZ:3002           XP28GHZ:0                    LISTENING
  TCP    XP28GHZ:3003           XP28GHZ:0                    LISTENING
  TCP    XP28GHZ:5180           XP28GHZ:0                    LISTENING
  TCP    XP28GHZ:netbios-ssn    XP28GHZ:0                    LISTENING
  TCP    XP28GHZ:2869           XP28GHZ.mshome.net:44823     TIME_WAIT
  TCP    XP28GHZ:2869           XP28GHZ.mshome.net:48656     TIME_WAIT
  TCP    XP28GHZ:4392           XP28GHZ.mshome.net:2869      TIME_WAIT
  TCP    XP28GHZ:8348           XP28GHZ.mshome.net:2869      TIME_WAIT
  TCP    XP28GHZ:12374          XP28GHZ:0                    LISTENING
  TCP    XP28GHZ:15402          XP28GHZ.mshome.net:2869      TIME_WAIT
  TCP    XP28GHZ:17802          XP28GHZ.mshome.net:2869      TIME_WAIT
  TCP    XP28GHZ:18324          XP28GHZ.mshome.net:2869      TIME_WAIT
  TCP    XP28GHZ:25804          XP28GHZ.mshome.net:2869      TIME_WAIT
  TCP    XP28GHZ:28535          XP28GHZ.mshome.net:2869      TIME_WAIT
  TCP    XP28GHZ:30279          XP28GHZ.mshome.net:2869      TIME_WAIT
  TCP    XP28GHZ:30955          XP28GHZ.mshome.net:2869      TIME_WAIT
  TCP    XP28GHZ:36589          XP28GHZ.mshome.net:2869      TIME_WAIT
  TCP    XP28GHZ:39371          XP28GHZ.mshome.net:2869      TIME_WAIT
  TCP    XP28GHZ:41260          XP28GHZ.mshome.net:2869      TIME_WAIT
  TCP    XP28GHZ:61625          XP28GHZ.mshome.net:2869      TIME_WAIT
  TCP    XP28GHZ:netbios-ssn    XP28GHZ:0                    LISTENING
  TCP    XP28GHZ:13409          XP28GHZ:0                    LISTENING
  TCP    XP28GHZ:netbios-ssn    XP28GHZ:0                    LISTENING
```

After you collect data from the volatile sources, you might have to shut down the system for transport. Or you might encounter a suspect computer that is already shut down. Proper shutdown is necessary to maintain the integrity of the original evidence. Deciding how to shut down a system can be a tough call. If you disconnect the power cord, you risk losing data, especially on Unix computers. If you shut down the computer through the normal shutdown method, you risk running destructive programs that will delete data upon shutdown.

Creating a Duplicate of the Hard Disk

Whether you choose to literally pull the power plug to immediately stop all disk writes or properly shut down the computer, after the system is off, you can begin the process of creating a duplicate hard disk. You should boot from a floppy boot disk and then create a bit stream of the hard disk. To create a bootable floppy disk, format the floppy and copy the system files to the floppy. To do this, type **c:\format a:\ /s**. These system files will be copied: io.sys, drvspace.bin, command.com, and msdos.sys.

Drive imaging can be performed in several ways:

- ◆ Disk-to-disk image, which is mainly used to test booting
- ◆ Disk-to-image file, which results in faster searches and is compressible
- ◆ Image file to disk, which is used to restore an image

forensically sound
Procedures whereby absolutely no alter-ation is caused to stored data so that all evidence is preserved and protected from all contamination.

Among network administrators, tools such as Norton Ghost are popular for disk imaging. However, this type of software does have some issues associated with it. Ghost does not create an exact duplicate of the disk by default. It re-creates the partition information and the file contents. A hash of the image will almost always result in a value that is different from the original disk and, there-fore, can be excluded from evidence because the Rules of Evidence generally require that you provide an exact duplicate of the original. If you have no other disk-imaging options available, use Ghost. It is better than having no image at all. A white paper on the use of Ghost as a forensic tool is available on the SANS website (`http://www.sans.org`).

forensic duplicate
A process used to copy an entire hard drive that includes all bits of information from the source drive and stores it in a raw bit stream format.

Regardless of whether the examiner performs a direct device-to-device copy of the media or creates forensic evidence copies for examination or restoration, the copy process should be *forensically sound* and the examination of media should be conducted in a forensically sound environment. A forensically sound environment is one in which the investigator has complete control. No proce-dures are permitted without the investigator approving them. The use of physical write-blocking devices or software write-blocking devices can be used to ensure that no writes impact the original media. These devices live between the operat-ing system and disk driver device or are plugged in between the disk controller and the physical disk to block any write requests. Nonforensic software can write to the drive, so using a write-blocking device eliminates this issue. Hard-ware and software write blocking and proper documentation were discussed in Chapter 3, "Computer Evidence."

------- **WARNING** -------

Disk imaging is not the same as using backup software.

mirror image
A process used to create a bit-for-bit copy from one hard drive to another.

Moving on, let's define some terms and features in regard to making full-volume copies of data:

The first step in the forensic examination of a computer hard drive is to create the bit stream copy or *forensic duplicate*. This bit stream image of the original media is then used for the analysis. Bit stream images allow you to capture the slack and unallocated space so the deleted files and file fragments can be recov-ered. Forensic duplicates can be created by using a hardware duplicator, such as the MASSter Solo-2 Professional Plus or the Forensic SF-5000. A *mirror image* can be used when time is of the essence, but you will end up creating a working copy of the mirror image for analysis. Besides hardware solutions, many of the common tools used for obtaining a forensic duplicate are built into the software. For example, the following figure shows this process using WinHex.

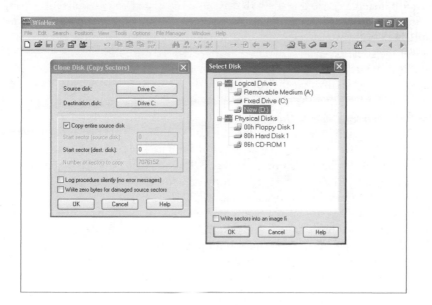

A suspect drive should be duplicated, and then only the copy should be used for investigation, thereby ensuring the integrity of the original drive. The integrity of the original media must be maintained throughout the entire investigation. In a computer investigation, there is no substitute for properly obtaining a good working copy. An investigator must duplicate a disk using sound practices before performing any analysis; otherwise, the investigation can be jeopardized. If not properly done, your analysis will almost certainly alter file access times. Examinations should be conducted on a forensic duplicate of the original evidence, or via forensic evidence files. You saw what happened when XCOPY was used to copy files. Using tools that are unsound can make it more to difficult get the evidence admitted in court.

As explained previously, forensic duplicating includes copying every bit of information on the disk regardless of whether or not it is part of the live data. This image provides a way for an investigator to do an in-depth analysis without fear of altering the original evidence. Keep in mind that the speed of the duplication process can vary greatly based on the physical state of the media, processor, and type of connection used to transfer the data. In addition, some products offer forensic compression and spanning options. *Forensic compression* reduces the image file by compressing redundant sectors. *Spanning across multiple discs* is used when the target media is smaller than the image file. For example, say that

forensic compression
The compacting of an image file by compressing redundant sectors to reduce the amount of space it takes up.

spanning across multiple discs
Breaks the image file into chunks of a certain size so the image file can be backed up onto multiple CD recordable discs or other media types.

you are imaging or cloning a 40GB drive and the drives you are currently using hold 10GB. You will need four drives to copy all the data. Spanning automatically breaks down the image into individual files. Certain programs allow you to preset file sizes, especially if you are using CD-Rs to store the image.

After an image has been made, how can you verify that it was made correctly? How can you be sure that the copy is exactly the same as the original? Verification will confirm that the original media was not changed during the copy procedure. Both the *cyclic redundancy check (CRC)* and the *Message Digest 5 (MD5)* confirmation ensure that the procedure did not corrupt the data. When MD5 is used, even a change to one bit of information on a large drive packed with data will result in a new message digest. By comparing the original disks and copies, these methods can be used in computer forensic examinations to ensure that an image is an exact replica of the original.

Recovering data from a physically undamaged disk can be done by simply hooking it into another system and taking a raw dump of the disk contents to a file. You can then examine the information without fear of damaging the original. Another method is to hook up a sanitized drive to an IDE slot and then image the data. This method is shown in the following graphic.

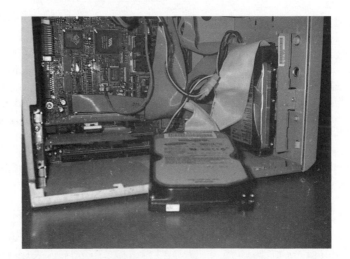

When you need to make an exact image of the hard drive, you should have a variety of tools in your lab. Each tool has its own strengths and weaknesses. You should work with as many tools as you can, and you should become familiar with them so that you know their strong points and how to apply each of them. When choosing tools, one important consideration should be whether or not the tool can detect the presence of a *hardware-protected area (HPA)*. These areas are created specifically to allow manufacturers to hide diagnostic and recovery tools. In essence, a portion of the disk is hidden and can't be used by the operating system. Neither the *Basic Input Output System (BIOS)* nor the operating system can see this hidden area. Companies such as Phoenix Technologies have developed products that can use this protected space to hold utilities for diagnostics, virus protection, emergency Internet access, and remote desktop rebuilds, but they also allow consumers to use this area to hide data. Technically savvy criminals may conceal their activity in this area.

Keep in mind that full imaging will copy each sector of the original media, including, data that is hidden, partially erased, encrypted, data contained in space that was swapped out of memory, and all of the unused space. A full image copy provides a wealth of information for the forensic examiner. When working with a suspect computer and making the image, here are a few steps to remember:

Basic Input Output System (BIOS)
Responsible for booting the computer by providing a basic set of instructions.

- ◆ Record the time and date reported in the BIOS. This can be an important factor, especially when time zones come into play.

- ◆ Remove the storage media (such as hard drives, etc.) before powering on the PC to check the BIOS.

- ◆ Do not boot the suspect machine's operating system, as booting it can destroy evidence.

- ◆ When making the bit stream image, be sure to document how the image was created. This includes recording the date, time, examiner, and tools that were used.

When making the image, make sure that the tool you use does not access the file-system of the target media containing the evidence.

——— *WARNING* ———

- ◆ Use tools that do not make any writes or change the file access time for any file on the evidence media.

After the image is made, the original evidence media should be sealed in an electrostatic-safe container, cataloged, and initialed on the seal. The container should then be locked in a safe room. Anyone who comes in contact with the container should initial it as well. Consider making a second bit stream image of your first image, especially if the seized machine was used in the workplace. The employer may want to put the machine back in service.

Extracting Data from PDAs

In addition to extracting images from hard drives, you can use tools for memory imaging and forensic acquisition of data from the Palm operating system family of personal digital assistants (PDAs). Obtaining a bit-for-bit image of the selected memory region can properly preserve evidence. During this process, no data is modified on the target device, and the data retrieval is not detectable by the PDA user. The memory image of the device includes all user applications and databases, passwords, and various other pieces of information that may be useful in a forensic investigation. One such tool, called Palm dd (or pdd), can retrieve and display the following:

- Card number, name, and version
- Palm OS version
- Manufacturer name
- Processor type
- RAM and ROM size

You can also extract the contents of the memory of a RIM Blackberry wireless PDA. Each device has either 512KB of SRAM or 4MB to 5MB of flash RAM. The SRAM is the same as the RAM on a desktop, and the flash RAM is actually the disk space used to store the file, operating systems, and the applications. In these devices, just as on a hard disk, you can hide databases, data between the application and file partitions, and data in unused filesystem space. A hacker can write a program that accesses a database upon synchronization of the device. The normal user or untrained investigator will have no idea it is there. A bit-for-bit image of the memory can be obtained by using a utility from the development kit called SAVEFS to dump the contents into a file that can be examined by a hex editor.

Image and Tool Documentation

Chapter 3 briefly described the evidence log documentation necessary to produce a good case. Let's go into a little more detail here and specify some particular items of interest that should be documented when you examine a system and make an image of the drive or memory contents:

- Collect the system date and time from the BIOS. You should compare it to a reliable known time source and note any differences.
- Record the drive parameters and boot order, along with the system serial numbers, component serial numbers, hardware component hashes, etc.
- On hard drives, record the number and type of partitions.
- On CDs, record the number of sessions.
- Note the operating and filesystems used on the media.
- Document installed applications.
- Make a full directory listing to include folder structure, filenames, date/time stamps, logical file sizes, etc.

As an investigator, you must be prepared to prove your methods and documentation. The case of United States v. Zacarias Moussaoui, Criminal No. 01-00455-A, is a good example in which a defendant's attorney disputed the authentication of hard drives submitted in discovery. The response explains that the FBI used three methods to image the drives. Page 2 of the response refers to methods approved by National Institute of Standards and Technologies (NIST). This brings up an interesting point. NIST does not approve imaging software. It tests it and publishes the results. The website for the Computer Forensics Tool Testing (CFTT) Project is http://www.cftt.nist.gov/. The "Imaging/Capture Tools" section references these tests for some of the tools.

To read the whole story about the drives in United States v. Zacarias Moussaoui, go to news.findlaw.com/hdocs/docs/terrorism/usmouss90402grsp.pdf **or** notablecases.vaed.uscourts.gov/1:01-cr-00455/docs/67282/0.pdf.

NOTE

Many of today's tools can capture all the information that is needed for an investigation. But as the size of hard drives increase, so does the time it takes to sort through the volumes of data acquired. When a case needs to move swiftly or your disk space is limited, what do you do? In the next section, we'll cover partial volume images and capturing individual types of information rather than doing a full volume image.

Partial Volume Image

With the advent of inexpensive storage, the ability to store large amounts of data and information has become common. A 200GB hard drive is no longer expensive. Larger hard drives and more storage space can cause issues for an investigator who might be working onsite or during emergency cases. Although some utilities include newer technology that speeds up the imaging process, there are times when a full volume image simply isn't possible. Such times might include situations in which data is stored on a mainframe computer.

Evidence is usually found in files that are stored on hard drives, storage devices, and media, so there may be instances in which you don't necessarily want or need the entire operating system. If your suspected criminal is not particularly techno savvy, you might only want the user-created files. Address books and database files can be used to prove criminal association, pictures can produce evidence of illegal activity such as counterfeiting, e-mail or documents can contain communications between criminals, and spreadsheets often contain drug deal lists. In these types of cases, copying only the directories or files that are pertinent to your case might be more efficient than copying the entire drive contents.

Remember that full imaging will copy each sector of the original media, including hidden data, partially erased data, encrypted data, and unused space. A full image copy also takes longer to make, and it will use more space. The full imaging process is less bandwidth-efficient than partial imaging because no matter how small the difference between the source and destination, the entire disk is copied. A partial image is quicker to copy and easier to work with and search.

However, by using a partial image, you run the risk of missing valuable data. If you do not image the whole drive, make sure that you have recorded the partition information.

Real World Scenario

Tales from the Trenches: Imaging

From time to time, I am called upon to image hard drives away from the comfort and security of my lab.

I have had to image hard drives at 2 o'clock in the morning. The reasons for the nocturnal timetables were simple. The employers needed to collect evidence of employee wrongdoing without the employees finding out that the bosses were on to them.

Although this type of exercise might seem extreme, it actually occurs quite often. CEOs and board chairmen have asked me to investigate senior-level executives when they thought that those executives were embezzling or violating Security and Exchange Commission (SEC) regulations.

The procedure to follow for acquiring evidence in this surreptitious manner is actually very straightforward. Don't get caught! For your career's sake, you must also check the company's policy to make sure that you have the legal authority to go into the office and that the company has a policy that shows that the employee has "no expectation of privacy" on his company computer.

Typically, I arrive at the corporate offices in the middle of the night and am met by the director of security, who escorts me to the executive's office and unlocks the door. Usually, I take a couple of "instant photos" of the office and desk to make certain that I leave the room exactly as I found it. I also begin my chain of custody by taking photographs of the computer, including the serial numbers on the case and the hard drive.

I then open up the executive's computer and image the hard drive using a portable forensics acquisition device known as the ImageMASSter Solo 2. Of course, I must "pull the plug" on the computer to power it off before I unplug the hard drive from the PC. After performing the forensics imaging, I then put the computer back together and leave the office exactly as I found it.

This method of forensics imaging requires that you "get it right" the first time. Make certain that you obtain an MD5 hash from the original drive and the forensics image, and that the two hash values match. Unlike performing a forensics image in your lab, you only get one chance to acquire the image successfully when you're in the field. If you don't capture the image successfully the first time, you might not get another chance to do so.

Don't attempt this type of forensics acquisition until you have some experience under your belt and you understand everything that can go wrong while imaging a computer.

When deciding which method to use, evaluate which of the following types of information you may need:

◆ Text documents, spreadsheets, databases, financial data, electronic mail, digital photographs, sound, and other multimedia files

◆ Previously deleted data, deleted folders, slack space data, and intentionally placed data

◆ Extra tracks or sectors on a floppy disk, or an HPA on a hard drive

◆ User settings, functionality of the hardware or software.

◆ Boot files, Registry files, swap files, temporary files, cache files, history files, and log files

The next section briefly describes some of the tools you will encounter in Chapter 8, "Common Forensics Tools." It goes into a little more in depth on some of the other tools that are available for capturing memory and disk images.

Imaging/Capture Tools

Just as with every other step along the way, the forensic software used during the examination should be documented by its version and should be used in accordance with the vendor's licensing agreement. The software should also be properly tested and validated for its forensic use. Several papers are available that document the NIST and the Department of Justice testing of various tools. You can find these papers on their websites. The link for NIST is http://www.cftt.nist.gov/ and the link for the Department of Justice is http://www.ojp.usdoj.gov/nij/sciencetech/cftt.htm. You also need to document all standard procedures and processes that you used, as well as any variations to or deviations from standard procedures. To reliably analyze any system, you must use unmodified, authentic tools. Remember, you should be prepared to testify to the authenticity and reliability of the tools that you use.

Be sure you have the proper tools to perform your investigation, including programs to collect evidence and perform forensic exams. Your tools should be on read-only media, such as a CD-R. In addition, make sure to have a set of tools for every operating system. Your set of tools should include the following:

◆ A program such as ps or PsService for examining processes and services running

◆ Programs such as arp and Netstat for examining the system state

◆ Scripts or programs to automate evidence collection

◆ A program for doing bit-to-bit copies

◆ Programs for generating checksums to verify the image

Forensic tools come in many different shapes and sizes. Besides programs and scripts of capturing data, there are handheld forensic imaging tools such as the one shown previously in this chapter. The successful use of forensic tools stems from being able to identify which are the most appropriate for your environment and becoming familiar with them before the need for an investigation arises.

Utilities

dd utility
Copy and convert utility. Originally included with most versions of Unix and Linux, versions now exist for Windows as well.

The *dd utility* is one of the original Unix utilities; however, it's now used in Linux and Windows as well. It has been around since the 1970s and is probably in every forensic investigator's tool box. The free dd utility can make exact copies of disks that are suitable for forensic analysis, and it can be used as a means to build an evidence file. Because it is a command-line tool, it requires a sound knowledge of Unix/Linux and the Windows command-line syntax to be used properly. You can use dd to copy and convert magnetic tape formats, convert between *ASCII* and *EBCDIC*, swap bytes, and force to uppercase and lowercase. Modified versions of dd intended specifically for use as a forensic utility are also available. The dd copy command has special flags that make it suitable for copying devices, such as tapes.

ASCII
Stands for American Standard Code for Information Interchange. It is a single-byte character encoding scheme used for text-based data.

WinHex is a universal hexadecimal editor for Windows 95/98/Me/NT/2000/XP. WinHex has minimal system requirements, operates very fast, and needs little memory. It is an advanced tool for inspecting and editing various types of files, recovering deleted files or lost data from hard drives or from digital camera cards. The disk and memory imaging features include:

EBCDIC
Stands for Extended Binary Coded Decimal Interchange Code. It is a character encoding set used by IBM mainframes. Most computer systems use a variant of ASCII, but IBM mainframes and midrange systems, such as the AS/400, use this character set primarily designed for ease of use on punched cards.

- Disk editor for both logical and physical disks, including hard disks, floppy disks, CD-ROM, DVD, Zip disks, and Compact Flash

- Supports FAT16, FAT32, NTFS, and CDFS filesystems

- RAM editor used to edit other processes' virtual memory

- Disk cloning

- Drive images that can be compressed or split into 650MB archives

Grave-Robber is part of The Coroner's Toolkit (TCT). The Coroner's Toolkit (TCT) is a collection of tools that are used for collecting and analyzing forensic data on a Unix system. Grave-Robber is a program that controls a number of other tools, all of which work to capture as much information as possible about a potentially compromised system and its files. Using it is an automated way to collect evidence. It gathers evidence, in this order:

- Memory

- Unallocated filesystem

- Netstat, arp, route

- Captures all process data

- Statistics and MD5 on all files and strings on directories

- Configurations and logs

Courts often accept evidence collected by tools that have been used in past trials. Tools such as The Coroner's Toolkit and commercially available forensic software are significant because the data collected by the tools is trusted and can be used as evidence.

NOTE

The Incident Response Collection Report (IRCR) is similar to TCT. The program is a collection of tools that gathers and analyzes forensic data on Windows systems. Like TCT, most of the tools are oriented toward data collection rather than analysis. IRCR is simple enough that anyone can run the tool and forward the output to a forensic investigator for further analysis.

The Legal Imager and reaSsembly Application (LISA) is a DOS-based disk-imaging tool, suitable for making images of hard disk drives for forensic analysis. LISA can clone a drive, validate images on either CD or disk, image a series of floppy disks, or image single partitions. LISA also maintains a database of all located disks. It will also image local disks across networks. In terms of security, LISA utilizes a 32-bit CRC fingerprint for all imaging and rebuilding actions.

Commercial Software

EnCase is a commercial software package that enables an investigator to image and examine data from hard disks, removable media, and some PDAs. It enables examiners to acquire and analyze volatile data, image drives, verify the copy is exact using MD5 and CRC, and mount evidence files of hard drives and CD-ROMs as local drives. It also includes the ability to boot the mounted drive in VMware. Many law enforcement groups throughout the world use EnCase. If an investigation might be handed over to the police or used in a court of law, you should consider using EnCase.

SafeBack is a commercial computer forensics program also commonly used by law enforcement agencies. SafeBack is used to create bit stream backup files of hard disks or to make a mirror-image copy of an entire hard disk drive or partition. It is used primarily for imaging the hard disks of Intel-based computer systems and restoring these images to other hard disks. It is a DOS-based program that can be run from a floppy disk and is intended only for imaging.

Access Data's Forensic Toolkit (FTK) takes a snapshot of the entire disk drive and copies every bit value for analysis. It provides a complete and thorough computer forensic examination of computer disk drives. Suppported filesystems include FAT 12/16/32, NTFS, NTFS compressed, and Linux ext2 and ext3. Like EnCase, it is a full suite of forensic applications.

ByteBack is a suite of tools requiring only a PC with a floppy drive and a DOS 5 or higher boot device. It allows you to block or write protect a device before performing any operation. It can be used to image a disk with a transfer rate of about 200MB per minute, and it supports DOS, Windows, Unix, and Linux filesystems.

The ILook Investigator is a set of computer forensic tools used to capture and analyze images created from computer system hard drives and other external storage media that run on Windows 2000 and Windows XP platforms. The newest version has two components. The IXimager is an imaging tool used to create an image from computers and related media. It is designed and constructed to follow forensic best practices.

ILook is provided free to qualifying agencies throughout the world. Eligible users must be involved in computer forensics and employed by one of the following:

◆ Law enforcement agency whose employees are sworn law enforcement officers

◆ Government intelligence agency

◆ Military agency with authority in criminal and or counter intelligence investigations

◆ Government, state, or other regulatory agency with a law enforcement mission

ILook is directly developed and supported by the IRS Criminal Investigation Division in conjunction with other federal agencies, including the FBI, ATF, and the Department of Defense.

Maresware is a set of programs frequently used by law enforcement, government intelligence agencies, computer forensics experts, and corporate internal security personnel. The NTIMAGE program was still in beta status as of January 2004. The NTIMAGE program is designed to create forensic images while running directly under the Windows NT, Windows 2000, and Windows XP operating systems so that it can image a drive when the system cannot be shut down. It has these additional capabilities:

◆ Creates a disk-to-disk clone or an output image file using either a single file or sections to write to CD

◆ Creates a compressed output file

◆ Creates a drive clone while simultaneously creating an image file

◆ Performs CRC32, MD5, SHA1, SHA2 (256-, 384-, 512-bit) hashes on the drive separate from the imaging, on specific sectors of the drive, or while imaging the drive

SnapBack DatArrest Forensic Suite is an easy-to-operate suite of tools used for forensic data seizures. It works on virtually all IBM-compatible computers and is used for making drive-to-drive or partition-to-drive images. It can perform the following copy methods:

◆ Server or PC hard drives to tape

◆ Server or PC hard drive to removable media

◆ Hard drive to hard drive

◆ Tape to tape

The captured image contains all system software, networking software, associated drivers, software applications, configurations, and data files as well as the BIOS settings for the system so that you have a complete copy of the drive including the operating system, applications, and all of the data.

PDA Tools

Palm dd (pdd) is a Windows-based tool for Palm OS memory-imaging and forensic analysis. The Palm OS Console mode is used to capture memory card information and to create a bit-for-bit image of the selected memory region.

PDAZap is a small application that, when placed on a SonyEricsson P800 (Symbian), will allow you to image the device's flash memory to a Sony Memory Stick Duo. This image in turn can be used by forensic investigators to analyze the data captured.

This is simply a list of the most common tools used to capture data for analysis. Remember that forensic tools come in many different shapes and sizes. The successful use of these tools stems from being able to identify the most appropriate tool for your environment and becoming familiar with them before the need for an investigation arises.

Terms to Know

Address Resolution Protocol (ARP)	forensically sound
ASCII	hardware-protected area (HPA)
Basic Input Output System (BIOS)	Message Digest 5 (MD5)
cyclic redundancy check (CRC)	mirror image
dd utility	Netstat
EBCDIC	Request for Comments (RFC)
forensic compression	spanning across multiple discs
forensic duplicate	traceroute

Review Questions

1. Why do you need to be careful about the utilities you choose to use for disk imaging?

2. What is an HPA?

3. How does a mirror image differ from a forensic duplicate?

4. How can you verify that in imaging the source media, the original media is unchanged?

5. Name a tool that can be used to image the data in the memory of a PDA.

6. What does the Netstat utility do?

7. When collecting evidence, which do you want to extract first: the information in memory or on the hard drive?

8. Why can choosing the method used to shut down a suspect computer be a difficult decision to make?

9. If you need to boot a suspect computer to make an image copy, how should you do it?

10. Name three programs or utilities that can be used to collect forensic images.

Chapter 6

Extracting Information from Data

After you capture the data image as described in the last chapter, what should you look for? How do you figure out what portion of what you have captured is useful to your investigation? What happens if you can't find what you are looking for? These are some of the questions that run through the mind of every forensic investigator.

After the data is imaged, the forensic examiner can search and index all contents of the drive without changing or modifying the data, thereby preserving the evidence. But what if the evidence is missing? Criminals or intruders can use programs to delete e-mail, pictures, and documents. Trained forensic investigators must have tools available that will help them recover this information and help them prepare the evidence for presentation.

In this chapter, you'll look at the process of divining the information you need from the data you have captured. You'll study the process of analyzing and organizing the information you have gathered. You'll learn when to grab the low-hanging fruit and when to dig deeper for data that may or may not exist. You'll study the various types of hidden and trace evidence. Finally, you'll move on to preparing and presenting evidence.

What Are You Looking For?

For a long time he remained there, turning over the leaves and dried sticks, gathering what seemed to me to be dust into an envelope and examining with his lens not only the ground, but even the bark of the tree as far as he could reach.

Dr. Watson on Sherlock Holmes

Finding what you are looking for in a computer forensics investigation can be likened to the preceding quote. There are so many places to look because operating systems vary, application programs vary, and storage methods differ. Computer evidence is almost never isolated. It is a result of the stored data, the application used to create the data, and the computer system that produced the activity. Systems can be huge and complex, and they can change rapidly. Data can be hidden in several locations. After you find it, you may have to process it to make it humanly readable.

Begin the discovery process by installing the disk in your analysis system on an open *IDE port* and boot the system using a floppy boot disk. Be careful not to damage the hard disk when you connect the disk to the IDE cable. IDE interfaces have ports for two devices on each cable. Ideally, you should connect this drive, and only this drive, to the IDE cable on the second IDE interface. Next, identify the partitions on the drive using *fdisk*. Exercise caution when you use `fdisk`; you don't want to risk modifying the partition table or disk label. In `fdisk`, you should select the Display Partition Information option to view the name/number, volume label, size, and filesystem associated with every partition on the hard disk. When you are ready to start examine the imaged data, you'll have many places to explore.

IDE port

The Integrated Drive Electronics (IDE) port is a system-level interface that allows the operating system to recognize a hard drive as part of the system.

Internet Files

fdisk

A utility that can be run from a bootable floppy disk that displays current disk partition information and allows you to repartition a hard disk.

To determine what it is you are looking for, you must first determine the type of intrusion or potential crime and the appropriate response. Let's start with a case that would involve the Internet and pictures. For example, an employee is suspected of illegally accessing and downloading pictures of proprietary designs from a competitor's internal website and using these designs in his own work. Due to the nature of the business, this is a serious offense and you have been called to investigate. After your imaged drive is ready to be examined, open your forensic software and start a case, as shown in the following graphic.

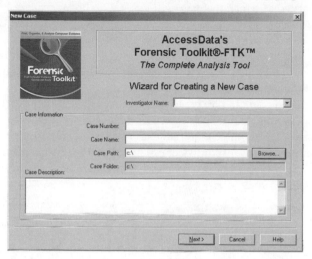

When a user logs on to a Windows NT, 2000, or XP system for the first time, a directory structure is created to hold that individual user's files and settings. This structure is called the profile, and it has a directory that is given the same name as the user. This profile contains several folders and files. Because this case involves searching for images that were downloaded from the Internet, you can begin by adding evidence from the folders where these files may be stored, as illustrated in the next graphic.

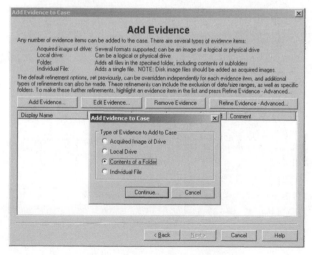

browser

An application that allows you to access the World Wide Web. The most common ones are Microsoft Internet Explorer and Netscape.

Before a *browser* actually downloads a web page, it looks in the Temporary Internet Files folder to see if the information is already there. This is done to increase the speed at which the page will load. Web browsers *cache* the web pages that the user recently visited. This cached data is referred to as a *temporary Internet file,* and it is stored in a folder on the user's hard drive. All of the *HTML* pages and images are stored on the computer for a certain amount of time, or they are deleted when they reach a certain size.

cache

Space on a hard disk used to store recently accessed data in an effort to improve performance speed.

Sometimes, while a user is viewing web pages, other pages pop up at random. These pop-ups can result in files being written to a user's hard disk without their knowledge. For example, many hacker sites have Trojan horses that automatically download objectionable material (that is, files) to an unsuspecting user's computer without the user's knowledge. The following illustration shows how the information in the Temporary Internet Files folder can be viewed through forensic software.

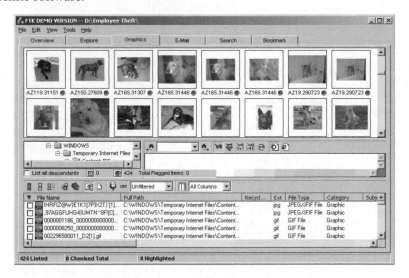

WARNING

Information found in the Temporary Internet Files folder could have been unintentionally downloaded by the suspect.

temporary Internet files

Copies of all the HTML, GIF, JPG, and other files associated with the sites a user has visited on the Internet.

For Netscape files, look in the folder `C:\Program Files\Netscape\Users\` *username*`\cache`. For Internet Explorer files, look in the folder `C:\Windows\ Temporary Internet Files`.

Besides the temporary Internet files, you may also find evidence in the History folder. The History folder contains a list of links to web pages that were visited. The following graphic shows an example of the data contained in this folder (left side of graphic). It also shows why this file may have little or no data. The History feature in Internet Explorer (right side of graphic) has an option for how long the list of visited websites should be kept. The default setting is 20 days. Computer-savvy people often change this default setting to a shorter period, or they click the Clear History button to erase where they have been before they log off the computer.

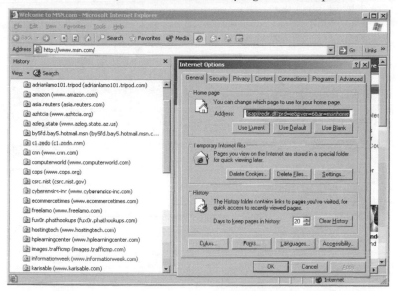

The Cookies folder is similar to the History folder. It holds *cookies* or information stored by Internet sites that were visited by the user. A number of utilities that work with forensic software display the contents of a cookie in an easily readable format. One such utility is CookieView, which you can download from `http://www.digital-detective.co.uk/freetools/cookieview.asp`.

Many applications create temporary files when the application is installed and when a file is created. These files are supposed to be deleted after the application is installed or when you close the document—but sometimes this doesn't happen. For example, each time you create a document in Microsoft Word, the software creates a temporary file (with a `.tmp` extension) such as those shown in the following example. The Properties dialog box, shown on the right side of the

HyperText Markup Language (HTML)
A web-based programming language used to create documents that are portable from one platform to another.

cookies
Small text files that are placed on your computer's hard drive when you browse a website. The file contains a simple unique number that identifies you to the website's computers when you return.

image, indicates that the ~WRL3206.tmp file was created quite a while ago. Temporary files can possibly provide some useful evidence.

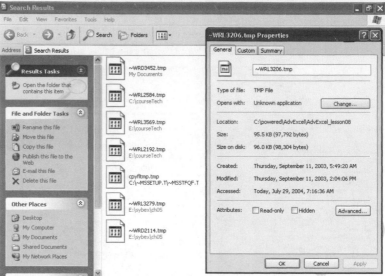

If, during your investigation of the computer, you find no history files, temporary Internet files, or temporary files in the expected folders, you can assume the data has been stored somewhere else so you'll need to dig deeper. Here are some file types you may want to look for:

◆ Files with strange locations

◆ Files with strange names

◆ Filenames with too many dots, or that start with a period (.) and contain spaces

◆ Files that have changed recently

MACtime is a common forensic tool that is used to see what someone did on a system. It creates an ASCII timeline of file activity. Other various tools are also available. You can use X-Ways Trace to analyze a drive to locate information about Internet-related files. Such tools can be very useful in gathering evidence (such as the site visited, last date visited, and cache filename).

E-mail Headers

e-mail header

Data contained at the beginning of an electronic message that contains information about the message.

Let's consider another example. Several employees in a company report that they've received e-mail messages from the support team requesting information to update the database. The e-mail instructs the user to send his logon and password back to the sender. Because IT staff would never request such information from users, you suspect that this is an attempt by an intruder to gain sensitive information. In this instance, one of the first items you may want to look at is the *e-mail header*. The following graphic shows an example of an e-mail header.

```
: Message Source                                                    _ □ ×
X-Message-Info: JGTYoYF78jFg/PDpgUHrmzEkk2Aj8+Qz
Received: from ds9-rml.wellsfargo.com ([159.37.7.78]) by mc11-f28.hotmail.com with Microsoft SMTP:
       Sat, 5 Jun 2004 18:13:48 -0700
Received: from adred.wellsfargo.com by ds9-rml.wellsfargo.com
          via smtpd (for mc11.bay6.hotmail.com [65.54.167.5]) with SMTP; 6 Jun 2004 01:13:48 UT
Received: from kush.wellsfargo.com (kush.wellsfargo.com [10.12.104.9])
      by adred.wellsfargo.com (8.12.9-20030924/8.12.10) with ESMTP id i561DdWp011993;
      Sat, 5 Jun 2004 18:13:39 -0700 (MST)
Received: from kush.wellsfargo.com (localhost [127.0.0.1])
      by kush.wellsfargo.com (Switch-3.0.5/Switch-3.0.0) with ESMTP id i561Daii016134;
      Sat, 5 Jun 2004 18:13:36 -0700 (PDT)
Received: from xcgi-aztem-03.wellsfargo.com (xcgi-aztem-03.wellsfargo.com [10.27.204.146])
      by kush.wellsfargo.com (Switch-3.0.5/Switch-3.0.0) with ESMTP id i561BPii014755;
      Sat, 5 Jun 2004 18:11:25 -0700 (PDT)
Received: by xcgi-aztem-03.wellsfargo.com with Internet Mail Service (5.5.2657.72)
      id <K5DJRRK9>; Sat, 5 Jun 2004 18:11:25 -0700
Message-ID: <2916C09CB2FC9245BF439173B02220A4060E1C2D@msgsw55mrmsp04.wellsfargo.com>
From: hauguelj@wellsfargo.com
To: juliev@messagegate.com
Cc: jessicar@messagegate.com
Subject: Web Conference on MEETING  COMPLIANCE - TUESDAY, JUNE 8, 2004 - 1
         0:00-11:00 AM
Date: Sat, 5 Jun 2004 18:11:16  0700
Importance: high
X-Priority: 1
MIME-Version: 1.0
X-Mailer: Internet Mail Service (5.5.2657.72)
Content-Type: multipart/alternative;
         boundary="----_=_NextPart_001_01C44B62.FF6113DB"
Return-Path: hauguelj@wellsfargo.com
X-OriginalArrivalTime: 06 Jun 2004 01:13:48.0710 (UTC) FILETIME=[85844460:01C44B63]

This message is in MIME format. Since your mail reader does not understand
```

The e-mail header shows the path the message took from its first communi cation point until it reached the recipient. The first point is the *IP address* of the e-mail sender as it was assigned by his or her *Internet service provider (ISP)*. We will go through and analyze the lines in the e-mail header, so you will know how to read and interpret them.

Before communication can begin, a software or device driver must be installed on the computer and a common method of communication or *protocol* determined. A protocol is a set of rules and conventions that governs how computers exchange information over the network medium. In simple terms, a protocol is the language that computers use to talk to each other. For example, if I only speak and understand English and you only speak and understand French, we will not be able to effectively communicate because we don't know what each other is saying or how to talk to each other. The same holds true for computers.

Computers need addresses and protocols to communicate. AN IP address is an identifier for a computer or device on a *Transmission Control Protocol/Internet Protocol (TCP/IP) network*. Networks using the TCP/IP protocol route messages based on the IP address of the destination. An IP address is 32 bits, or 4 bytes, long and is a decimal number between 0 and 255, which is expressed as four octets in dotted decimal notation. For example, 192.00.132.25 is a valid IP address.

IP address
An identifier for a computer or device on a TCP/IP network.

protocol
A set of rules and conventions that governs how computers exchange information over the network medium.

Transmission Control Protocol/ Internet Protocol (TCP/IP) network
A network that uses the TCP/IP protocol.

IP Address Classes

IP address space is divided into five classes: A, B, C, D, and E. The first byte of the address determines to which class an address belongs. The following information will help you understand the different classes of IP addresses:

- ◆ Network addresses with the first byte between 1 and 126 are Class A. They can have about 17 million hosts each.

- ◆ Network addresses with the first byte between 128 and 191 are Class B. They can have about 65,000 hosts each.

- ◆ Network addresses with the first byte between 192 and 223 are Class C. They can have 256 hosts.

- ◆ Network addresses with the first byte between 224 and 239 are Class D. They are used for multicasting.

- ◆ Network addresses with the first byte between 240 and 255 are Class E. They are used as experimental addresses.

Certain ranges are reserved for use on internal networks. These addresses are considered nonroutable on the Internet. Here are the private address ranges:

- ◆ **Class A 10.0.0.0 network**: Valid host IDs are from `10.0.0.1` to `10.255.255.254`.

- ◆ **Class B 172.16.0.0 through 172.31.0.0 networks**: Valid host IDs are from `172.16.0.1` through `172.31.255.254`.

- ◆ **Class C 192.168.0.0 network**: Valid host IDs are from `192.168.0.1` to `192.168.255.254`.

Guide to TCP/IP, Second Edition by Laura Chappell and Ed Tittel (2004) and *IP Addressing and Subnetting, Including IPv6* by J. D. Wegner et al. (1999) are two useful IP addressing references.

Internet service provider (ISP)
Provides a gateway to the Internet and other online services, primarily as a paid service.

Because of its routing ability, TCP/IP has become the protocol of choice for many internal networks as well as external networks, making it a standard. TCP/IP calls for data to be broken into *packets*. The packets are passed across the networks by devices called *routers*, which read the headers to determine if each packet belongs to its network or should be passed on to another network. This is analogous to sending a letter, and the zip code indicates the ultimate destination for the letter. For example, when a person sends a letter from California to New York, the letter may be transported to various post offices before it actually arrives in New York. If the zip code on the letter does not match the zip code for the area in which it arrives, the letter is forwarded on until it reaches its final destination.

You should become familiar with e-mail and web protocols other than TCP/IP. Here is a list of the most common ones you will see:

◆ Domain Name Service (DNS) resolves the names that users type into a web browser to their proper network addresses. DNS is most commonly used by applications to translate domain names of hosts to IP addresses.

◆ File Transfer Protocol (FTP) performs basic interactive file transfers between hosts, allowing files to be uploaded and downloaded.

◆ Simple Mail Transfer Protocol (SMTP) supports basic message delivery services between mail servers.

◆ Post Office Protocol (POP) is used to retrieve e-mail from a mail server. It downloads the messages to the client, where they are then stored.

◆ Internet Message Access Protocol (IMAP) allows e-mail to be accessed from a computer at home, at the office, and while traveling, without the need to transfer messages or files back and forth between computers.

◆ HyperText Transfer Protocol (HTTP) is a low-overhead web browser service protocol that supports the transport of files containing text and graphics.

That's a lot to absorb. But now, we can finally make sense of the e-mail header. Let's look at it again.

packets
Unit of information routed between an origin and a destination. A file is divided into efficient-size units for routing.

routers
Devices used to forward packets.

```
Message Source                                                          _ B X
X-Message-Info: JGTYoYF78jFg/PDpgUHnmzEkk2Aj8+Qz
Received: from ds9-rm1.wellsfargo.com ([159.37.7.70]) by mcii-r28.hotmail.com with Microsoft SMTP
        Sat, 5 Jun 2004 18:13:48 -0700
Received: from adred.wellsfargo.com by ds9-rm1.wellsfargo.com
        via smtpd (for mc11.bay6.hotmail.com [65.54.167.5]) with SMTP; 6 Jun 2004 01:13:48 UT
Received: from kush.wellsfargo.com (kush.wellsfargo.com [10.12.104.9])
        by adred.wellsfargo.com (8.12.9-20030924/8.12.10) with ESMTP id i561DdWp011993;
        Sat, 5 Jun 2004 18:13:39 -0700 (MST)
Received: from kush.wellsfargo.com (localhost [127.0.0.1])
        by kush.wellsfargo.com (Switch 3.0.5/Switch-3.0.0) with ESMTP id i561Daii016134;
        Sat, 5 Jun 2004 18:13:36 -0700 (PDT)
Received: from xcgi-aztem-03.wellsfargo.com (xcgi-aztem-03.wellsfargo.com [10.27.204.146])
        by kush.wellsfargo.com (Switch-3.0.5/Switch-3.0.0) with ESMTP id i561BPii014755;
        Sat, 5 Jun 2004 18:11:25 -0700 (PDT)
Received: by xcgi-aztem-03.wellsfargo.com with Internet Mail Service (5.5.2657.72)
        id <K5DJRRK9>; Sat, 5 Jun 2004 18:11:25 -0700
Message-ID: <2916C09CB2FC9245BF439173B02220A4060E1C2D@msgsw55mnmsp04.wellsfargo.com>
From: hauguelj@wellsfargo.com
To: juliev@messagegate.com
Cc: jessicar@messagegate.com
Subject: Web Conference on MEETING  COMPLIANCE - TUESDAY, JUNE 8, 2004 - 1
        0:00-11:00 AM
Date: Sat, 5 Jun 2004 18:11:16 -0700
Importance: high
X-Priority: 1
MIME-Version: 1.0
X-Mailer: Internet Mail Service (5.5.2657.72)
Content-Type: multipart/alternative;
        boundary="----_=_NextPart_001_01C44B62.FF6113DB"
Return-Path: hauguelj@wellsfargo.com
X-OriginalArrivalTime: 06 Jun 2004 01:13:48.0710 (UTC) FILETIME=[85844460:01C44B63]

This message is in MIME format. Since your mail reader does not understand
```

When a user sends an e-mail message, the message is transmitted to a forwarding server or an ISP's mail server. The mail server adds a `Received:` field to the header of the e-mail message. The message will then be passed through additional mail servers before reaching its final destination. As the message is transferred from server to server, each mail server adds its own `Received:` field to the message header on top of the one from the last server. In the preceding example, the e-mail message has six `Received:` fields, meaning that it passed through six e-mail servers before reaching the recipient. Reading the header from the bottom up, the information on the bottom line starts with an X. This entry is added by the sender's mail server, which records the time (in coordinated universal time, or UTC) the message was received by the mail server from the sender. Moving up the header, the next X entry shows Internet Mail Service and an ID (`5.5.2657.72`). This information indicates that the sender's mail server uses Internet Mail Service and assigned a unique ID to the message. The `Received:` entry, found several lines above, shows when the next server in the relay received the message. As you follow the information up through the message header, you can trace the path the message traveled through the mail servers (in this case, at wellsfargo.com). The entry at the top was inserted by the last server in the relay before the message was delivered to its destination.

This header was obtained from Microsoft Outlook Express. To view header information, click the Properties of the e-mail, click the Details tab, and then click the Message Source button, as shown in the following figure.

E-mail addresses and messages are stored in a file within the mail program's folder. This file usually has a `.pst` or `.pab` extension. Depending on your e-mail software, the steps may vary on how to expose the e-mail header. The following link offers instructions for some of the more popular programs: `http://www.spamcop.net/fom-serve/cache/19.html`.

Deleted Files

The Recycle Bin, which is present on Windows operating systems, is another place where you might find useful data. It acts as a halfway point for deleted files, so that files can be undeleted by the user if required. Information contained in the Recycle Bin includes the original location of files before they were deleted. The date and time of deletion are recorded in this file. When the Recycle Bin is emptied, this file is deleted along with the other files. You may still be able to recover a deleted file's contents if they have not been overwritten.

Most people believe that when they delete something from their computers, they actually erase the document. This is not necessarily true. When a file is deleted, the first character of the filename is changed to a hex E5. Chapter 2, "Preparation—What to Do Before You Start," discussed filesystems and explained that a filesystem keeps a table of contents of the files on the disk. When a file is requested, the table of contents is searched to locate and access the file. When a file is deleted, the actual file is still there, but the table of contents ignores it. We used the Davory Data Recovery utility to recover deleted files from a JumpDrive. The following graphic shows the results.

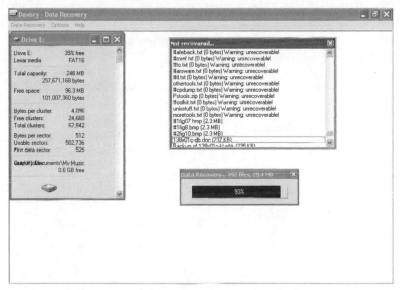

As you can see, the utility recovered 186 files that we thought were deleted. It also shows the names of files that it could not recover. They were unrecoverable mainly because we moved them instead of deleting them. When files are moved, they are simply placed elsewhere so they still exist. This example illustrates that, even when a file has been deleted or moved, you can still find information about that file.

Passwords

Let's examine one last scenario that involves password cracking to access systems. As an investigator, you should know what to look for when a system has been hacked.

Passwords are used for many purposes. Users are often untrained in methods for creating complex passwords, or they have trouble remembering more than one. Therefore, they create one easy-to-remember password and use it for everything.

NOTE

brute force
Systematically trying every conceivable combination until a password is found, or until all possible combinations have been exhausted.

Often, the password file is captured before it can be cracked. On a computer running Windows 98 or an early operating system, passwords are stored in a file with a `.pwl` extension and one is created for each user. On a computer running Windows 2000 Server or Windows Server 2003, the password file is stored in a database called the Security Accounts Manager (SAM). One of the most popular ways of obtaining passwords is by using a method called *brute force*. Several programs use this method. L0phtCrack, Crack, and John the Ripper are some of the more popular ones. If you search the Internet for password-cracking tools, you might be amazed at the amount of information you can find. So, where do you look on a computer after it's been broken into? Let's start with the log files.

All operating systems come with the ability to audit and log events. In the following example, the Windows computer was set up to log success and failed attempts at logons.

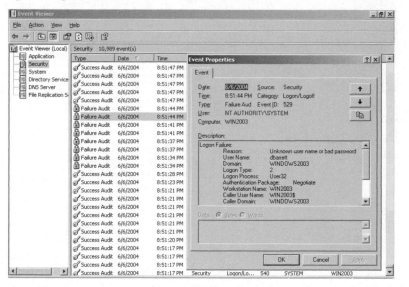

By examining the log, you can see that several failed attempts to log on as Administrator were made within 1 minute. This many failed attempts should alert you that someone could be trying to crack the password. Administrators frequently set the lockout threshold at three to five failed attempts. At the threshold point, the account becomes locked and will thwart further attempts to crack it.

NOTE **Password-cracking programs have legitimate uses. For example, when a network administrator suddenly quits, is fired, or dies, a password-cracking program can allow an authorized person access to the Administrator account.**

There are various other logs that can be reviewed to find evidence of computer entry. On Windows computers, most of these are stored in the `C:\Windows\Security\Logs` directory. In Linux, you will find security logs in the `/Var/Log/`

directory. This contains all root access allowed and all denied access. Other logs are stored in /Var/Adm/Syslog, /Var/Admmessages, and /Var/Adm/Kernel. Log files can be found on routers, intrusion prevention, and intrusion detection systems as well. Telltale signs can appear in logs, offering strong indications that something is amiss. When you are examining security logs to trace an attempt to crack the Administrator password, look for long entries of random characters, password changes, and repeated occurrences of three dots (. . .). These are all suspicious. Look through the log files to make sure you understand what has happened to a system.

Often perpetrators use tools such as *port scanners* to find open ports on a system and then upload a remote access program to take control of the system. The longer they can go undetected, the longer they can use the system as a conduit. Of course when this happens, you may be able to find evidence in the log files.

Your chances of turning up specific evidence might not be very good; therefore, you should look for anything and you might find something. You should be well-informed about recent exploit scripts and newly discovered vulnerabilities. Remaining current can help you identify popular means of attack. Become familiar with how systems work, what services are running, when log entries are created, and what the log entries represent. These areas are where evidence might be found.

port scanners
A program that attempts to connect to a list of computer ports or a range of IP addresses.

How People Think

When determining where the evidence you need might be located, understanding how people think can be helpful. You can't be a good forensics expert or good cop unless you know how criminals think.

According to experts, criminal behavior is often caused by a combination of environmental, psychological, and biological factors. Certain characteristics (such as short attention span, lack of impulse control, and poor home life) are likely predictors of criminal behavior. Although most crimes are committed by young men in their teens and twenties, this is not always the case where computer crimes are concerned.

You must understand your enemy. Hackers are usually unconventional thinkers who refuse to accept No. If they're told a computer wasn't meant to do something, they figure out a way to do it. Seeking to understand why hackers hack, Information-Week.com posted a series of questions on hacker bulletin boards and websites. It published the results in an article titled "The Mind of a Hacker," available online at http://www.informationweek.com/showArticle.jhtml?articleID=16000606. When asked about their motives for hacking, nearly 100 percent of the respondents said they hacked for intellectual challenge, to increase their knowledge, to learn about computers and computing, or to understand how things work. However, 14 percent cited that attacking authority and attacking the government were among their motivations. Seven percent said that they hacked to attack capitalism, break the law, or become famous.

So, what motivates criminal activity?

Anger or Revenge   An estimated 58 percent of companies surveyed reported authorized users and employees as the source of a security breach or corporate espionage act within the past year.

Network Disruption   A denial of service (DoS) attack does just that; it denies service. A DoS attack can completely shut down a network. High-profile sites are frequently hit with denial of service attacks.

Financial Gain   This includes the theft of customer data, corporate trade secrets, competitive information, and actual money.

Data Destruction   This includes the rerouting of data intended for a particular site and overloading a site with data not intended for it, thereby crippling the server and rendering a site useless.

Sexual Impulses   This includes active and passive pedophiles, S&M enthusiasts, serial rapists, and serial killers.

Psychiatric Illness   Personality disorders such as schizophrenia, bipolar disorder, aggression, and depression can motivate a person to hide their illness online where they can interact without physical contact.

signature analysis
A technique that uses a filter to analyze both the header and the contents of the datagram, usually referred to as the packet payload.

When searching for data, you need to realize that users who want to store data and hide its actual content from others may do so in a number of ways. One of the most common ways to hide data is to change the filename and the extension associated with a file so that it doesn't look suspicious. Although it can be difficult to determine if an original filename has been changed, most forensic software can detect a change made to the file extension. An altered file extension is detectable through a method called *signature analysis*. Although searching for text strings is the main method of obtaining digital evidence, using various types of forensic software, you can run searches on the evidence and perform signature analysis at the same time. Basically, signature analysis computes any hash value discrepancies between a file's extension and the file's header. When these two do not match, it may indicate that a more detailed analysis of the file is required.

Picking the Low-Hanging Fruit

The concept of low-hanging fruit comes from the idea that it is much easier to go after information that is readily available than to spend time digging for deeply rooted information; however, identifying the low-hanging fruit can be difficult. Most cybercriminals will walk away from a system that is too hard or takes too long to get into. In some instances, grabbing the low-hanging fruit may be nothing more than choosing the easiest part of the system to deal with at the time.

honeypot
A specially equipped system deployed to lure hackers and track their use of the system's resources.

The cybersecurity field is rife with low-hanging fruit. When a company doesn't install patches for operating systems, or enforce sound password and logoff policies, it leaves its systems vulnerable. Some people believe that if you leave your system unprotected, you deserve to be hacked. And it will happen, because the low-hanging fruit is the easiest to grab. As most network administrators know, more employees will attempt to access a network folder called `private` than a folder named `data`. In a way, this is similar to a *honeypot*. A honeypot is a security resource whose value lies in being probed, attacked, or compromised. In essence, you put low-hanging fruit out there, and then watch to see what happens.

As a forensic investigator, you will have to determine whether the low-hanging fruit provides enough evidence for your case. Let's start with the area that might provide you the evidence you need without doing an extreme amount of investigative work. This is evidence that is readily available, such as computer and log files, especially with unsophisticated criminals. People treat their computers as their own private storage facilities, even if they are the company's computers that they're assigned to use. What people keep in their computers can be incredible—everything from their sexual preferences to evidence of crimes.

Although you should strive to have more than enough evidence, you might be able to use low-hanging fruit to get the information you need. It is at least a good place to start.

Hidden Evidence

In the first section of this chapter, we explored the types of evidence you can look for on a computer. What happens when you can't find any evidence but you know it's there? Chances are it's either hidden, or somewhere in trace evidence. (We'll cover trace evidence in the next section.)

There are various types of hidden evidence. We'll start with document *metadata*. Virtually all applications produce some type of evidence that ordinary users aren't aware of. We will use a Microsoft Word document as an example. As a Word document is written and changed, these changes are normally tracked. To view this information, simply click the file and then choose Properties. The Properties dialog box is shown in the following graphic.

metadata
A data component that describes the data. In other words, it's data about data.

This information can be especially useful to a forensic investigator. For example, say you are dealing with a situation in which a system was compromised and intellectual property was stolen. If the criminal is unsophisticated, you could very well end up with a good lead just by looking at the properties of the new documents. Metadata can be found in most Word, Excel, and PowerPoint documents. Because metadata has become a visible issue, there are ways to delete it. Microsoft released a tool that removes personal or hidden data that might not be immediately apparent when you view the document in your Microsoft Office application. This tool is called `rhdtool.exe`, and it can be found at `http://www.microsoft.com/downloads/details.aspx?FamilyID=144e54ed-d43e-42ca-bc7b-5446d34e5360&displaylang=e`.

Although some metadata is readily accessible through the user interface of each Microsoft Office program, other metadata is accessible only through extraordinary means (for example, opening a document in a low-level, binary file editor such as HexEditor).

Real World Scenario

The Case of Exposed Data

A case in June 2003 involved the infamous British dossier, "Iraq's Weapons of Mass Destruction: the Assessment of the British Government," and how Saddam's intelligence services tried to conceal them from United Nation's inspectors. A good portion of the report was copied from three sources: (1) an article in the *Middle East Review of International Affairs* by Ibrahim al-Marashi, a research associate at the Center for Nonproliferation Studies in Monterey, California, (2) an article by Ken Gause (an international security analyst from Alexandria, Virginia), titled "Can the Iraqi Security Apparatus Save Saddam?" (November 2002), pp.8-13, and (3) an article by Sean Boyne, titled "Inside Iraq's Security Network," in two parts published during 1997. The articles by Gause and Boyne appeared in *Jane's Intelligence Review*. The original sources were exposed by studying the metadata in the document. Most Word document files contain a revision log, which lists the last 10 edits of a document, showing the names of the users who worked with the document and the names of the files under which the document was saved. Revision logs are hidden and cannot be viewed in Word. However, a researcher used a utility to extract and display the revision logs and other hidden information in the files, and then made it public. The researcher used a low-level binary editor to extract this information.

The next method of hiding data we will look at is *steganography*. The goal of steganography is to avoid drawing suspicion to the transmission of a hidden message. Steganography is a special kind of cryptography that makes the presence of secret data undetectable. It encrypts the original plaintext information into a digital image. The least significant bit of each byte of the image can be replaced with bits of the secret message. Such a message can be hidden in a sound file, a graphic file, or on unused spaces on a hard disk. Someone who saves pornography to their hard disk may choose to hide the evidence through this method. In some instances, steganography can be used as a means of covert communication for terrorists. Three of the more popular steganography programs include Hide and Seek and Stealth, which can be used on Windows-based systems, and Steganographic File System (SFS), which is used on Unix filesystems.

steganography
Passing information in a manner such that the very existence of the message is unknown.

You can readily view all the code for a web page simply by opening a web page and choosing the View Source option from the View menu on the toolbar (or right-click anywhere on the web page and choose View Source). The following graphic shows the result of viewing the source code for `http://www.msn.com`.

Most web pages are written in HTML. From looking at the previous graphic, you can see how easy it would be to hide messages or data in web page coding. For example, say I was stealing company secrets and wanted to allow a competitor to access them. I could set up my own website and hide the information in the source code. The competitor could then retrieve the information quite easily.

Most operating systems allow users to hide files based on extensions. Using this feature is as simple as changing the properties of a directory to Hidden on the General tab in the properties in Windows. An untrained eye might never see system files or even the extensions associated with files if the user chose to hide them.

You can hide Unix directories by putting them in existing directories that have a lot of files, such as in the `/dev` directory on a Unix implementation, or by making a directory that starts with three dots (`...`) instead of the normal single or double dot. To hide files on a Unix computer, put one dot in front of the file (for example, `.myfile`). This prevents the file from showing up in the output of a file listing. To see all hidden files, use the `ls` command with the `-a` parameter, like this: `ls -a`.

Hidden disk partitions are the last method of hiding data that we will cover in this chapter. We'll use the example of a *dual-boot system*, in which, essentially, one operating system is hidden from the other. One of our laptops (ComputerA) is set up for dual booting. It can boot to either Windows XP or SuSE Linux. When you view the system in Windows, the Linux partition doesn't show up, mainly because Windows doesn't understand the Linux filesystem. So, Windows acts as though it isn't there. If the bootloader is set up to know about the other operating system, you are given a choice of which operating system to use after a computer boots. This lets you know that more than one operating system is installed. However, some operating systems allow you to choose which operating system to boot to without user interaction. For example, another one of our computers (ComputerB) dual boots either Windows 98 or Windows Server 2003. An ordinary user would not know that Windows Server 2003 is installed because we configured the system to not display the operating systems upon boot. Because Windows 98 can't read the NTFS partition, the partition that Windows Server 2003 is installed on doesn't show when accessing data in Windows 98. This is another example of where an untrained person would have no idea that hidden data might exist. So, we can store files on the Windows 98 drive while booted to Windows Server 2003, and hide the directory so other users have no clue the files are even there. In this instance, the evidence you may be looking for could be stored partially on one partition and partially on another partition. If space allows, you could actually install more than two operating systems.

Several other methods, such as *covert channels*, can be used to hide data. A tool such as Loki can transmit valuable data in seemingly normal network traffic. Loki is a Trojan horse that looks like a stream of pings, but instead it provides a backdoor to the computer on which the client is installed. After the client is installed, it allows communication to occur without being controlled by a security mechanism. Tools such as Loki and other backdoor programs can be found at `http://www.antihackertoolkit.com/tools.html`. Data can also be hidden in the whitespace in documents, behind graphics in documents, and in host-protected areas (HPAs) on drives. These areas of a hard drive are created specifically to allow manufacturers to hide diagnostic and recovery tools, but they can be used to hide data as well.

dual-boot system
A system that has the ability to boot, or start, and run more than one operating system.

covert channels
A method by which an entity receives information in an unauthorized manner.

Real World Scenario

Tales from the Trenches: Hidden Evidence

While many technical methods exist for hiding data (examples include stenography, encryption, and digital watermarking), some of the cases that you work will involve data that was hidden using techniques so simple that any average Microsoft Office user could use them.

I once worked on a case involving two coworkers who transferred information to each other by embedding short messages at the end of Word documents. They changed the color of the text to white so that the message was white text on a white background and appeared invisible to anyone who saw the document.

Another simple technique is to use a nonstandard font to write a Word document. The person receiving the document knows which font is needed to view the text and has that font loaded on their computer. Anyone without that font would see only "garbage" on their screen when they viewed the document.

This last technique was used by an illegal drug supplier. He took a photograph of a handwritten sign that contained the instructions and location of how and where a drug transaction was to take place. The drug dealer hoped that anyone monitoring or "sniffing" his network traffic would be unable to "read" the message. A forensics examiner using the search functionality of any forensics utility would not see the message. The examiner would have to look at the graphics function of the tool to see the message.

These and many other techniques for finding hidden data are taught in the computer forensics course that Warren Kruse and Neil Broom teach for Intense School. For additional information about this training, please visit http://www.intenseschool.com or Neil's website at http://www.trcglobal.com.

Trace Evidence

Trace evidence is a term that applies to all types of physical evidence that may be circumstantial evidence in the trial of a case. Trace evidence, although often insufficient on its own to make a case, may corroborate other evidence or even prompt a confession. Tracing some piece of data present at a crime scene to its origin can assist in an arrest and conviction. Similarly, finding some trace of data from the victim or crime scene on a suspect's computer can have a strong impact on a case.

Computer evidence can be found in file slack and in unallocated file space called *slack space*. Sometimes a good portion of a computer's hard disk may contain data fragments from word processing documents, or almost anything that has occurred in the past. This space can be a valuable source of computer evidence because of the large volume of data involved and because most everyday computer users are unaware of it. In the following graphic, a utility called

trace evidence
Traces of data either left behind or found with a criminal that can be used to prove that a crime was committed.

slack space
The space on a hard disk between where the file ends and where the cluster ends.

Karen's Disk Slack Checker was used to check the slack space on a computer. As you can see, there is quite a bit.

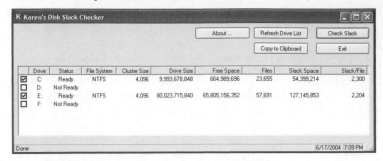

Slack space is a result of how data is written to disks. Operating systems normally write in clusters. Clusters are made up of blocks of sectors. Even if the actual data being stored requires less storage than the cluster size, an entire cluster is reserved for the file. For example, say that the cluster size is 32KB and you create a file that is 2KB. That 2KB file is allocated 32KB of space; therefore, 30KB is unused. Let's go a bit further and say that you create a 31KB file. You decide that you no longer need the file and delete it. At some point in the future, you create another file that is 4KB. When the system is looking for a location to write this new 4KB file, it finds the space from the old 31KB file that you supposedly deleted and places the data there. Now you have 4KB of the new data plus the remainder of the old data in the same space. So, to recover data, you would trace evidence from the first file in the new file. These pieces of files or file fragments can contain a significant amount of information.

swap file
Space on the hard disk used as the virtual memory extension of a computer's actual memory.

On computers running a Microsoft Windows operating system, large quantities of evidence can be found in the Windows *swap file*. In Windows 2000, XP, and Server 2003 the file is named PAGEFILE.SYS by the operating system. This is a memory management function within the Windows operating environment. It uses space on the hard drive to swap data in and out of memory in order to better utilize the memory. Swap space can be found on computers running Linux as well. In fact, when you install the operating system, you actually specify a Linux swap file partition.

Trace evidence can also be found on backup tapes. This option is frequently forgotten. If files are deleted from computers, they might still be available on backup tapes. Most companies have some type of backup tape rotation and perform full backups at least once per quarter. Third-party service providers might back up e-mail and keep the tapes of that e-mail backup for some period of time. Even though the files may be gone from the computer, in most cases, e-mail systems are backed up and you have the option of finding out how long the messages are kept.

Fax buffers, printer buffers, and floppy disks can hold trace data as well. Often people put one or two files on a floppy disk and tend to forget about them, usually accruing a sizeable number of partially filled disks. Floppy disks can be imaged and then processed. The following graphic shows a picture from The Legal Imager and reaSsembly Application (LISA).

Terms to Know

browser	IP address
brute force	metadata
cache	packet
cookie	port scanner
covert channel	protocol
dual-boot system	router
e-mail header	signature analysis
fdisk	slack space
honeypot	steganography
HTML	swap file
IDE port	trace evidence
Internet service provider (ISP)	temporary Internet file
Transmission Control Protocol/ Internet Protocol (TCP/IP) network	

Review Questions

1. What set of rules and conventions governs how computers exchange information over the network medium?

2. Name some factors that motivate criminal activity.

3. As a Word document is written and changed, these changes are tracked and produce a type of evidence that is called what?

4. What types of file should arouse your suspicion when you are examining data?

5. Why should you look at the header of an e-mail?

6. What is steganography?

7. What method can you use to determine if the extension of a file has been changed to avoid suspicion?

8. If you are investigating a case that involves the Internet and pictures, what three areas could reveal the Internet habits of the suspect?

9. What is a dual-boot system?

10. Name three types of trace evidence.

Chapter 7

Passwords and Encryption

Computer forensics is all about perspective and process. Your main perspective must be as a neutral party in all activities. You approach each investigation the same way, ensuring that it is repeatable and sound. After you identify and preserve the evidence, you analyze it to determine its impact on your case. In many situations, the actual evidence is protected from unauthorized disclosure. When searching for evidence, you, the investigator, might be unauthorized from the data owner's perspective. It all depends on who owns the computer and who hired you. You need to know how to exercise your granted authority and access data that is protected. The two most common controls used to protect data from disclosure are access controls and encryption. This chapter covers the most common type of access control, the password, and the general topic of encryption.

You'll learn basic techniques to obtain passwords and access encrypted data. This chapter won't cover the mathematics behind encryption in much detail. Such a discussion is beyond the scope of this book. However, it will cover the basic types and uses of encryption and how to "get to" data that has been encrypted.

Passwords

user ID
A string of characters that identifies a user in a computing environment.

Computer users must commonly provide a *user ID* to log on to a system. The user ID identifies the specific user and tells the security subsystem what permissions to grant to the user. Unfortunately, some computer users are disingenuous and will provide another person's user ID. By doing so, the new user can perform actions that will be traced back to the user ID owner's account.

Real World Scenario

Who Are You, Really?

Fred is an enterprising university student who enjoys testing the limits of his school's computer use policy. The policy clearly states that users can use only their own IDs to access the computer system. If Fred wants to create some mischief on the university's computer system, he could ignore the policy and use Mary's user ID to access the system. In effect, he could pretend to be Mary. With no controls in place to stop him, Fred could be quite mischievous and it would appear that Mary was the guilty party. A control would be anything that stands between Fred and Fred's unauthorized actions. Actually, there is one control to deter him. The university's computer use policy is an administrative control. Such controls dictate proper behavior and the penalty of noncompliance, but they do not stop unauthorized actions in Fred's case.

password
A string of characters used to authenticate a user by comparing the provided value to a value that has previously been stored and is associated with a specific user ID. Passwords are routinely stored when an account is created or the password is changed.

There is a simple solution. The user ID provides the identification of a user. Another piece of information, one that only the true user should know, provides the authentication that the user is who she says she is. The most common authentication item is the *password*. A user provides a user ID and the proper password. The security system validates that the password provided matches the user ID. If the two match, the user is authenticated and trusted.

During an investigation, investigators commonly need access to one or more computer accounts. When a suspect or other knowledgeable user is cooperating with the investigation, obtaining a user ID and password can be as easy as asking for it. Never forget to try the simple approach. Always ask for any passwords you need. When passwords are not readily available to you, you have three alternatives for acquiring them. You can:

1. Find passwords
2. Deduce passwords
3. Crack passwords

Understand when and how to use each of these techniques. Although passwords are the most common user authentication technique, they can be quite unsecure. The next sections look at each password recovery technique and show you just how available some passwords can be.

Finding Passwords

By far the easiest way to obtain a password is to simply ask someone who knows the password to provide it to you. If asking nicely doesn't work, try social engineering. Try an approach that builds trust with a person who knows information you want. The person could be anyone who knows the password. You could call and pretend to be a member of the network administrator team. A simple statement like, "Hi, this is Tom from network support. Your computer looks like it is sending out a virus to other computers. I need to log on to stop it. What is the user ID and password you used to log on this morning?" Far too many people would provide the requested information. As long as you have permission to conduct social engineering activities, you can proceed. As long as you abide by any applicable security policies, encouraging a suspect to give you the information you need is perfectly fine. Law enforcement officials are good at doing this. Ask them for help, especially if this is a criminal investigation.

If you cannot ask, or the person who knows the password is not cooperating, you can still use a simple approach. There are two basic types of passwords: those that are easy to remember and those that are hard to remember. With more people becoming aware of security issues, passwords tend to be more secure than in times past. Most people equate password complexity with security. That is, long, hard-to-remember passwords appear to be more secure than simple ones.

TIP

Longer passwords can be less secure than shorter ones. Passwords that expire frequently are less secure as well. The reason is that when a user must use a password that is too hard to remember, he will often write it down. The hassle of retrieving a lost password often encourages users to keep their own sticky notes with passwords written on them. When trying to create strong passwords, allow users to create ones they can remember.

Because a password is a string of characters that authenticates a user's identity, it is important that the user always have access to the password. The more complex a password is, the more likely it is that the user has it written down or otherwise recorded somewhere. Look around the computer for written notes. You will find sticky notes with passwords written on them in a surprisingly large percentage of the sites you investigate. Here is a list of common "hiding places" for password notes:

- On the monitor (front, sides, top, etc.)
- Under the keyboard

- In drawers (look under pencil holders and organizers)
- Attached to the underside of drawers
- Anywhere that is easily accessible from the seat in front of the computer but not readily visible
- Personal digital assistants (PDAs)
- Obvious files on the hard disk (such as `passwords.txt`)

Don't dismiss this important method of finding passwords. Few people trust their memories for important passwords. They are probably written down somewhere.

Deducing Passwords

So, you've looked all around the physical hardware and desk but you still cannot find the password you are looking for. You still have other options to obtain passwords. In spite of all the common rules to create "strong" passwords, the rules are routinely broken. If you are trying to guess a password, try the obvious ones. The more you know about the real user, the better chance you have of guessing the password. Try some of these ideas:

- User ID
- Birthdate
- Social security number
- Home address
- Telephone number
- Spouse/children/friend name
- Pet name
- Favorite team name or mascot
- Common word or name from a hobby

NOTE

Use this section as a lesson for creating your own passwords. Because so many people ignore password best practices, take it upon yourself to be unique. Take the time to create strong passwords and keep them secure.

Although guessing a password is possible, it is not very productive in most cases. Don't spend a lot of time guessing a password. Only try it if you have a pretty strong hunch that you'll be successful. I solved a password puzzle one time by piecing several pieces of information together. I found a note that read "me 4 her -7." I tried several combinations and hit on a password that consisted of the subject's initials, "ajd," and his wife's initials, "rgd." The password was "ajd4rgd7. (In case you are wondering, this was not the actual password. The initials were changed to protect the innocent.)

Even though you might get lucky once in a while, really "guessing" a password is not very common. It looks good in the movies, but it doesn't happen that often in the real world. Deduced passwords normally come from piecing several pieces of information together. For instance, when analyzing a subject's activity, keep track of visited websites and locally protected applications. You might find a cookie for a recently visited website that stores an unprotected password. Many people use the same passwords repeatedly, so if you find an unprotected password for one resource, try it in other areas.

As much as it violates good security practices and common sense, you'll find the same password often used to protect a secured server and to subscribe to a website's news services. If you can find a password, see if it is used elsewhere.

<table>
<tr>
<td>When you're poking around and guessing passwords, you might end up locking the resource you are attempting to access due to excessive failed logon attempts. Always make sure you have at least two copies of media. If you corrupt one copy, you can always make a new working copy from your second image. You never want to explain to the judge that you had to check out the original media from the evidence locker twice because you messed up the first copy.</td>
<td>*NOTE*</td>
</tr>
</table>

Up to now, our password discussion has focused on ambiguous strategies. Finding, guessing, or deducing a password is more of an art than a science. It involves knowing your subject and knowing how people think. It might take a lot of homework, but it is fun and can yield that gold nugget that opens up the evidence you need.

Cracking Passwords

The last method of obtaining a password is the most technical and complete. When you cannot find a password by any other means, you can try the process of *password cracking*. Cracking a password involves trying every possible password combination, or every combination in a defined subset, until you find the right one.

password cracking
Attempting to discover a password by trying multiple options and continuing until a successful match is found.

Different utilities allow you to crack passwords online or offline. The utilities employ several different methods. Because older Unix systems stored encoded passwords in a single file, the /etc/passwd file, several utilities emerged that would try different combinations of password strings until they found a match for each line in the file. All you had to do was copy the /etc/passwd file to your own computer, launch the password cracker, and let it run.

This approach became so popular and dangerous that newer flavors of Unix go to great lengths to hide encoded passwords in another file, the /etc/shadow file, that has highly restricted access permissions. If you have access to a computer running Unix or Linux, look at the /etc/passwd file. The x character between two colons indicates that the actual password is stored in the shadow file. For example, here is what a line from the /etc/passwd file would look like if you are using password shadowing (notice the "x" after the user name, msolomon):

Real World Scenario

The Contract Ends Now!

Several contractors were working at a manufacturing plant in southern California. We were hired to fill various functions, including project management and application development. The project goal was to modify a manufacturing software package to meet the client's specific needs. One morning the company's system administrator noticed that his assigned IP address was in use when he booted his computer. After a couple comments under his breath, he rebooted again and found that the IP address was available. He took note of the people who were in the office that morning and started doing a little investigative work on his own to find out if anyone was using his IP address. He found that a particular contractor had installed a common password cracker in his home directory. A further look at the contractor's history file showed that he had been engaging in attempts to crack the system's password file.

The system administrator immediately removed the contractor's access and had him terminated that very morning. The company's policy regarding appropriate use of computing systems forbade any use of password-cracking software and provided the grounds for immediate termination.

msolomon:x:517:644::/home/msolomon:/bin/bash

Take a look at some of these password-cracking utilities for more details on how they work (an Internet search for these utilities can provide up-to-date URLs):

◆ Jack the Ripper

◆ Crack

◆ LASEC

◆ L0phtcrack (LC4)

Anytime you find passwords stored in a file or database, you can use offline password-cracking techniques. If you cannot find the password repository or do not have access to it (it might reside on another system), you will need to try online password cracking. Online password cracking is much slower and may fail for more reasons that offline cracking. An online password-cracking utility attempts to pass logon credentials to a target system until it finds a successful user ID/password pair. The number of attempts that are necessary to find a password is the same as an offline cracking utility, but the act of passing the logon credentials to another process requires substantially more time. If the target computer is remote to the client password-cracking utility, network propagation further slows the process and adds to the possibility of failure.

Regardless of the type of utility you decide to use, there are three basic approaches, or "attack types," that password-crack utilities employ.

Unauthorized Password Cracking is Illegal

Never attempt to crack passwords unless you have specific, written authority to do so. The person or organization who owns the computer system can provide the necessary permission. Without written permission, you may be at risk of substantial civil and criminal penalties. Ensure that your permission is in writing, has been granted by someone with the authority to do so, and is specific as to what you are allowed to do. The main reason to crack a password is to obtain evidence that is protected by that password. You can obtain permission to crack a password from the computer owner or a court. In cases where the computer owner is unwilling to provide the permission to crack a password, a court order will suffice.

Dictionary Attack

A *dictionary attack* is the simplest and fastest attack. The cracking utility uses potential passwords from a predefined list of commonly used passwords. The list of passwords is called the password dictionary. The larger the dictionary, the higher the probability the utility will succeed. A little research on the Internet will yield several password dictionaries of common passwords.

dictionary attack
An attack that tries different passwords defined in a list, or database, of password candidates.

The reason such an attack works so well lies in human nature. People tend to use common, easy-to-remember passwords. Look through a password dictionary to see if you are using any common passwords. If your password is in a password dictionary, your password is too weak and should be changed.

Brute Force Attack

On the other end of the spectrum is the *brute force attack*. A brute force attack simply attempts every possible password combination until it finds a match. If the utility attempts to use every possible combination, it will eventually succeed. However, the amount of time required depends on the complexity of the password. The longer the password, the more time it will take to crack.

brute force attack
An attack that tries all possible password combinations until the correct password is found.

Brute force attacks should not be your primary method of cracking passwords for two reasons. First, brute force attacks are slow. They can take a substantial amount of time. If you do not know the length of the password, you will have to try many, many combinations that will not succeed.

Second, the location of the client, resource server, or authentication credentials (passwords) may be on different computers. If so, the brute force attack will generate a huge volume of network traffic. Excessive network traffic and multiple failed logon attempts may have a tangible impact on the network. Unless you can set up a copy of the suspect network in your lab, you may not be allowed to launch a brute force attack.

Hybrid Attack

hybrid attack
A modification of the dictionary attack that tries different permutations of each dictionary entry.

The final type of attack, the *hybrid attack*, combines the dictionary and brute force attacks. In a hybrid attack, the utility starts with a dictionary entry and tries various alternative combinations. For example, if the dictionary entry were "lord," the hybrid attack utility would look for these possible alternatives:

◆ Lord

◆ l0rd

◆ 1ord

◆ 10rd

And many, many others. As you can see from this list, it is common to obscure passwords from dictionary words by replacing the letter "l" with the digit "1," or replacing the letter "o" with the digit "0." Don't do this. Even simple cracking utilities know this trick. Regardless of the type of utility you choose, there is a tool that can help you get the passwords you need to access evidence.

The next section addresses one of the methods of protecting data from disclosure—encryption.

Encryption Basics

After you gain access to the files that contain evidence you need, you may find that the file itself is unreadable. As computer investigators begin to use more sophisticated tools to investigate, the bad guys, and good guys alike, have learned to take more sophisticated steps to hide information. One method used to hide information is to modify a message or file in such a way that only the intended recipient can reconstruct the original.

cryptography
The science of hiding the true meaning of a message from unintended recipients.

Cryptography is used to scramble the contents of a file or message and make it unreadable to all but the intended recipient. In the context of a computer investigation, the investigator is an unintended recipient. The word cryptography comes from the Greek word "krypto," which means "hidden," and "graphein," which means "to write."

encrypt
Obscure a message's meaning to make it unreadable.

Although cryptography's importance has become more widely acknowledged in recent years, its roots can be traced back 5,000 years to ancient Egypt. The Egyptians used hieroglyphics to document many rituals and procedures. Only specially trained agents could interpret these early hieroglyphics.

decrypt
Translate an encrypted message back into the original unencrypted message.

Later, around 400 B.C., the Spartans used an innovative method to *encrypt*, or hide, the meaning of military communication from unauthorized eyes. They would wrap a strip of parchment around a stick in a spiral, similar to a barber's pole. The scribe would write the message on the parchment and then unwind it from the stick. With the parchment stretched out, the message was unintelligible. In fact, the only way to read the message, or *decrypt* it, was to wrap the parchment around another stick of the same diameter and equal, or greater, length. The "secret" to reading the message was the dimensions of the stick and the knowledge of how to wrap the parchment. Anyone who possessed these two components could read a secret message.

Roman Emperor Julius Caesar was the first to use a cryptography method, or *cipher*, similar to the decoder rings that are popular as children's trinkets. He used the method, called a *substitution cipher*, to send secret messages to his military leaders. In this cipher, a message is encrypted by substituting each letter of the original message with another letter. A substitution table provides the static mapping for each letter. The recipient decrypts the message by reversing the process. The recipient translates each letter from the encrypted message to the original letter by reading the translation table backward. The resulting message is identical to the original. One must posses the translation table to encrypt and decrypt messages using a simple substitution cipher. The main weakness of the cipher is the table itself. Anyone who discovers or acquires the translation table can decrypt messages.

Although the algorithms used in today's encryption implementations are far more complex than the Caesar cipher, the basic approach and goals are the same. Let's look at some common practices in encryption.

cipher
An algorithm for encrypting and decrypting.

substitution cipher
A cipher that substitutes each character in the original message with an alternate character to create the encrypted message.

Common Encryption Practices

In general, encryption provides:

Confidentiality   Assurance that only authorized users can view messages

Integrity   Assurance that only authorized users can change messages

Authentication   Assurance that users are who they claim to be

Nonrepudiation   Assurance that a message originated from the stated source

To the computer forensics investigator, the most common exposure to encryption is when confronted with encrypted files. It is becoming more common for subjects to use encryption to hide the contents of files. Although there are other valuable uses of cryptography, such as securing communication transmissions and authenticating the originator of a message, they are beyond the scope of this discussion. Our main concern is to understand the basics of cryptography and how to react when you encounter encrypted files. Most commonly, you will recognize encrypted files when an attempt to open a file with a known extension fails. For example, you attempt to open an encrypted Microsoft Word document in Microsoft Word, but you receive an error. The text of the error tells you that you need a converter to read the file. In other words, Microsoft Word does not recognize the encrypted contents of the file. Another sign of encrypted files is a collection of meaningless filenames. Many encryption utilities change the filenames to hide the meaning and type of the file.

There are two main types of encryption algorithms. An algorithm is the detailed sequence of steps necessary to accomplish a task. The first type of encryption algorithm uses the same value to encrypt and decrypt the original text. Such algorithms are called "private key algorithms." The second type of algorithm uses one value to encrypt the text and another value to decrypt it.

These algorithms are called "public key algorithms." Each type has strengths and weaknesses, but they both serve the same function.

Encryption algorithms transform an original message, called *plaintext*, into an encrypted message, called *ciphertext*. The algorithm also generally provides a method for reversing the process by translating the ciphertext back into the original plaintext message. Here's an example. Suppose you want to send a message to a particular recipient that no one else can read. You choose to substitute each letter with an alternative letter. You take each letter in the original message and replace it with the letter that is three positions higher in the alphabet. So, you replace an "A" with a "D," and replace a "T" with a "W." To keep things simple, you rotate around the end of the alphabet so you replace a "Y" with a "B." This is exactly how Caesar's cipher worked.

Our plaintext message is: Hello there.

Our encrypted message is: Khoor wkhuh.

All you have to do to decrypt the message is to reverse the process. Take each letter and replace it with the letter that is three positions lower in the alphabet. By doing so, you end up with the original message. The only requirement for this method to work is that both the sender and the receiver must agree on the specific rules. You'll see how that can cause some problems in a later section.

All algorithms use some type of value to translate the plaintext to ciphertext. Each algorithm performs steps using the supplied value to encrypt the data. The special value that the algorithm uses is the encryption key. Some encryption algorithms use a single key, while others use more than one. In the Caesar cipher, the key value is 3. The key value tells how many positions to add to the plaintext character to encrypt and the number to subtract from the ciphertext character to decrypt. As long as the sender and receiver both use the same algorithm and key, the process works.

Private Key Algorithms

The easiest type of encryption to understand and use is the *private key algorithm*. This type of algorithm is also called a *symmetric algorithm*. It is symmetric because the decrypt function is a simple reversal of the encrypt function. It looks the same on both sides.

plaintext
The original unencrypted message.

ciphertext
The encrypted message.

private key algorithm
An encryption algorithm that uses the same key to encrypt and decrypt.

Symmetric Algorithm

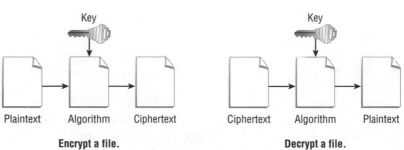

Encrypt a file.   Decrypt a file.

This type of algorithm is simple and fast. It is the type of algorithm most frequently used for file encryption. All you need is the key and the algorithm, and you can decrypt the file. Although this type of algorithm is common for encrypting files, it can be more difficult to use for message encryption. The problem is the management of the encryption key. You need the key to decrypt a file or message. You have to find a way to get the key to the recipient in a secure manner.

If someone is eavesdropping on all communication between you and your recipient, they will likely intercept the encryption key as well as any encrypted data. With the key, they will be able to decrypt files at will. For the purposes of computer forensics, you will more likely find encrypted files on media that were encrypted using a symmetric algorithm. The simple reason for this is that symmetric algorithms are fast and easy to use. Because you have only a single key, you don't need to specifically generate keys and then keep up with multiple values. That means you need the single key.

symmetric algorithm
Another name for a private key encryption algorithm.

Don't infer that computer investigators only deal with file encryption using symmetric keys. You can, and will, run into various types of encryption and algorithms. Encryption is a discipline in itself. This section just highlights the issues you are most likely to encounter.

NOTE

Key discovery is similar to password discovery. You need to find, deduce, or crack the encryption to get to the key. The biggest difference between cracking passwords and cracking encryption keys is that the latter is almost always harder and takes far longer. The simple explanation is that the plaintext for a password is generally limited to a couple dozen characters. The plaintext for a file could be gigabytes. Cracking the encryption key takes substantially longer than cracking a password.

Although many well-known symmetric encryption algorithms exist, here are a few of the more common ones:

- Data Encryption Standard (DES)
    - First published in 1977
    - Adopted by the U.S. government standard for all data communications
    - Uses 56-bit key (plus eight parity bits)
    - Old and weak by today's standards
- Triple DES (3DES)
    - More secure than DES
    - Uses three separate DES encryption cycles
- International Data Encryption Algorithm (IDEA)
    - International standards designed to be stronger than DES
    - Keys are longer than DES keys (start at 128 bits)

- Blowfish
  - Stronger alternative to DES and IDEA
  - Key size can vary from 32 bits to 448 bits
- Skipjack
  - Optimized for embedded operation in chips
  - Used in the Clipper and Capstone chips
  - Key size is 80 bits
- Advanced Encryption Standard (AES)
  - The latest, strongest standard
  - Based on the Rijndael cipher
  - Key sizes are 128, 192, or 256 bits

Each algorithm in the previous list can effectively encrypt files. The list is sorted in general algorithm strength order. For more security, use a newer algorithm and a secure key. Research some of the common encrypt/decrypt utilities and compare the algorithms they support.

Public Key Algorithms

public key algorithm
An encryption algorithm that uses one key to encrypt plaintext and another key to decrypt ciphertext.

passcode
A character string used to authenticate a user ID to perform some function, such as encryption key management.

The other type of encryption algorithm is the *public key algorithm*. This type of algorithm is also called an *asymmetric algorithm* because the decrypt process differs from the encrypt process. The asymmetric encryption algorithm addresses the issue of key distribution. Two keys are required to complete the encrypt-decrypt process.

The process starts with key generation. The software that encrypts plaintext will also have a utility to generate keys. When asked, the user supplies a *passcode* and the utility uses the passcode to generate a private key and a public key. You must keep the private key secret and not disclose it to anyone. You can distribute the public key to anyone. The encryption algorithm uses one key to encrypt plaintext and the other key to decrypt the resulting ciphertext.

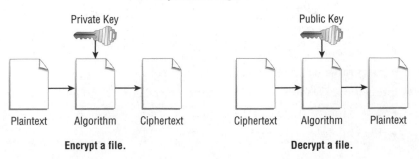

Asymmetric Algorithm

Private Key   Public Key

Plaintext → Algorithm → Ciphertext   Ciphertext → Algorithm → Plaintext

Encrypt a file.   **Decrypt a file.**

The resulting process allows you to encrypt data with your private key. Anyone who has the public key can decrypt the file or message. This process provides the ability to verify that a file or message originated from a specific person. If you can decrypt a file with Fred's public key, Fred had to encrypt it with his private key. Although this is great for sending messages and verifying the sender's identity, it doesn't provide much value if all you want to do is encrypt some files.

The most common type of encryption you will run into during evidence analysis is file encryption. For that reason, we focus on symmetric key algorithms.

asymmetric algorithm
Another name for a public key encryption algorithm.

Steganography

Both symmetric and asymmetric encryption algorithms share one common trait: you can tell a file is encrypted by examining its contents. The fact that a file is encrypted draws attention to its value. An investigator wants to decrypt a file just because it is encrypted and, therefore, probably contains some data of value.

There is another approach. Steganography is the practice of hiding a message in a larger message. The original message, or file, becomes the carrier and the hidden message is the payload. Large pictures and sound files make good carriers because they allow the payload to be inserted without changing the original file in an obvious way. Steganographic utilities insert the bytes of the payload into the carrier by slightly changing bytes in the carrier file. If the changed bytes in the carrier are separated by enough original data, the change is unnoticeable. If every 100th pixel in a picture were changed by a single shade of color, the resulting picture would appear identical to the original.

Steganography allows users to embed desired data into seemingly innocent files and messages. A secret message embedded in a picture file can be sent via e-mail as an attachment and raise no suspicion. The ease with which anyone can obtain steganographic utilities makes covert data communication and storage easy.

Real World Scenario

Keeping Secrets

Intelligence experts suspect that the terrorists who planned and carried out the attacks on New York and Washington, D.C. on September 11, 2001, may have used steganography to communicate with one another. They are suspected of embedding messages in digital pictures and then e-mailing the pictures (and embedded messages) as attachments to normal e-mail messages. The messages looked like common e-mails with attached pictures. The pictures could have been anything. Nothing was there to provide a clue that the pictures held secret messages. That's the power of steganography.

Detecting stegagnography is difficult. You either have to detect the changes to the carrier file or use statistical analysis to detect an anomaly. Detecting changes to the carrier file requires a noticeable difference that you can see or hear. Statistical analysis depends less on objectivity by comparing the frequency distribution of colors of a picture with the expected frequency distribution of colors for the file. For audio carrier files, a statistical analysis utility would use sound patterns instead of colors.

Another method of detecting steganography is by the presence of steganographic utilities on the suspect machine. Although the mere presence of such software does not prove steganography is in use, it provides the motivation to look harder for carrier files with embedded messages. Few people go to the trouble of acquiring and installing steganographic utilities without using them.

Here are a few steganographic utilities. Look at several of these for more information about and examples of how steganography works:

◆ Steganos Security Suite

◆ SecurEngine

◆ Hermetic Stego

◆ Xidie

◆ PhotoCrypt

Remember that the appeal of steganography is that its very nature masks the existence of the message. You can look at a suspect drive and overlook embedded data if you aren't careful. Look for utilities that create steganographic files. Also look for files that would make good carriers. If the circumstantial evidence points to hidden data, chances are steganography is in use.

Next, we'll look at the quality of encryption by considering key length and key management.

Strengths and Weaknesses of Encryption

Encryption is not an impenetrable safeguard. With some effort, you can access data that has been encrypted. Encryption is far from worthless, though. As a computer investigator, you will be called on to access information that a suspect has encrypted. You will have to break the encryption.

Before you are ready to defeat file encryption, you need to have a better understanding of the strengths and weaknesses of encryption. This knowledge will provide a better awareness of where to start and what steps to take for each unique situation.

Key Length

The length of the encryption key is directly related to the security of the encryption algorithm. Although there are differences in the relative strength of each algorithm, the key length choice has the greatest impact on how secure an encrypted object will be. Simply put, longer keys provide a larger number of possible combinations used to encrypt an object.

A key that is 4 bits in length can represent 16 different key values, because $2^4 = 16$. A key length of 5 bits allows 32 key values, and so on. Although it may be easy to try to decrypt a file or message with 32 different key values, larger keys mean more possible key values.

Some older algorithms that were approved for export by the U.S. government used 40-bit keys. These algorithms are considered to be unsecure by today's standards because of the small key length. A 40-bit key can hold one of 2^{40} values, or 1,099,511,627,776 (1 trillion). Assuming that you have a computer that can make 1.8 million comparisons per second, it would take about a week to evaluate all possible key values.

The DES algorithm uses 56-bit keys. Although DES is considered to be too weak for most security uses, it is far stronger than a 40-bit key algorithm. A DES key can store one of 2^{56}, or 72,057,594,037,927,936 (that's 72 quadrillion) values. Using the same computer as before, it would take about 1,260 years to evaluate all possible key values.

As key values increase in size, the computing power required to crack encryption algorithms becomes exponentially large. At first glance, it looks like an algorithm with a key length that requires over 1,000 years to crack is sufficient. Unfortunately, that's not the case. Today's supercomputers can evaluate far more than 1.8 million comparisons per second. When you introduce parallel-processing capability, you can realistically create a unit that can crack DES in a matter of minutes (or even seconds). That is the reason key lengths have grown to routinely be over 100 bits. Longer keys provide more security by reducing the possibility of using a brute force attack to discover the encryption key.

Key Management

Because the encryption key is crucial to the encryption process, it must be protected at all costs. After the key is disclosed, the encrypted data is no longer secure. Symmetric algorithms use a single key. The sender and receiver must both posses the key to encrypt and decrypt the data. For local file encryption, the same person is likely to encrypt and decrypt the data. The purpose of encryption in such a case is to protect file contents from any unauthorized access.

You may find encrypted files both on hard disks and removable media. In fact, suspects with a basic knowledge of security will often encrypt files before archiving them to removable media. In many such cases, you will find the encryption utility on the main computer. Look for a stored copy of the key. Many people keep copies of important information in ordinary text files. Look for a file with an obvious name (such as `key.txt` or `enc.txt`) or one that contains a single large number and little else. You can also look in personal notes or other personal information manager files for an unusually large number that seems to have no other meaning. Your task in such a situation is similar to finding passwords.

The next section addresses proper handling of encrypted data by first identifying encrypted files and then decrypting them to extract the data.

Handling Encrypted Data

At some point in your investigation, you will likely encounter encrypted data. Your course of action depends on the particular type of encryption and the value of the expected evidence once you decrypt the data. If you suspect the encrypted data holds a high value to your case, it will warrant more time and effort to get at the data. Decrypting data can require a substantial effort. Only pursue that course of action when necessary.

Identifying Encrypted Files

Identifying encrypted files is pretty easy. You try to access a file with the appropriate application and you end up getting garbage. The first step you should take is to find out the type of file with which you are dealing. Most operating systems make assumptions about file types by looking at the file's extension. For example, a file with the .doc extension is assumed to be a word processing document, and a file with the `.zip` extension is assumed to be a compressed archive file. You can't always trust extensions. One way to "hide" files from casual observers is to change their extensions to another file type.

For example, an easy way to hide pictures from standard viewer applications would be to change the extension from `.jpg` to `.txt`. Any extension would work, but the `.txt` extension would represent all such files as text files in most file browser windows. If you wanted to represent your hidden pictures as another file type, simply use another defined file extension. Alternatively, you could use an undefined file extension, but these files would likely attract more attention.

To ensure you are not simply looking at altered file extensions, always use a file viewer that is designed to look at the file extension as well as the file contents. Such a utility will notify you if it finds files that have been changed to a non-standard extension. If your file viewer finds such files, you may be dealing with files that were deliberately hidden.

Another telltale sign that you are dealing with encrypted data is the generated filename. Although many applications generate filenames, many encryption utilities have the option to obscure filenames as the plaintext file is encrypted. That makes it harder for an investigator to identify the file named `My Illegal Activities.doc`.

Instead, the encryption utility might name the file 100455433798.094. If you find a collection of files with obviously generated filenames, find out why. Those files might be encrypted.

In summary, when you find files that don't fit their extensions or have unknown extensions, consider them potentially encrypted. Look at their location in the file system, and check any path history of file accesses and encryption utility activity. The file encryption utility might keep track of recent write locations. Take hints wherever you find them.

Decrypting Files

Let's assume you have identified one or more files that appear to be encrypted. What do you do next? The simple answer is to crack the encryption. The full answer is a little more complex.

Before you even start thinking about exhausting your budget on the latest encryption busting utilities, take the simple approach. Ask the suspect. If you have not found encryption keys written down or otherwise recorded in obvious places, just ask. Your suspect might provide the keys. He might not. If asking does not work or you know the suspect is unlikely to cooperate, use social engineering. If you can convince a suspect to divulge secrets like encryption keys, you can save yourself a lot of work. Only resort to technical means when you have exhausted more conventional methods of collecting information.

NOTE

The suggestion to use social engineering in no way suggests that you should engage in activities that are questionable. Make sure all of your activities are documented and approved before you start. Evidence that is deemed inadmissible is worthless in court.

First, evaluate the type of encryption you have encountered. A common type of encryption is that provided by popular applications. Microsoft, WordPerfect, and PKZIP all provide options within the application to encrypt the contents of its data files. Although convenient, application-supported encryption tends to be very weak. You can find a wide variety of utilities that are specifically developed to crack application encryption. Here is a short list of utilities that help recover file contents of specific file formats:

- **PKZip Cracker** Decrypts ZIP archive files
- **Zip Crack** Decrypts ZIP archive files
- **Word Unprotect** Decrypts Microsoft Word documents
- **WP Crack** Decrypts WordPerfect documents

NOTE

There are many other utilities that will help you defeat application-specific file encryption. The ease of availability should point out that such encryption has far less value than generic file encryption algorithms. In short, don't rely on any application vendor to provide strong embedded encryption for your own privacy needs.

After ruling out embedded encryption, you will need to move to a more sophisticated method. Always begin by looking for the low-hanging fruit. Let's assume you are looking at an encrypted document. Find out as much as possible about the file's context. Here are a few questions to consider:

◆ Does the file have a defined extension?

   ◆ Unless you have information to the contrary, assume the file's extension is valid.

   ◆ Encrypting a file and then changing the extension to throw off an investigator is too much work for most people.

◆ Where is the file located?

   ◆ File location, especially unusual locations, may give clues to the originating application.

   ◆ If you find files stored in unusual locations, check the default document directories for installed applications. That information might tell you what application created the file.

◆ What application(s) likely created the file?

   ◆ If you know, or suspect, what application created the file, see if the application uses a cache or temporary files.

   ◆ Look at deleted files in the application's temporary directory. Any files here will likely be pre-encryption data.

◆ What is the last access time for the file?

   ◆ Look for any deleted files with access times just prior to the last access time of the encrypted file. Although good encryption utilities will not leave such obvious traces behind, the application that generated the file might not be so careful.

◆ Do installed applications create temporary files during creation/editing?

   ◆ Attempt to recover all of the files you can. Even the most innocent ones can be valuable.

◆ Are any files in the Recycle Bin?

   ◆ Don't laugh; it happens!

These questions will get you started. The best outcome of searching for deleted and unencrypted copies of files would be to find a pristine copy of the one file you need—before it was encrypted. Although you may find just what you are looking for, it is more likely that you will find another piece of the puzzle. Any unencrypted file or file fragment that you can relate to an encrypted file will increase your chances of successfully decrypting files. Let's look at a few attack methods to decrypt suspect files.

Real World Scenario

Tales from the Trenches: Opening Encrypted Files

The process of opening encrypted files is one that the computer forensics expert will be called upon to perform from time to time.

One day I was contacted by Bill, a previous client, who insisted I meet with him right away. I told him I would be right over. He said we needed to meet "away from the office" and suggested a local restaurant where we could talk in private.

As soon as I arrived, Bill told me he was having major troubles at work with a small group of employees who he thought were planning to leave the company and form their own firm, competing against him. Bill knew there was nothing he could do to keep the employees from leaving, but he wanted to ensure that they did not take any proprietary information belonging to his company with them when they left.

He was specifically concerned because the company's "network guy" came to him and reported that he had observed an unusually large amount of network activity by a few employees recently including accessing of the customer database and billing system. While this type of access was not against company policy and was within the employee's job description, it was unusual enough for the network guy to report it. Bill asked him to "keep an eye open" for any additional unusual activity.

A few days later the "network guy" informed Bill he had observed an increase in the amount and size of e-mail these same employees were sending through the company e-mail server. When he explored further, he noted these employees had sent a large number of e-mails to a former employee and that these e-mails were encrypted. He was, of course, unable to read the e-mails. Encryption was not a normal process used by the company, but it was not against the company policy to use encryption.

Bill needed proof that these employees were sending proprietary information out of the company to this former employee so that he could terminate their employment and so that he could obtain a "cease and desist" order against his former employee to prevent him from using the proprietary information.

As expected, while examining the employees' computers, I located a large number of encrypted files and attempted to crack the password protection so I could see the content of the files. The majority of files were protected with a very strong encryption utility known as PGP. I knew that the possibility of cracking a PGP-protected file was very slim, but I also knew that I had human nature working in my favor.

Continues

On one of the computers, I located a small collection of Microsoft Word documents that were password protected using the built-in Microsoft password-protection security. On another one of the computers, I located a small collection of Microsoft Word documents (created with Office 97) that were password protected using the built-in Microsoft password-protection security. This protection scheme can be very simple to crack using a variety of available commercial cracking utilities. I was able to open each of these files within a few minutes and review their content. None of these files had anything to do with the case, but I was not deterred. I had learned a long time ago that people are generally very lazy when it comes to choosing passwords and typically will use the same password over and over again.

I attempted to use the recovered password to open the PGP files and was able to access all of the information that was stored on this employee's computer. I located enough evidence to assist Bill in obtaining the "cease and desist" order and to terminate the employees without fear of being sued for wrongful termination.

Although this is one example of overcoming an encryption technology by using a weakness in the implementation of the technology (the human weakness of reusing passwords) and not a weakness in the technology itself, you will find many situations where a weak encryption technology will work in the investigator's favor.

Brute Force Attack

The brute force attack method of decrypting files is the worst choice. It uses the same approach as brute force password cracking. The utility tries every possible key value to see if the decryption results in an intelligible object. This option should be your last resort.

Known Plaintext Attack

known plaintext attack
An attack to decrypt a file characterized by comparing known plaintext to the resulting ciphertext.

The *known plaintext attack* is a method of cracking encryption that uses the plaintext and the associated ciphertext. If you have both the unencrypted and encrypted versions of a file, you can analyze the relationship between the two and deduce the encryption key. The PkCrack utility utilizes this type of attack. You provide an unencrypted file and an encrypted ZIP archive, and PkCrack will compare the two and attempt to find the key used in the encryption.

Even though the files you have access to may seem to be unrelated to the evidence you are looking for, they could help provide the key the suspect used to encrypt. Keeping track of multiple encryption keys is difficult, so you can probably use that key to decrypt other files the suspect encrypted.

Chosen Plaintext Attack

chosen plaintext attack
An attack to decrypt a file characterized by comparing ciphertext to a plaintext message you chose and encrypted.

You may have access to the encryption engine, but not the key. It is possible the encryption utility allows you to encrypt files using stored credentials without disclosing those credentials. In such cases, you may be able to discover the encryption key using a *chosen plaintext attack*. In a chosen plaintext attack, you encrypt a file of your choosing and compare it to the resulting encrypted file. After you create the plaintext and ciphertext, the attack progresses just as the known plaintext attack.

Which Way to Go?

Each type of attack requires different input, output, and access to the encryption utility. Always try the easiest methods first. If they don't work, move on to the more complex approaches. There are no guarantees that discovering a method to decrypt files will be successful within a reasonable timeframe. A brute force attack will always work eventually. But remember that "eventually" can mean several thousand years.

Use what you can and take the time to think about your evidence. Evidence collection and analysis is very much like assembling a puzzle. Forget about the picture; just look at how the pieces fit together.

Terms to Know

asymmetric algorithm	passcode
brute force attack	password
chosen plaintext attack	password cracking
cipher	plaintext
ciphertext	private key algorithm
cryptography	public key algorithm
decrypt	social engineering
dictionary attack	substitution cipher
encrypt	symmetric algorithm
hybrid attack	user ID
known plaintext attack	

Review Questions

1. What is a password?

2. What is the process of getting someone to carry out a task for you?

3. Are more complex passwords stronger or weaker than simpler passwords?

4. What method should you first use to get a password?

5. What type of password attack tries passwords from a predefined list?

6. Which type of password attack uses passwords from a list and then tries variations on each element from the list?

7. What is an algorithm for encrypting and decrypting data?

8. What term describes an encrypted message?

9. Which symmetric encryption algorithm is based on the Rijndael cipher?

10. Which symmetric encryption algorithm uses 56-bit keys?

Chapter 8

Common Forensics Tools

Chapter 4, "Common Tasks," covered the frequently performed tasks in an investigation. The first steps nearly always involve old-fashioned detective work. You need to observe and record first. You do not start looking for documentary evidence until after you survey the physical evidence. Once you start examining media contents, you'll need some tools to help you find and make sense of stored data.

Investigators and computer examiners need several different types of tools to identify and acquire computer evidence. Some evidence is hidden from the casual observer and requires very specialized tools to access. This chapter covers some of the more common tools available to carry out computer forensic tasks. This list is a sampling of the more popular tools available to the general public. Although every attempt has been made to provide a balanced list of forensics tools, there are several limitations to any static list of available tools. The list of tools in this chapter is not exhaustive. You'll likely find useful tools not listed here; however, the exclusion of any tool does not diminish its merit. You'll also find many web addresses in this chapter. They are provided for your convenience. Each one was valid at the time of writing, but web addresses do change and you may have to do a little investigative work to find a lost tool.

Disk Imaging and Validation Tools

After you identify the physical media you suspect contains evidence, you must make sure you preserve the media before you take any further steps. Preserving the media is absolutely necessary to provide assurance the evidence you acquire is valid.

Chapter 3, "Computer Evidence," and Chapter 4, "Common Tasks," both emphasize the importance of copying all media first and then analyzing the copy. Unless you must examine a primary, working copy of media, you should always create an exact image of the media and verify that it matches the original before you continue your investigation. It is rare to examine the primary media copy for any investigation that might end up in court. For other investigations, you might be asked to perform a targeted examination on the primary copy of media. For example, assume you are asked to examine a user's home folder for suspected inappropriate material. It might be impossible or extremely difficult to create a mirror image of the disk drive, but you could scan the disk for existing or deleted files while it is in use. Although examining media while it is in use might not always be the best practice, it is done frequently for informal investigations.

To Copy or Not to Copy?

Whenever possible, create a duplicate of the primary media, verify the copy, and then examine it. Always invest the time and effort to copy original media for any investigation that might end up in a court of law. For investigations that produce evidence that will not be presented in court, you might need to analyze the primary media copy directly. This is possible and desirable in cases where copying media would cause service interruptions.

Your choice of which tools to use depends on several factors, including:

- Operating system(s) supported
  - Operating system(s) in which the tool runs
  - Filesystems the tool supports
- Price
- Functionality
- Personal preference

Let's look at some tools you can use to create and verify media copies.

ByteBack

The first tool in our list is ByteBack, developed by Tech Assist, Inc. ByteBack is a data recovery and investigative tool that provides more functionality than just disk copying. The ByteBack tool runs in DOS and provides a simple interface for operations. Here is a sample of the cloning/imaging interface.

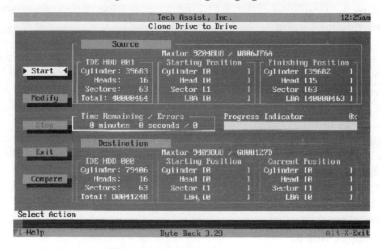

Some of the features of ByteBack include:

Cloning/Imaging   Quickly clones (to same media type) or images (to compressed files) physical sectors of many media types.

Automated File Recovery   Automatically recovers most files, including deleted files, on FAT and NTFS volumes including deleted files, files located in slack space, and old formats.

Rebuild Partitions and Boot Records   Automatically repairs FAT12, FAT16, FAT32, and NTFS volumes, boot records, and partitions. It can also recover individual files on these volumes.

Media Wipe   Quickly overwrites every sector of a drive.

Media Editor   Contains a powerful sector editor for viewing and searching raw data.

ByteBack also provides software write blocking for the source drive and automatic CRC and MD5 hash calculation to verify the copy operations. If you need more functionality, ByteBack provides a binary search feature that allows you to search for any character string on the drive, including slack space.

For more information on ByteBack and additional features, visit the company's website at http://www.toolsthatwork.com/byteback.htm.

dd

The *dd utility* copies and converts files. As briefly discussed in Chapter 5, "Capturing the Data Image: Memory and Disks," dd is commonly used in forensics to copy an entire environment. You can specify the input and output file, as well as conversion options. This utility takes two basic arguments—if and of. The if argument specifies the input file and the of argument specifies the output file. When using dd to copy individual files, the utility abides by the operating system file size limit, normally 2GB. Larger files will simply be truncated. For example, to copy a simple file from a source (such as /home/michael/sn.txt) to a destination (such as /tmp/newfile), you would issue the following command:

```
dd if=/home/michael/sn.txt of=/tmp/newfile
```

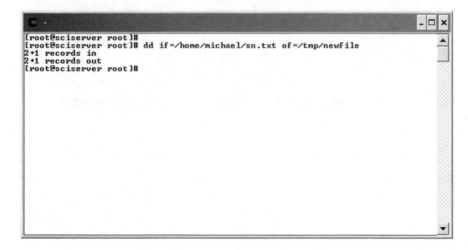

Using similar syntax, you can copy the hard disk drive located at /dev/hda to an image file named /dev/hdb/case_img using this command:

```
dd if=/dev/hda1 of=/dev/hdb/case_img
```

When using the dd utility with device files, you are not limited to a 2GB limit. The current Linux version is GNU dd. GNU dd is found in the fileutils collection, with the latest version at ftp://prep.ai.mit.edu/pub/gnu/fileutils-3.12.tar.gz. You can also find the dd utility on any computer running Unix or Linux. Type **man dd** in Unix or Linux for a man page entry that describes the command syntax. The Windows dd version is at http://users.erols.com/gmgarner/forensics.

DriveSpy

DriveSpy is a DOS-based forensic tool, developed by Digital Intelligence, Inc. Unlike ByteBack, DriveSpy is an extended DOS forensic shell. DriveSpy provides an interface that is similar to the MS-DOS command line, along with new and extended commands. The entire program is only 110KB and easily fits on a DOS boot floppy disk.

DriveSpy provides many of the functions necessary to copy and examine drive contents. All activities are logged, optionally down to each keystroke. If desired, logging can be disabled at will. You can examine DOS and non-DOS partitions and retrieve extensive architectural information for hard drives or partitions. DriveSpy does not use operating system calls to access files, and it does not change file access dates.

Additional functionality includes:

- Create disk-to-disk copy (supports large disk drives).
- Create MD5 hash for a drive, partition, or selected files.
- Copy a range of sectors from a source to a target, where the source and target can span drives or reside on the same drive.
- Select files based on name, extension, or attributes.
- Unerase files.
- Search a drive, partition, or selected files for text strings.
- Collect slack and unallocated space.
- Wipe a disk, partition, unallocated or slack space.

DriveSpy provides basic command-line functionality that is portable enough to carry on a single floppy disk and use at the scene. For pricing and more information, visit the Digital Intelligence, Inc. website at http://www.digitalintel.com/drivespy.htm.

EnCase

The EnCase product line from Guidance Software is one of the most complete *forensic suites* available. We cover more of EnCase's functionality and its different products in the "Forensics Tools" section later in this chapter. EnCase is included in this section due to its drive duplication function.

forensic suite
A set of tools and/or software programs used to analyze a computer for collection of evidence.

In addition to providing tools and a framework in which to manage a complete case, EnCase includes a drive duplicator. The drive imager creates an exact copy of a drive and validates the image automatically. It either creates complete images or splits drive images to economize storage. EnCase can copy virtually any type media, creating an identical image for analysis. EnCase calls this *static data support.*

———————————
TIP
———————————

EnCase Enterprise Edition also supports *volatile data support.* **This feature takes a snapshot of Random Access Memory (RAM), the Windows Registry, open ports, and running applications. It provides potentially valuable information that is lost when a machine is shut down.**

It is also worth mentioning that Guidance Software sells hardware disk-write blockers. Their FastBloc products provide the extra measure of assurance that no writes occur on the device. You can use the write blocker with EnCase or just rely on EnCase to use its own software write blocking to protect the original media if you boot to DOS and not Windows. You can also use FastBloc with non-EnCase software.

The EnCase products currently run on Windows 9*x,* Windows 2000, Windows XP, and Windows Server 2003. For more information on the EnCase product line, visit the Guidance Software website at `http://www.EnCase.com`.

Forensic Replicator

Forensic Replicator, from Paraben Forensic Tools, is another disk imaging tool that can acquire many different types of electronic media. It provides an easy-to-use interface, as shown in the following graphic, to select and copy entire drives or portions of drives. It also handles most removable media, including Universal Serial Bus (USB) micro drives. Replicated media images are stored in a format that can be read by most popular forensic programs.

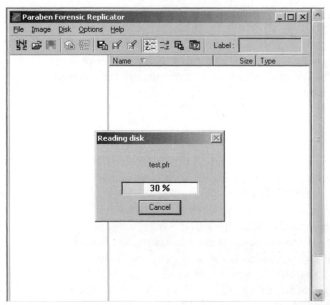

Forensic Replicator also provides the ability to compress and split drive images for efficient storage. The ISO CDRom option allows you to create CDs from evidence drives that can be browsed for analysis. This option can make drive analysis much easier and more accessible for general computers. You don't need to mount a copy of the suspect drive on a forensic computer. You can use searching utilities on a standard CD-ROM drive. Forensic Replicator also offers the option of encrypting duplicated images for secure storage.

Paraben also sells a Firewire or USB-to-IDE write blocker, called Paraben's Lockdown, as a companion product. Forensic Replicator requires a Windows operating system to run. You need to boot into Windows to use the product. For additional information about the Paraben forensic tools product line, see the "Forensics Tools" section later in this chapter. For more information on the Forensic Replicator product, visit the Paraben Forensic Tools website at `http://www.paraben-forensics.com/replicator.html`.

FTK Imager

FTK (Forensic Toolkit) Imager from AccessData Corporation is a set of forensic tools that includes powerful media duplication features. The "Forensics Tools" section later in this chapter covers more FTK features. FTK can create media images from many different source formats, including:

◆ NTFS and NTFS compressed

◆ FAT12, FAT16, and FAT32

◆ Linux ext2 and ext3

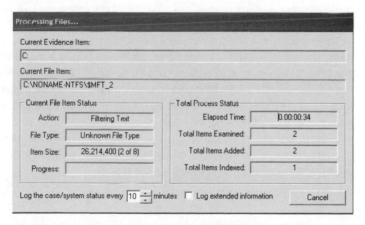

FTK generates CRC or MD5 hash values, as do most products in this category, for disk-copy verification. FTK provides full searching capability for media and images created from other disk imaging programs. Image formats that FTK can read include:

◆ EnCase

◆ SMART

◆ SnapBack

◆ SafeBack (not V3.0)

◆ Linux dd

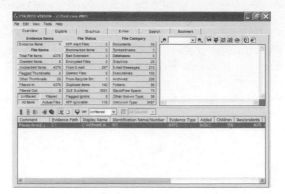

FTK Explorer is a Windows-based utility and, therefore, requires that the user boot into a Windows operating system. For more information about FTK Explorer, visit the AccessData Corporation website at `http://www.accessdata.com`.

Norton Ghost

Norton Ghost, from Symantec, is not a forensic tool, but it does provide the ability to create disk copies that are *almost* exact copies of the original. You can verify the copies you make and ensure each partition is an exact copy, but a complete drive image that is created by using Ghost commonly returns a different hash value than a hash of the original drive. Although Ghost is a handy tool, it may not provide evidence that is admissible in a court of law. The most common uses for Ghost include backup/restore and creating installation images for multiple computers. Even though Ghost's primary use is not forensics, its utility value merits a place in our list of useful tools.

Norton Ghost is a Windows application and requires a Windows operating system. For more information on Norton Ghost, visit the Symantec website at `http://www.symantec.com/sabu/ghost/ghost_personal/`.

ProDiscover

ProDiscover, from Technology Pathways, is another forensic suite of tools. As with other forensic suites, we will cover additional features in a later section. Also like other forensic suites of software, ProDiscover provides disk imaging and verification features.

ProDiscover provides the ability to create a bit stream copy of an entire suspect disk, including hidden hardware protected area (HPA) sections (patent pending), to keep original evidence safe. As discussed in Chapter 5, the HPA is an area of a hard disk drive that is not reported to the BIOS or the operating system. Some disk drive manufacturers use the HPA to store utilities that are hidden from the operating system. It also automatically creates and records MD5 or SHA1 hashes of evidence files to prove data integrity.

Technology Pathways provides several different versions of ProDiscover, depending on your particular forensic needs. One interesting feature of ProDiscover is that it allows you to capture a disk image over a network. You don't have to be physically connected to the suspect computer. All of Technology Pathways products provide disk imaging and verification and require a Windows operating system. For more information on ProDiscover, visit the Technology Pathways website at http://www.techpathways.com/DesktopDefault.aspx?tabindex=4&tabid=12.

SafeBack

SafeBack, licensed through New Technologies Inc., creates bit stream images of hard disk drives and drive contents. Although SafeBack is a very good backup and installation image utility, it really shines as a forensic tool. One of the design goals of SafeBack was to produce evidence-grade backups of hard drives. It accomplishes this through its self-authenticating disk imaging process. Version 3.0 of SafeBack implements two hashing processes that are based on the SHA256 algorithm. SHA256 hash values are stored internally to protect them from alteration. All operations are logged and output to an audit file.

SafeBack is a DOS-based utility. For more information on SafeBack, visit the New Technologies Inc. website at `http://www.forensics-intl.com/safeback.html`.

SMART

SMART, from ASR Data Acquisition & Analysis, LLC, is another forensic software suite. The suite is comprised of several tools that are integrated into a full-featured forensic software package. Two tools in the package are SMART Acquisition, which provides disk imaging, and SMART Authentication, which provides verification functionality.

SMART runs in Linux and provides a graphical view of devices in a system. The first step in creating a disk image is to calculate a hash value for the source device.

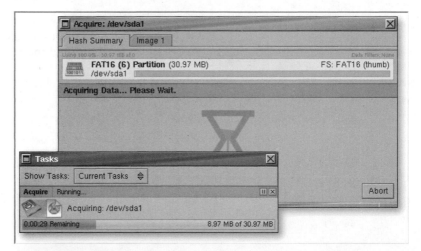

After SMART generates and stores the hash value, it can create one or more device images. SMART can create multiple image files, use compression, split images to fit on smaller devices, and associate images with existing case files.

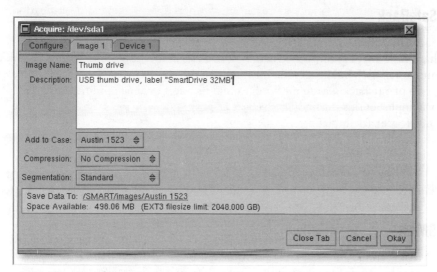

We will cover more SMART functionality in a later section. For more information on SMART, visit the ASR Data Acquisitions & Analysis website at `http://asrdata.com/SMART/`.

WinHex

WinHex, from X-Ways Software Technology AG, is a universal hexadecimal editor and disk management utility. It supports recovery from lost or damaged files and general editing of disk contents. Its disk cloning feature is of the most interest for this section.

WinHex can clone any connected disk and verify the process using checksums or hash calculations. WinHex runs in Windows operating systems.

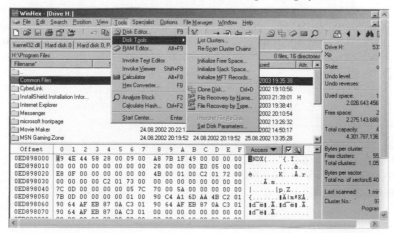

WinHex provides many more features beyond disk imaging and verification. For starters, WinHex provides the functionality to examine, and optionally edit, disk contents. You can also search disks for text strings using WinHex's search engine. Its support of various data types and its ability to view data in different formats make WinHex a valuable forensic tool.

For more information on WinHex and its additional capabilities, visit the X-Ways Software Technology website at `http://www.x-ways.net/winhex/index-m.html`.

Forensics Tools

After you have a verified copy of original media, you're ready to begin the analysis process. You can use the tools discussed in the following sections to perform many forensics functions. Your choice of tools depends on your specific needs. The following sections include common software and hardware tools and briefly discuss their capabilities.

As with the disk imaging tools, your choice of which tools to use depends on the following:

◆ Operating system(s) supported

◆ User interface preference

◆ Price

◆ Functionality/capabilities

◆ Vendor loyalty

Software Suites

Several companies specialize in developing and providing forensic tools. These companies produce software and/or hardware with diverse functionality. Some suites of forensic software are tightly integrated and have mature user interfaces. Other forensic suites are little more than a collection of useful utilities. Consider the following tools and try out the ones you like. Your final choice of forensic tools should provide the functionality to perform the examinations you will encounter. Although all the bells and whistles are nice, get what you really need.

EnCase

Guidance Software produces the EnCase product line. The products were originally developed for law enforcement personnel to carry out investigations. The product line has grown to support commercial incident response teams as well as law enforcement. The EnCase product is built around the general concept of the case. The first action you take is to create a case file. All subsequent activities are related to a case.

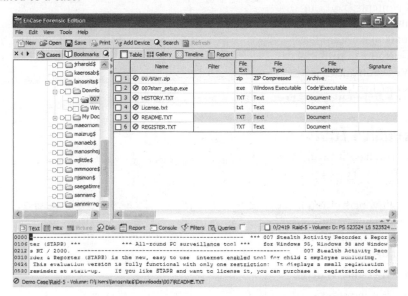

EnCase is an integrated Windows-based graphical user interface (GUI) suite of tools. Although the EnCase functionality is impressive, you will likely need another utility at some point. Fully integrated solutions can increase productivity, but don't hesitate to use another tool when you need it.

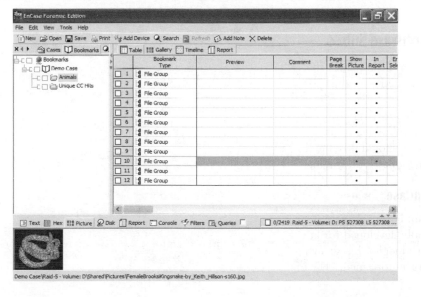

Here are just a few features of EnCase:

◆ Enterprise Edition provides centralized monitoring and real-time investigation with no service interruptions

◆ Snapshot enables investigators to capture volatile information including:

    ◆ RAM contents

    ◆ Running programs

    ◆ Open files and ports

◆ Organizes results into case files and manages case documents

◆ Helps maintain the chain of custody

◆ Provides tools for incident response team to respond to emerging threats

◆ Supports real-time and postmortem examinations

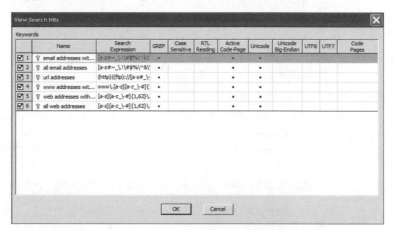

EnCase provides the functionality to acquire and examine many types of evidence. The organization around a case provides the structure to keep information in order. All in all, EnCase is one of the premium suites of software you definitely want to evaluate when selecting your forensics tools. For more information on EnCase, visit the Guidance Software website at `http://www.encase.com`.

Forensic Toolkit (FTK)

Another forensic suite that provides an integrated user interface is AccessData's Forensic Toolkit (FTK). FTK runs in Windows operating systems and provides a very powerful tool set to acquire and examine electronic media. As discussed earlier in this chapter, FTK contains a disk imaging tool. This imaging tool provides one or more copies of primary evidence for analysis.

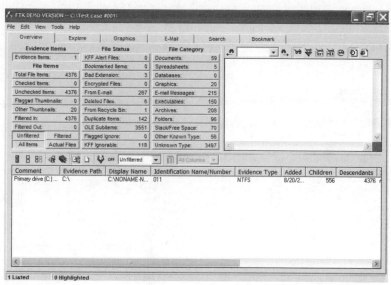

FTK provides an easy-to-use file viewer that recognizes over 270 types of files. FTK also provides full text indexing powered by dtSearch. We will cover dtSearch's features later in this chapter. The integrated file viewer and search capabilities provide the ability to find evidence on any device.

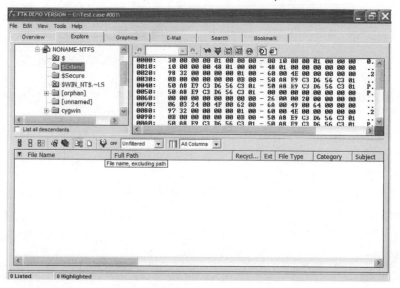

FTK works with media images created by several imaging utilities, including:

◆ FTK

◆ EnCase

◆ SMART

◆ SnapBack

◆ SafeBack (not V3.0)

◆ Linux dd

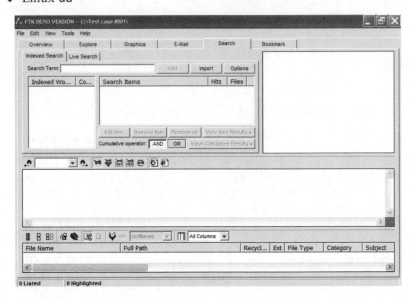

The searching capabilities of FTK include e-mail and Zip file analysis. FTK supports searching through many e-mail formats, including:

◆ AOL

◆ Netscape

◆ Yahoo

◆ EarthLink

◆ Eudora

◆ Hotmail

◆ MSN

FTK can quickly examine archive files in different formats as well. Files these programs generated are supported:

◆ PKZIP

◆ WinZip

- WinRAR
- GZIP
- TAR

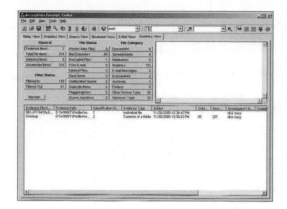

All results are organized by case and are presented in the case content summary. For more information on FTK, visit the AccessData website at http://www.accessdata.com.

Maresware

Maresware Computer Forensics software, developed by Mares and Company, is really a collection of tools useful to the forensic investigator. Like many of the forensics tools available, these tools were originally developed for law enforcement personnel. The tools in the set are the ones forensic examiners routinely use during an investigation.

Maresware features are similar to competitive products. The software provides tools to acquire and verify media images and examine the images. Core functionality includes searching and hidden file identification. The most notable difference from other forensic software suites is that the Maresware tools are stand-alone tools and can be called as needed. There is no set method or processing order you must follow. Maresware is flexible enough to allow you to use the tools you need in the order you need them.

Although the core functionality is similar to other competing products, at least four programs in the Maresware tool set bear individual description:

Declasfy A disk wiping program that overwrites the contents of physical media in compliance with U.S. Department of Defense (DoD) standards. The resulting media meets strict regulatory requirements for media reuse.

Brandit A utility that brands hard disks with identifying ownership information. This utility is useful to trace and identify stolen hard drives.

Bates_no This program assists in managing records and files by adding identifying numbers to document filenames. Identifying numbers, such as case-related numbers, makes it easier to group files together.

Upcopy A copy program that makes it easy to copy entire directories from a source location to a destination without changing any attributes or time/date stamps.

For more features or information on Maresware Computer Forensics software, visit the Mares and Company website at http://www.dmares.com/maresware/software.htm.

Paraben

Paraben Forensics Tools, produced by Paraben Corporation, is another collection of stand-alone tools. The Paraben forensic product line is actually made up of 10 individual software tool sets that make up the entire forensic suite. Each of the products can be purchased individually, and the pricing structure provides discounts for purchasing multiple tools.

Paraben's tools are frequently used with personal digital assistants (PDAs) and cell phones. Although this company's other software products are fine products, examine Paraben's products first if you want to examine PDAs or cell phones. Paraben has extensive experience in cell phone and PDA forensics tools. PDA and cell phone forensics is an area that has its own nuances. Paraben knows the ropes and can share a lot of knowledge. Here is a brief list of the Paraben Forensics tools:

Forensic Replicator A disk imaging and verification tool. Details of this product were discussed earlier in this chapter.

Forensic Sorter A tool that classifies data into one of 14 different categories, making examinations more productive. Organized data is easier to handle in groups of like data.

Network E-mail Examiner A tool that examines network e-mail archives.

E-mail Examiner A tool that examines e-mail files from over 15 mail types.

Decryption Collection A set of tools that help recover passwords and decrypt encrypted data.

Text Searcher A fast tool that searches media for desired text strings.

Case Agent Companion A set of tools that includes a file viewer capable of viewing over 225 file formats, along with searching and reporting tools. The tools help an examiner organize examination results by case.

PDA Seizure   A tool used to acquire, view, and reports on evidence from PDAs.

Cell Seizure   A tool used to acquire, view, and report on evidence from cell phones.

For more information on any of the Paraben product line, visit the Paraben Forensic Tools website at

`http://www.paraben-forensics.com/products.html`.

The Coroner's Toolkit (TCT)

The Coroner's Toolkit (TCT) is the first of two open source forensic software suites in our list. It was designed by Dan Farmer and Wieste Venema. TCT is a collection of programs written to support a postmortem analysis of Unix and Linux systems.

Unlike many other forensic tools, TCT was written more for incident response than law enforcement investigations. Due to its origins, TCT was not designed around the stringent requirements to produce and manage courtroom admissible evidence. As a result, it's up to you to manage your case files and properly maintain the chain of custody.

The documentation is straightforward and brutally honest. Because TCT is not encumbered by encouraging prospective buyers to purchase a product, the authors can cut right to the heart of operational details. In fact, they begin by telling you the most obvious shortcomings of TCT. That being said, the TCT tutorial provides a nice introductory primer on handling incidents and conducting investigations. Take a look at the tutorial at `http://www.fish.com/tct/help-when-broken-into`.

TCT includes four main features. Although other lesser programs are included with the package, these four features are core to TCT's functionality:

Information Capture   The grave-robber program collects a large amount of information from a machine. It can take hours to run, and it returns a lot of information.

File Analysis   The `ils` and `mactime` programs analyze and display access patterns of files from a historical perspective or from a running system.

Deleted File Recovery   The `unrm` and `lazarus` programs support the recovery of deleted files and file fragments.

Cryptography Key Recovery   The `findkey` program examines files and running processes to recover keys.

One of the key features that sets TCT apart from many other forensic tool sets is that is can operate on a live system and return information about live processes and open files. Although the high-end commercial packages support this type of real-time analysis, few others have the ability to examine volatile RAM. For more information on TCT, visit one of the two primary TCT websites at `http://www.fish.com/tct` or `http://www.porcupine.org/forensics/tct.html`.

The Sleuth Kit (TSK)

The Sleuth Kit (TSK) is the other open source forensic software suite on our list. Built on TCT, TSK is a collection of command-line tools that provides media management and forensic analysis functionality.

TSK has a few features that deserve separate mention. In addition to general functionality, TSK supports Mac partitions and can analyze files from Mac filesystems. TSK has been tested to run on Mac OS X as well. TSK also has the ability to analyze volatile data on running systems in a manner similar to TCT.

The core toolkit contains six different types of tools.

File System Layer   The fsstat tool reports filesystem details, including inode numbers, block or cluster ranges, and super block details for Unix-based systems. For FAT filesystems, fsstat provides an abbreviated FAT table listing.

File Name Layer   The ffind and fls tools report allocated, unallocated, and deleted filenames.

Meta Data Layer   The icat, ifind, ils, and istat tools report on file meta data (file details) stored in filesystems.

Data Unit Layer   The dcat, dlc, dstat, and dcalc tools report file content information and statistics.

Media Management   The mmls tool provides information on the layout of a disk.

hfind   The hfind tool looks up hash values.

mactime   This tool uses fls and ils output to create timelines of file activity, such as create, access and write activity.

sorter   This tool sorts files based on file type.

For more information on TSK, visit the main TSK website at http:// www.sleuthkit.org/sleuthkit/index.php.

Autopsy Forensic Browser

The Autopsy Forensic browser is a GUI front end for the TSK product discussed earlier. In addition to providing a graphical presentation of TSK tools, it also adds case management features to TSK. Like TSK, Autopsy runs in Unix/Linux and Mac OS X and provides a nice alternative to commercial Windows-based forensic tools.

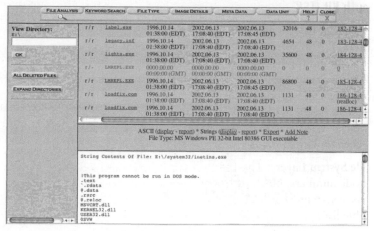

Here are a few features the Autopsy Forensic Browser adds to TSK:

Dead Analysis   Analyzes on a machine or device in a trusted environment

Live Analysis   Analyzes on a system that is up and running

Case Management   Organizes activities by case

Even Sequencer   Helps discern patterns by organizing system events chronologically

Notes   Offers easily accessible notes organized by case

Image Integrity   Verifies the integrity of any media images created for an investigation

Reports   Creates reports of activities, organized by case

Logging   Creates audit logs for activities, organized by case

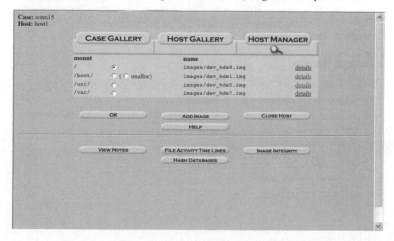

For more information on the Autopsy Forensic Browser, visit the Autopsy website at http://www.sleuthkit.org/autopsy/index.php.

ProDiscover

ProDiscover, from Technology Pathways, is another forensic suite of tools. Technology Pathways provides several different versions of ProDiscover, including Forensics, Investigator, Incident Response, Suite, and Windows, depending on your particular forensic needs. All ProDiscover products run in Windows operating systems and provide an integrated GUI for their forensic tools. The ProDiscover Suite combines the features of the entire family of forensic tools. Here are some notable features:

- Allows live system examination
- Identifies Trojans and other software intended to compromise the security of your system
- Utilizes a remote agent that allows centralized examination and monitoring, along with encrypted network communication to secure analysis data
- Creates a bit stream copy of an entire suspect disk, including hidden HPA sections (patent pending), to keep original evidence safe
- Ensures integrity of acquired images using MD5 or SHA1 hashes
- Supports FAT12, FAT16, FAT32, all NTFS, dynamic disk and software RAID, and Sun Solaris UFS filesystems
- Generates reports in eXtensible Markup Language (XML)

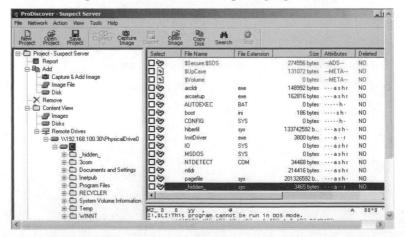

ProDiscover provides similar functionality to other full-featured forensic software suites listed in this section. Take a look at the full product line for a more detailed look at specific features. For more information on ProDiscover, visit the Technology Pathways website at http://www.techpathways.com/DesktopDefault.aspx?tabindex=4&tabid=12.

Vogon Forensic Software

Vogon International provides imaging, processing, and investigative forensic tools. The company's software products provide integrated tools that provide the majority of the functions a computer forensic examiner requires. Vogon Forensic Software runs in the Windows operating system. Their software product line consists of:

- Imaging software
  - Creates drive images with verification
  - Creates images from SCSI, IDE, and S-ATA hard disk drives.
  - Provides audit trail of imaging activities

- Processing software
  - Creates file hashes
  - Processes multiple image files in a session
  - Provides file identification and grouping
  - Automatically handles archive and compressed files
- Investigative software
- Supports fast and flexible text searches
- Handles 19 file system formats, including most common Windows, Unix/Linux, and Macintosh file systems
- Logs all activities
- Produces multiple views of suspect data and reports of activities and results

For more information on the Vogon International product line and pricing, visit the company's website at http://www.vogon-forensic-hardware.com/.

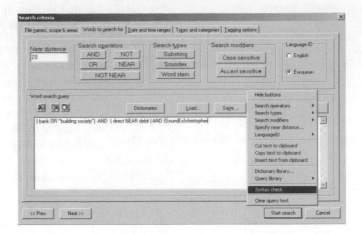

X-Ways Forensics

X-Ways Forensics, from X-Ways Software Technology AG, is a collection of several forensic tools that assist in examining media images. Compared to some of the other forensic suites in this section, it is a little more lightweight. However, it does provide a nice collection of forensic tools that include some large package features at a very reasonable price.

Some of the X-Ways features include:

◆ Case management

◆ Automatic activity logging

◆ Automated reports in HyperText Markup Language (HTML)

◆ A display of existing and deleted files, sorted by file type category

◆ Gallery view for graphics

◆ Skin color detection helps in isolating pictures that may contain pornography

◆ File extension/file type mismatches detection

◆ EnCase media image support (read)

This is only a short list of X-Ways features. For more information on this product, visit the X-Ways Software & Technology website at `http://www.x-ways.net/forensics/index-m.html`.

Miscellaneous Software Tools

In addition to drive imaging software and complete forensic software suites, many smaller tools and utilities that are of value to the computer examiner are available. No matter how many features your forensic suite of choice may be, you might have specific needs that require another special tool.

The following sections detail a few special-purpose tools that provide specific functionality. As with the previous sections, consider each of these tools and choose the best ones for your specific needs.

DiskJockey File Viewer

DiskJockey File Viewer, from Clear & Simple, is a general-purpose file viewer. It allows you to view files in over 220 formats (232 formats in the Deluxe Edition). You do not need to own the application that created the file to view it in DiskJockey. Forensic examiners can use DiskJockey to scan media and view files without having to open the files in a native application.

You can find many more details on DiskJockey by visiting the Clear & Simple website at http://www.clear-simple.com/.

DriveSpy

We discussed DriveSpy in the "Disk Imaging and Validation Tools" section. It is included here as well to remind you that DriveSpy does a lot more than just duplicate drives. For instance, it allows you to select files based on name, extension, or attributes. It also allows you to view the sectors and clusters in its built-in hex viewers. Another useful DriveSpy feature is a search engine that allows you to search a partition or drive for specific text strings. DriveSpy provides basic command-line functionality that is portable enough to carry on a single floppy disk and use at the scene. After you create an image of a drive, DriveSpy can assist you in examining the image's contents.

The discussion in the "Disk Imaging and Validation Tools" section covered some of its features. For pricing and more information, visit the Digital Intelligence, Inc. website at http://www.digitalintel.com/drivespy.htm.

dtSearch

After you create an image of suspect media, you'll need to search it for possible evidence. You'll need some tool to assist you in your search efforts. The dtSearch product line, from dtSearch Corporation, provides several solutions that allow you to search gigabytes of text in a short amount of time. Although not strictly a forensic tool, dtSearch provides the tool to perform a necessary forensic function.

The dtSearch website lists several features that set the product apart, including:

- Offers over 12 search options, including indexed, unindexed, felded, and full-text search options
- Converts results to HTML with search results highlighted (makes it easy to see search results context)
- Supports distributed searching for high performance

The dtSearch product line includes several different products for different needs, including:

dtSearch Desktop   Searches stand-alone machines

dtSearch Network   Searches across networks

dtSearch Web   Supports instant text searching for online documents

dtSearch Publish   Publishes an instant searchable database on CD/DVD

For the forensic examiner, the Desktop and Network products provide the capability to find possible evidence on multiple machines. For more detailed product information, visit the dtSearch Corporation website at http://www.dtsearch.com/.

Quick View Plus File Viewer

Quick View Plus, from Avantstar, is a general-purpose file viewer, similar to DiskJockey. Quick View Plus allows you to view files in over 225 formats. Quick View Plus also allows you to view parts of files and print them or cut and paste into your own applications.

From a forensic perspective, Quick View Plus provides examiners the ability to search many types of files for text strings and view the results in the context of the original file.

You can find many more details on Quick View Plus by visiting the Avantstar website at http://www.avantstar.com/solutions/quick_view_plus.

Text Search Plus

Text Search Plus, from New Technologies Inc., is a DoD-tested and certified text-searching tool. This tool was designed specifically for forensic examiners. Although other search tools were developed for a general market, Text Search Plus started off as a forensic tool.

Text Search Plus provides the following features beyond most general-purpose searching tools:

- Searches files, slack space, and unallocated file space
- Is approved for use in classified facilities
- Searches at the logical level (filesystem) or physical level (disk sectors)
- Searches up to 120 search strings at one time

Text Search Plus operates in DOS and is small enough to fit on a DOS boot floppy disk. Many commercial examiners, government, law enforcement, military, and intelligence agencies use the product. For more product details, visit the New Technologies Inc. website at `http://www.forensics-intl.com/txtsrchp.html`.

ThumbsPlus File Viewer

ThumbsPlus File Viewer, from Cerious Software Inc., is a general-purpose file viewer and editor. It allows you to view files in many formats. A good file-viewing tool makes browsing through several graphics files far easier. ThumbsPlus makes it easy to collect and browse most common graphic formats.

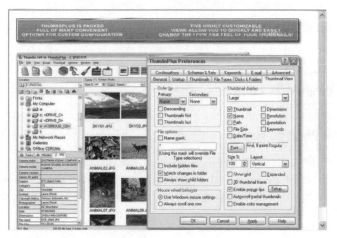

You can find many more details on ThumbsPlus by visiting the Cerious website at `http://www.cerious.com/`.

Hardware

Up to this point, we have ignored the fact that all software tools must run on hardware of some type. Although forensic tools run on general-purpose machines, using dedicated computers for forensics investigations is often advisable. Using dedicated hardware decreases the possibility of accidental contamination by nonforensic applications.

Although actual evidence contamination cannot occur to the primary media when analyzing an image of the original media, other applications can possibly affect the evidence image you are examining. Your forensic machine probably has special-purpose hardware elements such as a disk-write blocker, keystroke logger, or multiple format disk controllers.

Because forensic examination computers tend to support special-purpose hardware and software, several companies offer hardware devices and complete computer systems that are built from the ground up as forensic hardware devices. Some of the systems can be expensive, but if you need a prebuilt forensic hardware platform the cost is probably justified. Carefully consider your needs based on:

- Where will you analyze media?
  - At the scene
  - In the lab
- How often do you use forensic software?
- What type of operating system and hardware must you analyze?
- Will the evidence you collect be presented in a court of law?

Answers to these questions will help you to decide whether you need special-purpose forensic hardware and what features you need. The following sections describe some forensic hardware providers.

Forensic Recovery of Evidence Device

Digital Intelligence, Inc. produces a line of specially designed forensic workstations called Forensic Recovery of Evidence Device (F.R.E.D.). The company offers several different F.R.E.D. options, depending on your specific needs. Each system in the F.R.E.D. line is a purpose-built computer for forensic analysis. Whether you need a portable lab or a full-featured system that supports nearly every known hard drive interface, there is probably a F.R.E.D. computer that will satisfy your requirements.

In addition to the F.R.E.D. product line, Digital Intelligence, Inc. sells a line of other forensic hardware including:

- Forensic hardware kits with write blockers, power supplies, and interface cables
- The "shadow" device that caches all writes as a suspect's system boots
- Stand-alone write blockers
- Imaging chassis

Digital Intelligence, Inc. provides a complete line of hardware for forensic examiners. For more information on the Digital Intelligence, Inc. product line and pricing, visit the company's website at `http://www.digitalintel.com/`.

Vogon Forensic Hardware

Vogon International provides purpose-built forensic hardware, including both specialist imaging systems, forensic workstations through to scalable custom laboratory solutions. Vogon offers a range of forensic solutions for differing needs. Their product line includes:

- Imaging systems for IDE, SCSI, S-ATA, and PCMCIA and RAID
- A range of laboratory-based imaging and processing systems
- Custom high-end enterprise imaging systems
- Automated systems for high-volume forensic imaging and processing
- Password-cracking hardware for hard disk drives
- Integrated network-based forensic solutions
- Custom forensic solutions

(Photograph Courtesy of Vogon International 2004)

(Photograph Courtesy of Vogon International 2004)

For more information on the Vogon International product line, visit the company's website at `http://www.vogon-forensic-hardware.com/index.php`.

Your Forensics Toolkit

Now that you have seen a selection of the tools available for the forensic examiner, you need to decide which tools work best for you. Every forensic examiner has slightly different needs. The particular tools you acquire depend on many factors, including:

- Expected types of investigations
  - Evidence to be presented in a court of law
  - Evidence for internal reporting/auditing
- Operating system needs and preference
- Background and training
- Budget
- Status
  - Law enforcement
  - Private organization

Consider your specific forensic needs and then carefully consider the products available. In general, you should only acquire the functionality you need and nothing more. The problem is that it can be difficult to know exactly what functionality you need. Each investigation is different and may call for different approaches. In such cases, tool needs change. To the best of your ability, develop a list of forensic tool needs.

Real World Scenario

Tales from the Trenches:
Forensics Tools

The care and maintenance of your computer forensics tools begins well before you are asked to perform a forensic evaluation.

Each time you purchase a new hard drive, you must complete a procedure to sanitize the drive to ensure that there is no data on the drive prior to using it in the imaging process. This is a process that can require many hours to complete.

The CEO of a company once asked me to perform a forensics evaluation of a very senior employee's computer to look for evidence that this employee was planning to leave the company. The CEO was so concerned because this employee had access to very sensitive trade secrets that would put the company at a great disadvantage if they were obtained by a competitor.

The CEO wanted me to go into the employee's office in the middle of the night and image the hard drive without his knowledge and leave everything as I had found it so the employee would not know I had been there. I had only one problem. The CEO wanted the imaging done that night and I didn't have a hard drive with me that had been sanitized to the U.S. Department of Defense specification DoD 5220-22M standard.

I was out of town teaching a forensics class when the request was made. If I had been at home, I would have simply opened the safe at my lab and taken out one of the many sanitized hard drives (of varying sizes) that I keep prepped and ready to go. As a matter of procedure, each time I purchase a new hard drive, I use the Image MASSter Solo 2 Forensics unit to sanitize the drive and then I store the drive in my safe and complete an entry in a log to begin the chain of custody for that drive.

Because I did not have a prepped drive, I drove to one of the local computer super centers and purchased a drive. I had previously asked the CEO what size hard drive he thought the employee had in his computer and he told me the company standard was an 80GB hard drive. Of course, I purchased a 120GB hard drive to make sure I was buying a large enough drive.

Then, the real issue began. I went back to my hotel and began sanitizing the drive, which takes many hours to complete on a 120GB hard drive. The CEO told me he would meet me at the office whenever I was ready. The process completed at 4 AM and I called the CEO. We went to the office, and I was able to image the employee's computer and leave the building before any of the other employees arrived for work. After inspecting the hard drive, we discovered evidence that the executive was planning to leave and was collecting data to take with him. We were able to prevent him from taking the data with him. Very soon after, he did leave the company and, because of his actions, did not receive a severance package.

From this experience, I learned to always bring a sanitized 250GB hard drive with me when I travel out of town—just in case. From this story, you should learn that you will need to purchase a variety of hard drives and sanitize them before you ever talk to your first customer about performing a forensics examination.

Although it's important to be adequately prepared, one common pitfall is to over buy. The impulse in all things is to pack any acquisition with the maximum number of options. Think about it. Have you ever used all of the options on your video camera? Take a look at the owner's manual, and see all the cool things you can do with your camera. You probably heard about the features when you bought the camera and promptly forgot about most of them when you started using it. Forensic tools may include options you simply don't need. Avoid paying for options you'll never use.

Each Organization Is Different

In choosing a forensic tool set, consider how your organization approaches investigations. Do you need the ability to remotely examine machines? If so, you can narrow your search to a few options. Are you a Unix shop with a small budget? Open source tools might fit the bill in this situation.

There is no "one size fits all" forensic toolkit. Ask questions. Take the time to attend training and view tutorials. Test as much software as possible. Investing a substantial amount of time in this process will help you make more informed decisions. Thoroughly consider how your organization conducts investigations, what kind of investigations you will need to participate in, and what features you will need to get the job done.

Most Examiners Use Overlapping Tools

Unless a single set of forensic tools satisfies all of your needs, consider selecting multiple tools while weighing the costs involved. When you do select multiple tools, they will most likely overlap. That's okay. Get what you need. There is nothing wrong with having three disk imaging tools. Use the one that makes the most sense.

Most forensic examiners use tools from several vendors. Some may use commercial and open source tools. The source is not important. The important points are that you have the tools that get the job done, you know how to use them, and you have verified that the tools do what they are supposed to do before you use them on a real case.

One last point, get the necessary training to properly use the tools you acquire. Great tools can hamper or ruin an investigation if you don't know how to use them. Forensic tools can be highly effective or highly destructive, all depending on the knowledge of the user. Get the tools, and then get the training.

After you have built your toolbox and know how to use the tools in it, you are ready to tackle the next investigation.

Terms to Know

forensic suite

Review Questions

1. Which utility, originally created for the Unix platform, copies and converts files using two basic arguments (if and of)?

2. Which software suite provides an Enterprise Edition that specifically supports volatile data analysis on a live Windows system?

3. Which disk imaging software operates as an extended DOS command shell?

4. What are two common algorithms used to create hash values for drive images?

5. Which forensic software suite integrates the dtSearch engine in its searching function?

6. What two software suites are free?

7. What are two of several vendors of forensic computers?

8. After creating an image of a drive, what must you do to ensure that the copy matches the original?

9. You have many factors to consider when choosing appropriate forensic software. Name two.

10. Which utilities provide comprehensive forensic functionality?

Chapter 9

Pulling It All Together

In the last chapter, you learned about the various types of forensic tools used to gather evidence. Prior to that, you learned about capturing and extracting data. Through each step of the way you should be documenting what you are doing along with the evidence you find. Besides being familiar with the process of gathering information, data, and material that may be related to criminal activity, forensic investigators must also be skilled in the area of documentation. Throughout the forensic process, the investigator has the ability to extract and examine mounds of information. At times, this can be intimidating as well as overwhelming. Somehow, in the end, all of this information has to be processed into a succinct report that is understandable to a judge and jury.

Properly documenting the steps taken during the evidence-gathering process must be a top priority. Good documentation, along with sound forensic procedures, is essential for success in prosecuting computer crime cases. Crucial evidence is subject to question, and the qualifications of the expert witness can become an issue if the computer evidence was not documented systematically. This is why being able to accurately reconstruct an investigation is a critical skill.

It's time to look at what information you might need and how to put all this information together in an analysis report that is concise yet detailed enough to explain your findings. This chapter examines this process and looks at several sample reports so you can get an idea of the type and quality of documentation you will need for your case.

Begin with a Concise Summary

A small hard drive is 10GB. If the contents were printed, it would create a stack of paper approximately 1,111 feet tall. Even though you can't have too much documentation, when it comes to presenting the case, you need balance. You won't want to weed through tons of evidence again later, and you don't want to appear incompetent. For example, if you are asked about log events or a specific activity, you don't want to respond, "I know that I saw that somewhere." If the activity is in the Tcpdump log file, you'll need to be able to locate it again.

Often lawyers may want to have electronic evidence produced for them in paper format. A complete forensic analysis report can usually be stored on a single CD-ROM. Evidence is much simpler to handle in electronic form, where it can be filed, cross-referenced, and indexed. Most law firms now have the technology to do this. Various software programs, such as Summation, allow the evidence to be processed in a more efficient way than paper format. Additional information on Summation can be found at `http://info.summation.com/products`.

Kroll Ontrack is another software program that attorneys use. It provides software tools that allow you to view, search, sort, bookmark, and generate reports on the data after the evidence is extracted. Kroll Ontrack offers ElectronicData-Investigator free of charge to all of its computer forensics customers. For more information on the services that Kroll Ontrack provides, go to `http://www.krollontrack.com`.

Evidor serves as an automated forensic examiner. It can come in handy during civil litigation when one party wants to examine the other party's computers. Both WinHex and Evidor are products of X-Ways Software Technology AG. You can find them at `http://www.sf-soft.de/evidor/index.htm` and `http://www.sf-soft.de/winhex/index-m.html`.

When you are formulating a concise report, it is important to:

- Understand the importance of the reports
- Limit the report to specifics
- Design the layout and presentation in an easy-to-understand format
- Understand the difference between litigation support reports and technical reports
- Write clearly
- Provide supporting material
- Explain the methods used in data collection
- Explain results

The basic guidelines for your reports should be to document your steps clearly, organize the report by using a template, and be consistent. Documenting in a clear and concise manner helps ensure that the details can be recalled or conveyed when the need arises. In order to do this though, the scope of your original documentation must be broader and you should document every step of the process.

Document Everything, Assume Nothing

As an investigator, the better you understand a case, the better you'll be able to sense the next logical step. An experienced investigator knows that the success of a forensics investigation relies not only on the ability to uncover evidence but also on the ability to follow good methodology during the course of evidence collection and handling so that the evidence can be used in court. Under *Federal Rule of Civil Procedure 26(a)(2)(B)*, the parties involved in legal cases are required to disclose the identities of their forensics experts or risk not being able to call them to testify at trial. This rule states that testimony is to be accompanied by a written, signed report. The report is to contain:

- A complete statement of all opinions and the basis and reasons for such
- Any data or other information considered in forming the opinions
- Any exhibits to be used in support of or summary for the opinions
- The qualifications of the witness, including a list of all publications authored by the witness within the last ten years
- Amount of compensation to be paid for the study and testimony
- A listing of any other cases in which the witness has testified as an expert at trial or by deposition within the last four years.

Under Rule 30(b)(6), an organization's designated agent shall testify to matters known or reasonably available to the organization. This could include providing some additional items of more specific information, such as:

- Quantity and locations of computers in use
- Operating systems and application software installed and dates of use
- File-naming conventions and what directories data is saved to
- Backup disk or tape inventories and schedules
- Computer use policies
- Identities of current and former employees responsible for systems operations
- E-mail with dates, times, and attachments
- Word documents, tables, graphs, and database files
- Internet bookmarks, cookies, and history logs

You begin the documentation process long before you start dealing with the data evidence in a case. Prior to seizing equipment or data, make sure you have the necessary paperwork filed and have proper permission to seize the computer or equipment in question. Remember that the Fourth Amendment limits the ability of government agents to search for evidence without a warrant, but consent

Federal Rule of Civil Procedure 26
Federal Rule 26 states the General Provisions Governing Discovery and Duty of Disclosure. Section (a) states Required Disclosures and Methods to Discover Additional Matter.

is the most applicable exception to this Amendment. When a proper computer use policy is in place, it can cover an employee's consent to searching their system. If you have any doubts as to whether on not a warrant is needed, see the *Searching and Seizing Computers and Obtaining Electronic Evidence in Criminal Investigations* manual on the Computer Crime and Intellectual Property Section Criminal Division of the United States Department of Justice website at http://www.cybercrime.gov/s&smanual2002.htm.

NOTE

Although the excitement of working in the computer forensics field is experienced while performing the investigation and "catching the bad guy," the "real work" is achieved when the examiner "kills a few trees" and completes the paperwork. As a computer forensics examiner, you must remember that the job is not complete until the report is filed.

Document everything carefully, consistently, and neatly. As discussed in Chapter 3, "Computer Evidence," you need to record the who, what, when, where, why, and how of the case. You'll also want to pay special attention to procedural details. You may want to start with a bound paper notebook, making notes in pen with dates and initials. This type of documentation can provide a good point of reference for jogging the memories of the forensic examiners when the case is lengthy. Chapter 3 provided a brief explanation of documentation and a sample log sheet. The National Institute of Justice offers a document titled "Forensic Examination of Digital Evidence: A Guide for Law Enforcement." Appendix C in that document has a wide variety of sample forms that you can tailor for your needs. The document, with sample forms, is located online at http://www.ojp.usdoj.gov/nij/pubs-sum/199408.htm.

A large percentage of your time will be spent writing reports and completing logs. All the documentation that you create can be used at a later time by the courts. When you write the report, remember that it will likely take a few years for the case to reach the courts. The better detailed the report you write now, the easier it will be for you to recall facts about the case when you have to testify in the future.

Interviews and Diagrams

If you interviewed anyone, you should create a list of who you interviewed, including their names, e-mail addresses, what they saw, when, where, and how. In cases such as the release of malware or denial of service (DoS) attacks, you can sometimes obtain more information than you expect just by asking. You might even end up with a confession.

Using diagrams is another method of documenting a case. Remember that jurors might not know about the workings of computers and networks, so you may want to use pictures or drawings to get your point across. For example, if you are asked to prove that the data presented has not been altered, you will have to present documentation that you made the image of the original evidence correctly. Let's say that you used MD5 verification to ensure that the procedure did not corrupt the data. You explain that when using MD5, even a change to one bit of information on a large drive packed with data results in a new message digest. By comparing the original disks and the copy, you can ensure that an image is an exact replica of the original. By using a drawing like the following one, you can help the jury better understand how this procedure works.

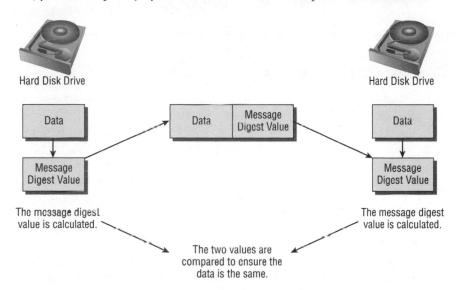

The message digest value is calculated.

The message digest value is calculated.

The two values are compared to ensure the data is the same.

When it was time to testify, the opposing attorney was very well briefed on the details of the case and on forensics procedures. If I had not properly prepared my report during that investigation, I would have performed poorly while I was "being grilled." I was properly prepared to testify because I had reviewed my report before the deposition and because I had written an extremely detailed report at the time of the investigation. This particular investigation had occurred three years and many investigations earlier, but I was able to easily recall the necessary facts just by reviewing the report.

Keep in mind that the work you do today to prepare a report may very well more than pay for itself many years down the road.

Videotapes and Photographs

If at all possible, videotape the entry of all persons into the crime scene. By taping the actual entrance of a forensics team into the area, you can help refute claims that evidence was planted at the scene. You might also want to take photographs of the actual evidence and take notes at the scene. For example, in the case of an intrusion, you may want to take a photograph of the monitor. However, time is usually of the essence. Consideration should be given to the possibility of destructive processes running in the background or a time-delayed password-protected screen saver. The computer most likely will be moved to a secure location where a proper chain of custody can be maintained and the processing of evidence can begin.

Pictures of the computer should be taken from all angles to document the system hardware components and how they are connected. Be careful to label each wire so that the original computer configuration can be restored. Remove the case cover of the PC or server, and carefully photograph the inside. Note the serial number, internal drives, and peripheral components. Documentation should include a physical description and detailed notation of any identifying markings or numbers. Make sure you document the configuration of the cables and connection types as well. Next, label the evidence and then once again photograph the evidence after the labels have been attached. It may be a good idea to use a 35mm camera to take the photographs. Digital images are easy to manipulate; therefore, should you be questioned whether the images have been altered, the negatives from the film can help your case.

electrostatic discharge (ESD)
Buildup of electrical charge on one surface that is suddenly transferred to another surface when it is touched.

Ideally, one person documents while another person handles the evidence. Document everything that goes on. The designated custodian for the chain of custody should initial each item after double-checking the list you have created. It is important to do this at the scene to eliminate the possibility of evidence tainting at a later date. You want to be able to prove that you did not alter any of the evidence after the computer came into your possession. Such proof will help you refute allegations that you changed or altered the original evidence.

Transporting the Evidence

The next step in the documentation process is to document the transporting of the evidence to the lab. Photograph or videotape and document the handling of evidence leaving the scene to the transport vehicle. Be careful to guard against *electrostatic discharge (ESD)*. Although ESD won't kill you, it can certainly kill your computer components. Integrated circuits (such as processors, memory, and expansion cards) are especially sensitive to ESD. During transportation, *electromagnetic fields* created by magnets and radio transmitters can alter or destroy data as well. To ensure the integrity of the data stored on the media, also avoid conditions such as moisture, high humidity, and excessive heat or cold. At the examination facility, videotape or photograph and document the handling of evidence from the transportation vehicle to the lab.

The original evidence should be left untouched unless extenuating circumstances exist. Do not leave the computer unattended unless it is locked in a secure location. You don't want to risk the destruction of any crucial evidence. New Technologies, Inc. (NTI) produces a program called *Seized*, which locks the seized computer and warns the computer operator that the computer contains evidence and should not be operated. You can find additional information at `http://www.forensics-intl.com/seized.html`.

electromagnetic fields
Produced by the local buildup of electric charges in the atmosphere. They can be damaging to computer components. They are present everywhere in our environment but are invisible to the human eye.

Seized
A program developed by New Technologies, Inc. (NTI) that locks a seized computer and warns the computer operator that the computer contains evidence and should not be operated.

Documenting Gathered Evidence

When gathering and preparing evidence, keep in mind that normal computer operations can destroy evidence in memory, in the file slack, or in the swap file. When documenting physical evidence such as floppy or hard disks, put one copy in a bag and seal it with tape that can't be unsealed without leaving a mark. Clearly mark the bags with the case information. The Legal Imager and reaSsembly Application (LISA) can record this type of evidence right in the software. (LISA is available at `http://www.blackcat.demon.co.uk/lisa/`.) See the following illustration for an example of how you can enter case details into LISA. Be sure to have extra plastic bags with ties to store evidence and additional copies of all incident-handling forms.

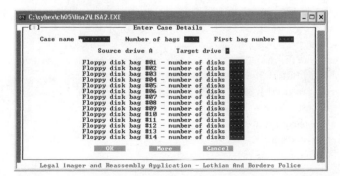

International Association of Computer Investigative Specialists (IACIS)
An international volunteer corporation comprised of law enforcement professionals, including federal, state, local, and international law enforcement, who are committed to education in the field of forensic computer science.

Complementary Metal Oxide Semiconductor (CMOS)
An on-board semiconductor chip used to store system information and configuration settings when the computer is either off or on.

The *International Association of Computer Investigative Specialists (IACIS)* has established a guide for forensic computer and digital evidence examinations. This guide lists examples of items to be documented. You can find it at `www.cops.org/html/forensicprocedures.htm`. You should document all standard procedures and processes used in the examination of the evidence and note in detail any deviations from the standard procedures. All recovered data should be properly marked.

Timelines of computer usage and file accesses can be valuable sources of computer evidence. Computer investigators rely on evidence stored as data and the timeline of dates and times that files were created, modified, or last accessed by a computer user. If the system clock is one hour different because of Daylight Saving Time, then file time stamps will also reflect the wrong time. To adjust for these inaccuracies, documenting the system date and time settings at the time the computer is taken into evidence is crucial. The accuracy of the time and date stamps on files is dependant on the accuracy of the time and date stored in the *CMOS* chip of the computer. It is important to document the accuracy of these settings on the seized computer to validate the accuracy of the times and dates associated with any relevant computer files. Compare the current time and date with the date and time stored in the computer. The current time can be obtained form official time sites such as `http://wwp.greenwichmeantime.com/` or `http://www.worldtimeserver.com/`. Normally, the date and time are checked by using a floppy boot disk to boot the computer and then checking the time and date in the BIOS settings. The following graphic shows how to display the date and time in the BIOS.

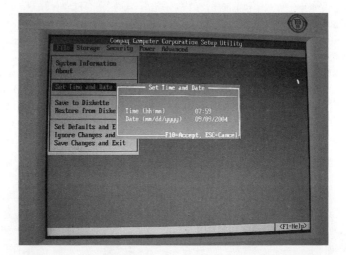

File dates and times are important in documenting the backdating of computer files. Sometimes criminals purposely change the date and time on their computers. They do this for several reasons; one of the most common is to defeat proper software licensing. Another reason the computer date and time may not be current is because the CMOS battery is dead. When a CMOS battery dies, the computer no longer keeps correct time, causing the computer date and time to be inaccurate. When the settings on the computer are inaccurate, the times and dates associated with relevant files can be established by a computer forensic specialist. Get Time from NTI can be used to document the time and date settings on a computer. A program called Afind is available from Foundstone's website (`http://www.foundstone.com`). Afind lists the last access time on files without tampering with the data. Remember to make a bit stream backup of the computer hard drive before running the computer or checking the time and date. It's important.

Activity timelines can be especially helpful when multiple computers and individuals are involved in the commission of a crime. The computer forensics investigator should always consider timelines of computer usage in all computer-related investigations. The same is true in computer security reviews concerning potential access to sensitive and/or trade secret information stored in the form of computer files. The time and date that files were created can be important in cases involving computer evidence. Forensic software, such as Guidance Software's EnCase, allows you to build a timeline in your casework. See the next graphic for an example.

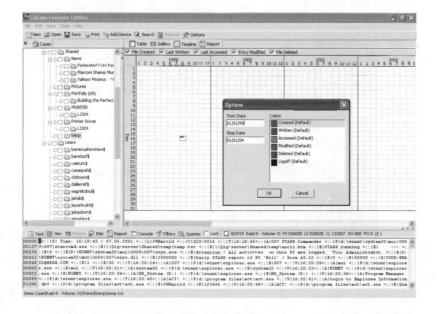

In your forensic software, you can create a case and then enter details such case description, examiner name, organization, and comments. The next section will discuss these in finer detail. When working in a case file, you have the option of logging all your actions, including exact dates and times and screenshots of dialog windows. The following graphic shows how to set these options in WinHex. WinHex was discussed in Chapter 5, "Capturing the Data Image" and Chapter 8, "Common Forensics Tools."

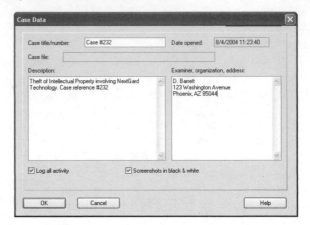

Documenting the process from entering the scene to gathering the evidence is important. You aren't done yet, though. A couple of additional pieces of documentation might need to be gathered before the report is actually written.

Additional Documentation

If someone intends to prosecute for damages caused to an organization, all losses the organization suffered as a result of the incident should be documented. Have the organization provide such data as:

- Estimated number of hours spent in response and recovery
- Cost of damaged equipment
- Value of data lost
- Amount of credit given to customers because of the inconvenience
- Loss of revenue
- Value of any trade secret information

The basic rule of evidence is that it must be the best available, which means evidence that is primary or first-hand. Computer forensics involves the use of tools and procedures to guarantee the accuracy of the preservation of evidence. Most computer forensic specialists use multiple software tools, developed by separate and independent developers, to help them accurately preserve evidence.

By using different, independently developed tools to validate results, inaccuracies due to software design flaws or bugs can be avoided. By validating your evidence with software tools and procedures, you help eliminate the possibility that lawyers will challenge the integrity of the results based on the accuracy of the software tool used. By documenting everything, you should be able to refute any claims that you mishandled evidence or that the tools used in your investigation were not acceptable.

Hacker Acquitted

Aaron Caffrey, 19, was acquitted after a jury unanimously decided he was not guilty of unauthorized computer access related to an attack on the Port of Houston's web-based systems in September 2001. Caffrey claimed that the evidence against him was planted on his computer by attackers who used an unspecified Trojan to gain control of his PC and launch the assault. A forensic examination of Caffrey's PC found attack tools but no trace of a Trojan infection. The case was dependent on whether the jury accepted the argument that a Trojan could remove itself or accepted expert testimony from the prosecution that no such technology existed.

Now that you are familiar with all the information you should document, it's time to decide how to put all this information into a report format that a judge and jury can easily understand.

Formulating the Report

As noted in the Tales from the Trenches, you might have to use the report you prepared to recall events years after the fact. Therefore, your report should contain information that is focused. Each forensic examiner has his or her own way of formulating reports, but establishing a standardized template is important. This way your work will be consistent. The more you use the template, the more proficient you will become. You will also want the items you refer to in your report to be consistent so you don't confuse your audience. For example, if you are discussing a hard drive in your report, be sure that all instances refer to it as just that. Using the terms hard disk, hard drive, and fixed disk interchangeably in the same report can cause confusion to the reader. In fact, including a glossary can help define the items listed in your report. Here are some items the report should contain:

- Name of the reporting agency and case investigator
- Case number
- Date of the report
- List of the items examined

- Description of the examination process
- Results and/or conclusion

A typical report format consists of several independent sections, which include the preceding information. These sections are broken down in the following order:

Executive Summary or Summary of Findings   The summary is a brief explanation of the circumstances that required the investigation and a short detail of the significant findings. Include the names of all persons involved in the case and the date.

Objectives   This section states the specific purpose for the investigation—for example, to determine if the subject used a laptop computer as an instrument in the crime of identity theft and/or as a repository of data related to that crime. Include the name of the reporting agency and investigator.

Analysis   This section provides a description of the evidence and the steps taken to process the evidence.

Findings   The findings include specific information listed in order of importance or relevance. This can include data and graphic image analysis, Internet-related evidence, and techniques used to hide data.

Supporting Documentation   This section includes how you arrived at the findings in the previous section. The supporting documentation is usually the longest section of the report. It can also contain the printouts of items of evidence and chain of custody documentation.

Glossary   Can be used with the report to help the reader understand technical terms contained in the report.

Now that you have some idea of the format the report should take, let's look at a few sample reports.

Sample Analysis Reports

In this section, you'll look at some sample analysis reports. Most of them are taken from the various software programs described in Chapter 8, "Common Forensics Tools." The reports in this section show samples of different sections of the reports. In addition to these reports, you can find two sample reports and case summaries in Appendix A of the "Forensic Examination of Digital Evidence: A Guide for Law Enforcement" document by the National Institute of Justice at www.ncjrs.org/pdffiles1/nij/199408.pdf.

This next sample report starts with a case brief explaining the particulars of the incident.

Case #234—NextGard Technology Copyright Piracy Summary

On May 7, 2004, a concerned citizen contacted the police department regarding possible copyright piracy. He explained that he searched the Internet looking to purchase NextGard Technology accounting and finance software. He purchased the software from a website called Cheepware.com that advertised this software as "authentic," but was unable to register the software he purchased. When the police department contacted NextGard Technology, they were informed that several other buyers complained about their inability to register NextGard Technology software bought from the same website. The case arose from a fourteen-month investigation led by U.S. Immigration and Customs Enforcement in cooperation with the Department of Justice Computer Crimes and Intellectual Property Section.

The investigation was conducted by the Bureau of Immigration and Customs Enforcement. After making an undercover purchase of software from the website through the Customs Cyber Center, the agents obtained a warrant to search the suspect's residence for computers and materials used in making counterfeit software and other evidence related to the theft charges. The agents submitted a desktop computer to the computer forensic laboratory for analysis.

Now let's move on to the objective of the case. As you follow along, note some of the particulars of the case, such as:

- Computer type
- Operating system
- Offenses committed with the computer
- Case agent
- Where the exam took place
- Tools used

Objective

Determine if the suspect used the desktop computer as an instrument in the crimes of criminal copyright infringement and/or as a repository of data related to those crimes.

- **Computer type:** Compaq Deskpro desktop computer
- **Operating system:** Microsoft Windows 2000 Professional
- **Offenses:** Criminal copyright infringement
- **Case agent:** Customs Cyber Center investigator, D. Brown
- **Where examination took place:** Computer Forensic Laboratory
- **Tools/Software used:** AccessData's Forensic Toolkit (FTK) and Password Recovery Toolkit

Initial Assessment

This section of the report gives an initial assessment of the case. It establishes that the proper documents were provided, the goals of the examination were set, and that the case was assigned.

1. The initial documentation provided by the investigator was reviewed. This review determined that:

    a. Legal authority was established by a search warrant obtained specifically for the examination of the computer in a laboratory setting.

    b. Chain of custody was properly documented on the appropriate departmental forms.

    c. The request for service and a detailed summary explained the investigation, provided keyword lists, and provided information about the suspect, the counterfeit software, and the Internet web address.

2. The computer forensic investigator met with the case agent and discussed the investigative avenues and potential evidence being sought in the forensic examination.

3. Evidence intake was documented:

    a. The computer was marked and photographed.

    b. A file was created and the case information was entered into the laboratory database.

    c. The computer was properly stored in the laboratory's property room.

4. The case was assigned to a computer forensic investigator.

Disk Imaging

The next section of the report documents the analysis. It explains how the evidence was assessed, how the drive was imaged, and how the data was analyzed.

1. The desktop computer was examined and photographed.

    a. The computer cover was removed and the hardware was examined and documented.

    b. A controlled boot disk was placed in the computer's floppy drive. The computer was powered on, and the BIOS setup program was entered. The BIOS information was documented, and the system time was compared to a trusted time source and documented. The boot sequence was checked and documented; the system was already set to boot from the floppy drive first.

    c. The desktop computer was powered off without making any changes to the BIOS.

2. Access Data's FTK was used to create an evidence file containing the image of the desktop computer's hard drive.

   a. The desktop computer was connected to a laboratory computer through a null-modem cable, which connected to the computers' parallel ports.

   b. The notebook computer was booted to the DOS prompt with a controlled boot disk.

   c. The laboratory computer, equipped with a hard drive with the same storage capacity, was booted to the DOS prompt with a controlled boot disk. FTK Imager was started, and evidence files for the desktop computer were acquired and written to the laboratory computer's hard drive.

   d. When the imaging process was completed, the computers were powered off. The desktop computer was returned to the laboratory property room, and the hard drive containing the FTK evidence files was write-protected and entered into evidence.

Analysis

This section of the report describes the evidence and the steps taken to process the evidence.

1. A laboratory computer was prepared by the investigator using licensed copies of Windows 2000 Professional, AccessData's FTK version 1.43, and WinHex version 10.45 SR-2.

2. The FTK evidence files from the desktop computer were copied to the laboratory computer's hard drive.

3. A new FTK case file was opened, and the notebook computer's evidence files were examined using FTK.

   a. Deleted files were recovered by FTK.

   b. File data, including filenames, dates and times, physical and logical size, and complete path, were recorded.

   c. Keyword text searches were conducted based on information provided by the investigator. All hits were reviewed.

   d. Graphics files were opened and viewed.

   e. HTML files were opened and viewed.

   f. Data files were opened and viewed; four password-protected and encrypted files were located.

   g. Unallocated space and slack space were searched.

   h. Files of interest were copied from the FTK evidence file to a compact disk.

4. Unallocated clusters were copied from the FTK evidence file to a clean hard drive, which had been wiped to U.S. Department of Defense recommendations (DoD 5200.28-STD). WinHex was then used to carve images from unallocated space. The carved images were extracted from WinHex, opened, and viewed. A total of 3,592 images were extracted.

5. The password-protected files were copied to a 1.44MB floppy disk. AccessData's Password Recovery Toolkit was run on the files, and passwords were recovered for the password-protected files. The files were opened using the passwords and viewed.

Findings

This section summarizes the findings that are valuable to the investigation.

The analysis of the desktop computer recovered 265 files of evidentiary value or investigative interest. The recovered files included:

1. Ninety document files including documents containing the suspect's name and personal information. Text in the files included names of customers who had purchased the software, their methods of payment, and shipping information. In addition, text that described the counterfeit software and pricing structure was found.

2. Fifty-seven graphics files including high-resolution image files of software labels and packaging materials, certificates of authenticity, registration cards, and copies of checks made out to Cheepware. Most graphics were scanned.

3. Eighty-three HTML files including Hotmail and Yahoo e-mail inquiries about the software including e-mails between the suspect and customers (which included the concerned citizen corresponding about the inability to register the software purchased).

4. Thirty-one graphics files carved from unallocated space depicting copies of checks.

5. Four password-protected and encrypted files.

   a. Microsoft Word 2000 document containing a list of personal information about several individuals including names, addresses, dates of birth, credit card numbers and expiration dates, and other information. Password: [gotya].

   b. Microsoft Word 2000 document containing information on how to crack the license for the NextGard software products. Password: [crack].

   c. Microsoft Excel spreadsheet containing the dates and dollar amounts of payments made through PayPal and eBay. Password: [money].

   d. Microsoft Excel spreadsheet containing a list of various software and their licensing key numbers. Password: [moremoney].

Supporting Documentation

This section contains the most detailed information. It describes how you arrived at the conclusions in the findings sections. It includes documents and tables that outline all the steps you took to meet the objective. You can start the section by providing details about the media analyzed and then move on to subsections showing string searches and log file analysis.

    The following graphic is the file overview. It summarizes the number of items included in the case.

```
Aug 6, 2004
Evidence Items
Evidence Items: 4

File Items
Total File Items: 5002
Flagged Thumbnails: 0
Other Thumbnails: 2025/

File Status
KFF Alert Files: 0
Bookmarked Items: 1645
Bad Extension: 394
Encrypted Files: 0
From E-mail: 13
Deleted Files: 0
From Recycle Bin: 0
Duplicate Items: 880
OLE Subitems: 277
Flagged Ignore: 0
KFF Ignorable: 180

File Category
Documents: 679
Spreadsheets: 0
Databases: 0
Graphics: 2025
E-mail Messages: 13
Executables: 198
Archives: 26
Folders: 0
Slack/Free Space: 0
Other Known Type: 150
Unknown Type: 1924
```

The following graphic is a sampling of the evidence list. These are some of the items you would include in the supporting documentation part of the report.

```
Aug 6, 2006
Display Name: Cookies
Evidence File Name: Cookies
Evidence Path: C:\Documents and Settings\Diane Barrett
Identification Name/Number:
Evidence Type: Contents of a folder
Added: 8/6/2004 12:53:47 PM
Children: 17
Descendants: 17
Investigator's Name: D. Barrett
Comment:

Display Name: Documents and Settings
Evidence File Name: Documents and Settings
Evidence path: C:
Identification Name/Number:
Evidence Type: Contents of a folder
Added: 8/6/2004 1:01:46 PM
Children:
Descendants: 4659
Investigator's Name: D. Barrett
Comment:

Display Name: Favorites
Evidence File Name: Favorites
Evidence path: C:\Documents and Settings\Diane Barrett
Identification Name/Number:
Evidence Type: Contents of a folder
Added: 8/6/2004 12:53:52 PM
Children: 3
Descendants: 7
Investigator's Name: D. Barrett
Comment:

Display Name: Temp
Evidence File Name: Temp
Evidence path: C:\Windows
Identification Name/Number:
Evidence Type: Contents of a folder
Added: 8/6/2004 12:53:50 PM
Children: 2
Descendants: 17
Investigator's Name: D. Barrett
Comment:
```

As you can see, this is the starting point for your reports. From here you formulate a report that is understandable to a judge and jury.

Additional Report Subsections

Often your reports may include additional subsections, especially if the case is quite extensive or contains data from many devices and computers. If the report becomes too long, include a table of contents so that everything is organized in a logical fashion. The audience can scan it and get a better idea of the purpose of the report.

If the event you are investigating is an intrusion, you could include a methodology section on attacks to help the audience understand how attacks are conducted or how the particular attack in the case took place. If the case involves an employee illegally accessing confidential information on a vendor website, a section on Internet activity could be added to show the browsing history and Internet activity of the employee. This section could also be used to show the download of malicious tools or evidence erase programs. When an employee has illegally accessed confidential information on a vendor website, a user applications section is usually included. The applications section should include a list of all installed applications such as "hacker tools" or malicious software and a description of what they do.

Sometimes a final summary and/or conclusion is included with a report. In the copyright piracy case, the final summary and conclusion might look like the following ones.

Summary

Based on the information revealed by the computer analysis, several new avenues of investigation were opened. By contacting the victims listed in the password-protected Microsoft Word document, investigators learned that the victims had all purchased software from the suspect through either his website or direct mail. The Hotmail and Yahoo e-mail found on the suspect's computer provided information on additional victims. The password-protected Microsoft Excel spreadsheet containing the dates and dollar amounts of payments made through PayPal and eBay documented that the suspect had sold 2,578 illegal copies of NextGard software with a retail value of $750,250.00.

Conclusion

The suspect eventually pled guilty and was incarcerated for 5 years.

Instead of a final summary or conclusion, your report can contain a section on recommendations. This can be especially helpful if the case probably won't end up in court—for example, when the company doesn't want to prosecute and just wants to know how to reduce its risk in the future.

You can use a glossary to define technical terms that the average person might not understand. You might also want to include an appendix for detailed information that would interrupt the flow if it were included in the report proper. When investigating accounting fraud, you will frequently come across large spreadsheets. These sheets are hard to print in a format that is easily viewable. In instances such as this, you will want to attach an electronic appendix.

Using Software to Generate Reports

Nearly all commercial forensics software will produce a report for the beginning of your documentation. Let's look at a sample report from Paraben's Case Agent Companion. To save space, most of the bookmarks have been deleted, but this will give you a general idea of what a generated report looks like.

Case #234—NextGard Technology Copyright Piracy Summary

Header

>   Agent: Customs Cyber Center

>   Examiner: D. Brown

Notes

>   Subject: Software Evidence

>   Body: The bookmarked files are part of a program that is used to generate software labels.

>   Author: D. Brown

>   Created: Fri Sep 10 13:42:28 GMT-07:00 2004

>   Modified: Sat Sep 11 06:16:35 GMT-07:00 2004

Analysis Logs

1. A laboratory computer was prepared by the investigator using licensed copies of Windows 2000 Professional, AccessData's FTK version 1.43, and WinHex version 10.45 SR-2.

2. The FTK evidence files from the desktop computer were copied to the laboratory computer's hard drive.

3. A new FTK case file was opened, and the notebook computer's evidence files were examined using FTK.

   a. Deleted files were recovered by FTK.

   b. File data, including filenames, dates and times, physical and logical size, and complete path, were recorded.

   c. Keyword text searches were conducted based on information provided by the investigator. All hits were reviewed.

d. Graphics files were opened and viewed.

e. HTML files were opened and viewed.

f. Data files were opened and viewed; four password-protected and encrypted files were located.

g. Unallocated space and slack space were searched.

h. Files of interest were copied from the FTK evidence file to a compact disk.

4. Unallocated clusters were copied from the FTK evidence file to a clean hard drive, which had been wiped to U.S. Department of Defense recommendations (DoD 5200.28-STD). WinHex was then used to carve images from unallocated space. The carved images were extracted from WinHex, opened, and viewed. A total of 3,592 images were extracted.

5. The password-protected files were copied to a 1.44MB floppy disk. AccessData's Password Recovery Toolkit was run on the files, and passwords were recovered for the password-protected files. The files were opened using the passwords and then viewed.

Bookmarks

Images Excluded

Contraband Images Included

Full Text Excluded

nero.exe

Description:

Name = nero.exe

Path = C:\Program Files\Ahead\Nero

Created = Sun Dec 16 13:40:06 GMT-07:00 2001

Modified = Wed Feb 20 10:53:58 GMT-07:00 2002

Last Accessed = Sun Apr. 11 13:40:06 GMT-07:00 2004

Size Actual = 18421

Size Allocated = 18421

PFS Type = 10000709

MD5 Hash = fc3031a83d9d82add69ab5df15a0d338

Cluster Map = []

Incident Counter = 0

Deleted = false

Encrypted = false

FOCH Hit = false

Volume = Volume0

System = Windows 2000

Author: D. Brown

Created: Fri Sep 10 13:49:23 GMT-07:00 2004

Modified: Fri Sep 10 13:49:23 GMT-07:00 2004

NeroCmd.exe

Description:

Name = NeroCmd.exe

Path = C:\Program Files\Ahead\Nero

Created = Sun Dec 16 13:40:06 GMT-07:00 2001

Modified = Wed Feb 20 10:53:58 GMT-07:00 2002

Last Accessed = Sun Apr. 11 13:40:06 GMT-07:00 2004

Size Actual = 71266

Size Allocated = 71266

PFS Type = 10000708

MD5 Hash = fe45230445a0b16fb0c3b483b21aa0c5

Cluster Map = []

Incident Counter = 0

Deleted = false

Encrypted = false

FOCH Hit = false

Volume = Volume0

System = Windows 2000

Author: D. Brown

Created: Fri Sep 10 13:49:23 GMT-07:00 2004

Summary

The analysis of the desktop computer recovered 265 files of evidentiary value or investigative interest. The recovered files included: 90 document files including documents containing the suspect's name and personal information; text in the files included names of customer who had purchased the software, their methods of payment, and shipping information. Text describing the counterfeit software and pricing structure was also found. Fifty-seven graphics files including high-resolution image files of software labels and packaging materials, certificates of authenticity, registration cards, and copies of checks made out to Cheepware. Most graphics were scanned. Eighty-three HTML files including Hotmail and Yahoo e-mail inquiries about the software including e-mails between the suspect and customers (which included the concerned citizen corresponding about the inability to register the software purchased). Thirty-one graphics files carved from unallocated space depicting copies of checks. Four password-protected and encrypted files.

The software allows you to add or remove sections and sort them to suit your needs, as shown in the following graphic.

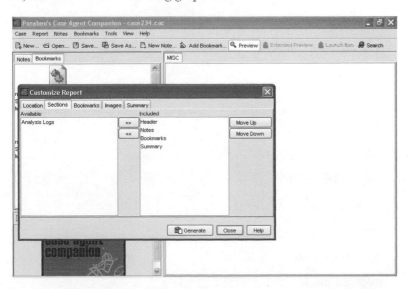

No matter whether you choose to use a reporting method similar to one demonstrated here, or create your own, your report should document facts in a manner that is easily understood. The goals of the report are to accurately account the details of the case in an understandable format while containing the required information to explain your findings and still withstand legal examination.

Terms to Know

CMOS	Federal Rule of Civil Procedure 26(a)(2)(B)
electromagnetic fields	International Association of Computer Investigative Specialists (IACIS)
electrostatic discharge (ESD)	Seized

Review Questions

1. What set of rules states the General Provisions Governing Discovery and Duty of Disclosure?

2. What are some of the items of information that a forensic examiner might be requested to provide under Rule 30(b)(6)?

3. Why is a template recommended for reports?

4. Where can you find out how to properly document and sample log sheets?

5. When should you consider using diagrams as a method of documentation?

6. Why should you videotape the entry of all persons into the crime scene?

7. Why is it important to be cautious when you are transporting evidence from the crime scene to the lab for analysis?

8. When formulating a concise report, what are some items you should consider?

9. Why are timelines of computer usage and file accesses important when processing computer evidence?

10. What are some items that your report should contain?

Chapter 10

How to Testify in Court

As a computer forensics professional, you collect evidence with the sole purpose of discovering the truth. After you collect evidence, you must be prepared to present it to someone to convince them of the truth of a matter. Some evidence you collect may be destined only to grace the pages of a summary report to your boss. At other times, you may be asked to testify in court. This chapter covers the basics of how to present yourself and your evidence in a court of law.

All of the material covered in this chapter is applicable to more informal proceedings, but your understanding of basic evidence presentation matters most when in court. Our goal is not to provide legal advice. You can research to find specific laws that govern your actions as a witness. This chapter is going to cover only the most important things you need to understand for you to be an effective witness.

Preparation Is Everything

The best way to be a successful witness is to be a prepared witness. You probably won't be successful if you arrive at the last minute and attempt to answer questions off the top of your head. You'll likely appear to be unprepared and unprofessional. Never allow yourself to be unprepared to present your evidence.

NOTE

In all things, act in an impeccably ethical manner. Never sacrifice your personal or professional ethics by participating in questionable actions. Remember that all actions and statements must adhere to strict ethical standards.

expert witness
A person called to testify in a court of law who possesses special knowledge or skill in a specific area that applies to a case.

In many cases, your role in a trial will be as an *expert witness*. If you want to be considered an expert witness, you need to acquire or demonstrate special knowledge of computers and computer evidence and skill at retrieving evidence from computers. You can achieve the status of "expert" through education and experience. You become an expert witness when you appear in court for the purpose of presenting evidence or opinion. Most witnesses are allowed to testify only to facts they have perceived first-hand. That is, a regular witness can tell only what she has seen, heard, touched, felt, and smelled. After you are accepted as an expert in your field, your status as an expert witness allows you to provide an opinion.

Be aware that you will be required to justify your status as an expert in your field. You probably will have to produce documented qualifications, including education and practical experience from valid sources. This information will be provided to both parties. In other words, the opposing counsel will receive a copy of your credentials and justification as an expert witness. Generally speaking, your resumé is not enough. You will need to provide additional information, such as:

◆ Education received and degrees earned

◆ Professional training received

◆ Certifications held

◆ Experience details

◆ Other times you testified as an expert

summons
A court order that compels a witness to appear in court and answer questions.

You are generally requested to appear in court by either receiving a *summons* or by client request. In either case, your testimony should be completely unbiased and independent. The weight of your testimony depends on your credibility. When you receive a summons, make sure you are prepared before you appear in court.

Most attorneys recognize that an expert in a particular field is not necessarily skilled in presentation skills. Being able to convey information is almost as important as possessing the information. If you are uncomfortable speaking in front of audiences, spend some time with a member of the legal team working on delivery skills. Take the time necessary to ensure you are effective at getting your message across.

Both the legal team and all expert witnesses must spend time preparing for a case. Attorneys usually want to meet with witnesses early in the process. Expert witnesses are sought only when they are needed to explain evidence or strengthen its impact. As an expert, you will be asked to provide information on your experience in one or more areas of expertise. You will also be asked about other times you have testified as well. Be prepared to answer at least the following questions:

- What is your educational background, including degrees earned?
- What experience do you have in the area in which you are an expert?
- How are you qualified as an expert in this area?
- Are you aware of any conflicts of interest with respect to this case?
- Have you ever testified in court?
  - Were you called as an expert witness?

In most cases, this initial contact and interview takes place before a formal agreement to testify is in place. Put another way, you're not being paid yet. If you want to work as an expert witness, collect as much background information as possible before the initial interview so you won't waste uncompensated time during initial conversations. If you are ultimately hired, the initial conversation is billable time.

After you are hired as an expert witness, the legal team should question you thoroughly to uncover any issues that could hurt their case. Such issues could include past complaints or claims filed against you, conflict of interest issues, or involvement in activities that reduce your objectivity. Although you have already stated that you are not aware of any conflicts of interest, some questions could arise during the trial that warrant a third party's attention.

Conflict of Interest

We've all heard the rules of radio giveaways: "Employees of Mega Radio Corporation and their families are not eligible to win this contest." Avoiding a conflict of interest is the reason for this restriction. If Mega Radio Corporation gave prizes to its employees and their families, many eyebrows would be raised. It would look as if the advertisers' money were being used for employee bonuses. As a result, listeners might lose interest and start tuning to other radio stations that give them a chance to win prizes. Fewer listeners mean advertisers get less return on their advertising investments. Such situations are a result of allowing the interests of one party (the employees' desire for bonuses) to conflict with the interests of another party (the advertisers' desire to entice more listeners by using contests). When you find yourself in a situation in which you have incentive to make a decision in one particular direction, a conflict of interest probably exists.

deposition
Testimony that is reduced to
written form.

Your first opportunity to share your knowledge should be before the trial. Many case preparation activities include taking *depositions* from witnesses. During a deposition, you are asked questions that pertain to your area of expertise and aspects of the case. You can have a material impact on the case at this point. If you provide strong testimony and speak with authority, you may influence opposing counsel to explore a settlement without going to trial. On the other hand, a weak and unsure testimony can encourage the other side to pursue a trial.

NOTE

The section titled "What Matters Is What They Hear" in this chapter discusses techniques to get your point across.

direct examination
Initial questions asked to a witness to
extract testimony.

When a case goes to court, you will participate in two basic phases of the trial—direct examination and cross examination. *Direct examination* is where attorneys ask questions that allow a witness to provide testimony. Your legal team should provide a list of direct examination questions they plan to use. The opposing counsel then has the opportunity to question you. Their line of questioning is called *cross examination*. The purpose of cross examination is generally to weaken your testimony through several means. The best approach to handling cross examination is to be fully prepared with answers to likely questions.

Understand the Case

cross examiniation
Questions asked by opposing counsel to
cast doubt on testimony provided during
direct examination.

As early as possible before your court appearance, meet with the legal team to discuss the case. The goal of such a meeting is to understand the basic facts of the case. Although you may have been integral in the evidence collection effort, you may not know about other critical aspects of the case. Becoming an expert in every detail of the case is unnecessary, but knowing about the case as a whole will help you testify for your own piece of it. Such knowledge can also keep you from conflicting with other witness testimony. We'll come back to the topic of saying too much later in this chapter.

Many attorneys who work with technical cases understand their intricacies and want the whole team to be well informed. If you work with an attorney who seems to guard case information, think long and hard before agreeing to participate. If you do proceed with limited awareness of the case, you may be surprised by some of the questions you will be asked when it is your turn in court.

Another reason to understand the case is that you may not be the only expert witness. Other expert witnesses may have been called on both sides. You need to understand what each expert will testify to before you prepare your own testimony. This knowledge will not change any of the facts in the case, but it will help you scope your own testimony. For example, if you know your own counsel will use a database expert, you can focus on other areas. Likewise, knowing that the opposing counsel has hired an expert to counter your testimony will direct your preparation. You should talk with your counsel to understand likely questions, or at least a general direction, that you may face during cross examination.

Understand the Strategy

After you have a grasp of the general facts of the case, talk with the legal team about their strategy for arguing the case. They may want to emphasize the technical details of the case. Or, they may want to simply touch on the technical evidence and focus more on other aspects. Your involvement is dependent on the strategy the legal team chooses.

These techniques are applicable to noncourtroom presentations as well. If your investigation is part of an incident response effort, your "courtroom appearance" might be a presentation on the incident. The rules and environment might be different, but the general goals are the same. Your goal is to present the evidence and provide an expert opinion as to what it means.

Remember what part you play in the courtroom. You are the witness. The attorneys are the primary players. They direct the action and call you when its time for you to contribute to the case. You were hired for a specific role. Let's talk some more about what that role really is.

Understand Your Job

The primary purpose of a trial is to provide a forum for an impartial individual or group of individuals to decide which party prevails in a conflict. In some cases, the facts of the case are plain enough for an ordinary individual to understand them. For example, in cases that involve traffic accidents, most people are familiar with traffic laws and the operation of an automobile. Unless unusual circumstances exist, many attorneys will present the facts directly to a judge or jury.

Cases that involve technical aspects tend to be different. They will commonly involve details that most people do not understand. A case that involves ballistics and traditional forensics evidence normally requires an expert to present and explain the evidence. We've all seen the televised court proceedings with the expert on the stand testifying as to the forensic methods employed. They are necessary to explain the intricacies to the judge or jury.

Your job is often harder, though. Few ordinary citizens will profess to understand how *ballistics* or *DNA* analysis takes place. Although they are familiar with the terms, most will agree that an expert is required to perform the actual analysis. Computers are different. Nearly everyone has a home computer. What's worse, many home computer owners think they are computer security experts. Your first job is often to explain basic security concepts and how popular concepts may differ from reality.

For example, most people know what *spam* is. Few know how it originates and just why it is so difficult to stop. Similarly, malicious code is not understood by most in the general public. Far too few people understand the differences between a virus, a Trojan horse, and a worm.

ballistics
The science of flight dynamics; often used to determine the flight path of weapons.

DNA
Deoxyribonucleic acid. DNA is a code used within cells of living organisms. Its uniqueness is useful in investigations to link individuals with substances found in specific locations.

spam
Unsolicited "junk" e-mail often sent to a large number of people.

As an expert in the field of computers and computer forensics, you possess a level of knowledge that is beyond the common experience in our society. Your value to a case is to share your experience and explain how the evidence proves facts in the case. You are a teacher as well as a witness. Simply put, the legal team would not be able to successfully convince the court that the facts presented are true without your help.

Appearance Matters

Although we often hear that we shouldn't "judge a book by its cover," we all do. Judges and juries do as well. Your credibility will be influenced by your appearance. As unfair as it may seem, you really do have to care about what you wear and how you carry yourself. Your knowledge and the weight of your testimony will mean little if you do not appear to be credible. Let's look at a few aspects of your courtroom appearance.

Clothing

First and foremost, dress appropriately. Wear clothes that you would wear to a conservative office. For men, wear a suit. Darker colors (such as blue, black, and dark green) tend to exude confidence and authority. Although you may make a fashion statement with more vibrant colors, conservative colors create an aura of credibility. For women, a business suit or dress will give the court the impression that you can be taken seriously.

Even though you may work in jeans and a T-shirt, you would never wear them to court. The way you dress gives the judge and jury an impression of how trustworthy you are. When you walk into the courtroom, you will be judged by the clothes you wear. Remember that we're not talking about fairness here—we're talking about making the most of your courtroom appearance. Regardless how you may dress the rest of the time, always dress to impress the court. It will serve you well.

When choosing your clothing for a court appearance, don't overdo it. Keep jewelry (for women) to a minimum, and wear only tasteful pieces. Men should avoid jewelry as much as possible. A dozen gold necklaces do little to enhance your testimony. All in all, dress conservatively.

Grooming

Grooming is as important as clothing. Your clothes should be pressed and clean. Your physical appearance should match your crisp, clean clothes. Don't show up to court looking disheveled. You are going to testify that you seized evidence, or accepted seized evidence, and handled it in a responsible manner. Responsible people comb their hair. If you are disheveled, you will have a difficult time convincing a jury that you are responsible.

Men, a 5-o'clock shadow gives the impression that you are sloppy. It doesn't matter if you rarely shave before going to the lab; in court, you must impress a judge and jury. Your job is to present yourself as credible and responsible. The way in which you present yourself says a lot about your ability to be responsible.

Attitude

When you take the stand, remember that the judge and jury are watching and listening to you. Getting them on your side is imperative. A poor attitude can hurt your testimony. It can actually turn the jury against you. When you alienate someone, you make it very difficult for them to believe you.

While you are testifying, be aware of your attitude. The jury will read your emotions and your *body language*. They will watch you to decide if you are being sincere. Look at the judge and jury as you speak. Ignoring the jury may appear as if you are being untruthful. Watch your body language as well. When you cross your arms, you become "closed off" and unapproachable. This action gives many people a feeling of inferiority, which is not the best way to convince a jury.

Avoid being sarcastic or overly confident. Such attitudes tend to alienate jurors. You must strive to be sincere, but not overly confident. Avoid common phrases such as:

body language
Communication using body movements, gestures, and facial expressions.

- Ummm
- You know
- Sure
- Wow
- Other colloquial sayings

As you deliver your testimony, be willing to help the judge and jury understand what you are saying. You are as much a teacher as a witness. Avoid being rude or condescending; instead, be as helpful and respectful as possible. Remember that you are the expert who is trying to present evidence in layman's terms to make it understandable. Let's look at how you can get the message across to make your evidence understandable.

What Matters Is What They Hear

You could have the most eloquent delivery ever presented in a courtroom, but if the jury does not hear what you have to say, it's all wasted effort. Although you may present a topic using sophisticated presentation aids, the actual success depends on the recipient. Your responsibility is to ensure that the target of your presentation "gets it." Far too many presenters focus on the presentation and not the perception of the presentation.

Take the time to really sell your presentation. Whether you are teaching a jury how a disk drive works, or answering cross-examination questions, get your message across.

Communication involves three critical components:

◆ Sender

◆ Message

◆ Receiver

The sender is the party who prepares and sends the message. The sender is responsible for all aspects of the actual message. The sender chooses the message's content, tone, style, delivery medium, and recipient.

The message is the actual content of what you are sending. The sender creates and sends the message to the receiver via the chosen media. The message itself consists of the body of the message, along with "tone" of the message. The tone of a message can be influenced by the choice of vocabulary, punctuation, and structure. For example, the following two messages are identical except for their tone:

1. Please come to my office.

2. PLEASE COME TO MY OFFICE!!!

Clearly, the second message creates more anticipation (and dread). You can create the same distinction using your vocal tone. You can add emphasis to certain words or phrases to make them stand out. Don't overdo it, though—you still must remain believable and credible. If you rely on theatrics to make your points, you will lose credibility in the long run.

Listening

Listening is an important and often overlooked skill. Use your listening ability to take in as much as you can in the courtroom. The judge's statements and actions can tell you a lot about how you should act. It may change daily, too. Judges and juries are regular people who have bad days just like you and I do.

Listening allows you to "test the waters" without making a mistake by charging ahead in the wrong direction. Both legal teams can direct you through the questions they ask. As a rule of thumb, go with the direction your own legal counsel is leading you in. If the opposing counsel leads you in a particular direction, place close attention to what's going on. They could be trying to trip you up.

Listening always helps you to be more prepared when you do take the stand. To communicate well, use your ears more often than your mouth.

Tone

Because you are the expert, you will be perceived to have superior knowledge in one or more specific areas that pertain to the case. Many people can be intimidated by people with superior knowledge or experience. Always avoid using tones in your voice that can be interpreted by others as being haughty. You will never gain any respect, but you risk losing it if you use a tone that infers superiority.

Try to switch into "teacher mode." Take the time to explain topics that are not clear to one or more people in the courtroom. A good teacher evaluates where students are and approaches them to move them toward understanding. An expert witness cannot interact directly with jurors in the same manner as a teacher does, but you can still be respectful and try to convey the essence of your message. Any time you talk "down" to a judge or jury you risk invoking feelings of resentment. Jurors who resent you may not be very favorable to you during deliberations.

It looks like mom and dad were right when they said, "It's not what you say, it's how you say it that counts." Make sure the jury has an opportunity to perceive you as pleasant. It will matter.

Vocabulary

As previously discussed, the job of the expert witness is to explain complex topics or procedures to laypeople. You must use words and phrases that explain and do not confuse judges and juries. Avoid using too many industry-specific terms and acronyms. For instance, talking about the "TCP and UDP packets traveling between the server and the client" will likely confuse most people. To use such an example, you will have to explain:

- ◆ How information travels across networks
- ◆ How networks split messages into smaller chunks, called packets
- ◆ What a server is and what is does
- ◆ What a client is and what it does
- ◆ Networking protocols (basic introduction)
- ◆ TCP and UDP protocols

That's a lot of explaining to do just to address a fairly simple concept. Well, that's your job as an expert witness. Make the complex seem simple and be careful of which words you choose. The more successful you are at using common words in your explanations, the more effective your presentation will be.

Know Your Forensics Process and Tools

You are a computer forensic examiner. If you are called as an expert witness, you will likely be asked to explain your process of collecting evidence. Many jurors will find this process interesting, but tedious as well. Most people are unfamiliar with the processes necessary to acquire and store digital evidence in a manner that preserves the state of the evidence. You will have to educate them.

You must know your own process and your toolset like the back of your hand. It is imperative that you know, and can clearly explain, the steps you take and the tools you use in an investigation. You will be asked to explain each of your steps as you collected and analyzed evidence. If you need to use notes in your testimony, get permission from the judge first. He or she will usually ensure that your notes have already been admitted into evidence and then allow you to look at them to assist in the accuracy of your testimony. Don't just read your notes to the court—your credibility will suffer if you appear to lean too much on your notes.

The opposing counsel will certainly hammer you if you are unsure about your own practices. Don't provide the opportunity.

Best Practices

A good place to start in explaining your own forensic process is by referencing industry best practices. A wealth of information that outlines best practices in most security areas is available online. There are several very good websites that discuss current computer forensic best practices. Look at several of these websites to make sure your processes and tools are consistent with current best practices:

- **SANS Reading Room** `http://www.sans.org/rr/`
- **United States Secret Service** `http://www.ustreas.gov/usss/ electronic_evidence.shtml`
- **CERT Coordination Center** `http://www.cert.org/tech_tips/ win-UNIX-system_compromise.html` (mostly related to incident response)
- **Enterprise Systems** `http://www.esj.com/news/article.asp? EditorialsID=826`

Many more useful websites are available for additional best practices information. Take some time to explore several of them. They will help your investigation practices, as well as your ability to be accepted as an expert in court.

Your Process and Documentation

The primary source of information for the testimony explaining your forensics process is your evidence documentation. You should have an activity log that shows every action taken with respect to evidence during your investigation. The activity log should commence with evidence acquisition and be current up through the current day.

Complete documentation gives the jury the impression that you have been careful. Although it is possible to win a case without appropriate documentation, it makes your job far more difficult. Make sure you are meticulous in documenting the investigation process. You will need the logs if you are called to appear in court. Organized written information gives judges and juries the impression that you are responsible and meticulous.

Your Forensic Toolkit

Be prepared to explain the contents of your forensic toolkit. Include all hardware and software you use during an investigation. For each component, explain why you have it in your toolkit, what function it performs, and how you used it for the current investigation. Corroborating third-party information may be helpful.

For instance, your forensic software tools vendor might maintain information on the reliability of its product. Many commercial products provide online resources that make the use of their product more accepted in a court of law. Showing how your product maintains the chain of evidence gives some jurors the answers they were seeking.

Know exactly what tools you have and which ones you use. Be ready to justify your choice of tools and explain why your choice was sufficient get the job done.

Say Only What Is Necessary

Brevity is the soul of wit.
—*William Shakespeare*

Be careful with the words you choose. They may come back to haunt you. Talking too much is a common mistake. The more you talk, the more you risk becoming a bore and the more information you divulge. Although it may appear that the primary purpose for an expert witness is to divulge information, that's missing the point. Your main job is to provide an expert's view or interpretation, not to dump memory. The most common type of information a person divulges when talking too much is that of weaknesses. When you are on the stand, answer all questions succinctly. Only add enough details to fully answer the question. Resist the urge to say more than is necessary and do not try to answer questions that aren't asked.

Be Complete, But Not Overly Elaborate

Although you want to avoid saying more than is necessary, you can't answer all questions with "Yes" or "No." When you are asked a question, provide a full answer. If more information is needed, the person asking the questions should ask for more information. Incomplete answers leave the appearance that there is something to hide.

If you cannot answer a question with a single word, use an answer that is still short. For example, look at the following exchange between an attorney and an expert in the area of firewalls:

Attorney: Mr. Jones, do firewalls stop all "bad" messages coming into a system?

> Mr. Jones: No.
>
> Attorney: Well then, do firewalls stop any "bad" messages at all?
>
> Mr. Jones: In most cases, they can be set up to stop messages that you define as "bad."

Although your second answer is not exhaustively complete in a technical sense, it does answer the question. The attorney might ask you to explain how firewalls work and how they can block messages. In contrast, here is a poor answer for the second question:

> Attorney: Well then, do firewalls stop any "bad" messages at all?
>
> Mr. Elaborate Jones: Firewalls examine all packets that are designated as of interest in the internal configuration. The specific action the firewall takes is contingent upon the rule set and connection status at the time the packet is received. We can block networks, IP addresses, ports, and actual variant packets at will. Most firewalls that are worth using can do all this dynamically. The days of static ACLs are long gone.

How many nontechnical jurors would understand Mr. Elaborate Jones' answer? Here are a few things that are wrong with his elaborate answer:

- It was too long. He wasn't asked to explain how firewalls work. He was asked for a general positive or negative answer.

- He used technical vocabulary. Most people aren't comfortable with terms such as internal configuration, rule set, and variant packets.

- He used technical acronyms. Don't use IP or ACL unless you explain what they mean.

- He expressed an inappropriate opinion. He could have just offended a juror who happens to be a junior system administrator for a company that does use static tables in a firewall.

In short, get to the point and only use elaboration to explain your answer, not to deliver it. You always must consider the target of your communication. Let's look at the importance of your audience.

Remember Your Audience

Never forget who the audience is for your testimony. You are speaking to the court. Specifically, you are speaking to the judge and jury. Your attorneys have heard you before. They should be comfortable with some shortcuts. Because you have met with them on several occasions, you may feel comfortable enough to drop some of the communication formalities. Don't make the mistake of being too informal in court.

To convey your message in the most effective manner, always speak to your audience. Remember their level of technical expertise is more limited than your

Real World Scenario

Tales from the Trenches: Testimony

The computer forensics expert will from time to time be called upon to testify about the actions they took and the findings they found while performing a forensics investigation.

Although the majority of cases worked in the field of computer forensics never reach a courtroom, having the ability to present information in a legal proceeding will be very helpful to your career.

The best advice that I can give to any investigator who is called upon to testify in a legal proceeding is to thoroughly review all the documentation associated with the case and then answer each question that you are asked in a direct and polite manner. Do not offer any additional information during the questioning except to answer the question. In other words, provide an answer for the question asked and nothing more.

If you feel that additional information needs to be presented because it is relevant to the case, discuss the details with the attorney you are working for before offering the information in open court or at a deposition. Let your attorney lead you into the testimony. Don't rush to present all the details of the case in your first answer. Remember that the attorney you are working with will be trying to tell a story to the jury and your job is to "complete" that story with details of the case as you are asked questions.

The first time that I testified in court, I was unaware of this "storytelling" approach that attorneys use. Each time that I was asked a question about the case, I provided an answer to the question asked but would then continue presenting additional information. I wanted to make sure that the jury understood exactly what had happened, and I was anxious to get in all the information. The problem was that instead of helping to "tell the story," I was distracting the jury with too many details. I was not giving the attorney the opportunity to "set the stage" and prepare them to receive the detailed information.

After the case was over, I made an appointment with the attorney to get her opinion of how she thought the testimony had gone. That was when I learned about the storytelling approach to presenting evidence to a jury. Since then, each time I testify, I remember to slow down and let the information flow and let the story be told.

own. If the jury were composed of computer forensic examiners, there would be no reason to call you in as an expert. You are there to make the complex technical details of the case accessible to the judge and jury. Always be aware of how your delivery sounds to your audience. It's a good idea to have someone on your legal team monitor your testimony from the perspective of a nontechnical person. Comments from such a monitor can be invaluable in helping you tailor your testimony style to make the most impact.

Keep It Simple

Always use the KISS method. The old Keep It Simple, Stupid acronym reminds us that simple is always better than complex. In fact, almost everyone will reject information that is confusing. If you want to be believed by the judge and jury, make your explanations simple. You'll have to walk a fine line between keeping your explanations accessible and making them too simplistic.

Explaining Technical Concepts

Humans are associative thinkers. We take new information and associate it with information we already know. If we establish a strong enough association, we remember the new information. We can remember information in isolation, but only for a short time. Here's a simple test to make my point:

1. What are Newton's three laws of motion?

2. Write the quadratic formula from memory.

3. What are the Spanish (or French) words for cat, house, and bread?

4. Diagram the first sentence in the preceding paragraph.

At one time, you could probably answer all these questions. If you're like most people, you could do it on the day of the test. But the memory faded after a few days because the information was isolated. If you currently speak Spanish or French, the third question is a snap. The moral is: your audience will retain information longer if you help them associate it with something they already know. They will also understand it far better. Try to explain technical concepts using analogies where appropriate.

Let's assume you are asked to explain how a firewall works. You can start with something like: "A firewall is similar to a toll plaza. All traffic must pass through a toll booth in the plaza. Traffic is sorted by payment method: fast pass, exact change, and change provided." This starts off with a mental picture your audience can build on. Take time to develop analogies to explain technical concepts. They can go a long way to get a nontechnical audience to understand technical concepts.

Use Presentation Aids When Needed

In addition to having your audience use mental pictures, bring some of your own. The old adage "A picture is worth a thousand words" is absolutely true. When appropriate, use various presentation aids to clarify your point. Don't use presentation aids just to look impressive. Some speakers use PowerPoint only because it is expected; however, use what works for you. Some speakers deliver effective presentations with old-fashioned overhead projectors and cellophane slides.

If you believe a picture will help your audience understand or remember something, use it. In many cases, having a picture on a screen while you explain a topic helps to cement the topic in the audience's mind. Pictures, however, are only one of the many presentation aids available. When they help your testimony, use some of the following:

- Pictures (including crime scene photos)
- Illustrations
- Animation
- Charts

The preceding list is not exhaustive. Use the presentation aid you think will make the most impact. That impact is measured in how well your audience understands the points you are making, not how impressive your presentation looks.

Watch for Feedback

One of the most crucial factors during testimony is audience feedback. Because you are making eye contact with the judge and jury, you can see how they react to you. Read their facial expressions and body language. You can tell when you are boring someone. Too few people care, though. When you are presenting any type of information, watch to see what your audience is "saying" to you. If you are boring, move to another topic, take a break, or change tactics. Anytime you lose your audience, do something.

If you see that you are losing the jury as you explain how firewalls work, ask for a break. Talk the problem over with your legal team. They may suggest you try a different approach. You may have no other alternative but to push on through. Regardless, try to react to your audience. You might not be able to make the technical exciting, but you can try. Simply responding to the facial expressions and body language of your audience can increase their trust in you.

Be Ready to Justify Every Step

Your own legal team will lead you through justifications and explanations of each step through your investigation. Be prepared to stop at any point and answer "Why" questions. You should prepare these questions and answers during trial preparation. Although tedious, you will have to provide very detailed explanations that satisfy the most skeptical listeners as to why you performed some action.

The real challenge comes during cross examination. Your own legal team questions you from the perspective that you performed your job appropriately and acquired evidence that proves facts. The opposing counsel will take the opposite approach. To the other side, the evidence does not prove the facts as they are presented or was not acquired properly. You will be asked to defend your actions at each step in the process. Be prepared to justify each action and explain precautions you took to preserve the evidence. Your investigation notebook will be invaluable. Make sure you keep your notebook up-to-date during an investigation and available during a trial.

Summary

As long as you have done your homework and have documented everything in an investigation, your testimony can positively affect the outcome of a case. Of course, if you are poorly prepared, you can have a positive impact for the opposing counsel. Do your homework, know your stuff, and be prepared. You'll have a much more pleasant experience, and you may be asked to do it all again.

Terms to Know

ballistics	DNA
body language	expert witness
cross examination	spam
deposition	summons
direct examination	

Review Questions

1. How does an expert witness differ from a regular witness?

2. What condition should exist before you appear in court as an expert witness?

3. Will your resumé validate you as an expert witness?

4. What condition exists when you have personal or business reasons to find in favor of one party over the other?

5. What is the process of taking testimony and reducing it to written form for admission into court?

6. What term describes the process of opposing counsel asking questions to cast doubt on your testimony?

7. Why should you bother dressing up when going to court?

8. What are the three components of communication?

9. Should you be explicit in your testimony?

10. What should you do when you see that your are losing you audience?

Appendix A

Answers to Review Questions

Chapter 1

1. What is electronic discovery?

   Answer: The process whereby electronic documents are collected, prepared, reviewed, and distributed in association with legal and government proceedings.

2. Name some examples of electronic discovery items.

   Answer: Examples of electronic discovery items are e-mail, word-processing documents, plaintext files, database files, spreadsheets, digital art or photos, and presentations.

3. The recovery of data focuses on what four factors?

   Answer: Identifying the evidence; determining how to preserve it; extracting, processing and interpreting the evidence; and being sure the evidence is acceptable in a court of law.

4. Who works under more restrictive rules, law enforcement officials or corporate employees?

   Answer: Law enforcement officials work under more restrictive rules than agents of an employer and corporate employees.

5. What is incident response?

   Answer: The actions taken to respond to a situation that can be recovered from relatively quickly.

6. What is the difference between a virus and a worm?

   Answer: Worms do not need user intervention.

7. Why aren't incidents in many corporate environments reported?

   Answer: Negative publicity is the reason many corporations don't disclose security breaches to law enforcement agencies.

8. What law was passed to avoid future accounting scandals such as those involving Enron and WorldCom?

   Answer: The Sarbanes-Oxley Act.

9. Name some factors that will determine which criminal cases get priority.

   Answer: Frequency, the amount of harm inflicted, crime jurisdiction, and success of investigation.

10. Name a good resource for computer forensics training for law enforcement.

    Answer: International Association of Computer Investigative Specialists (IACIS).

Chapter 2

1. What is the difference between a server and a PC?

   Answer: A server has the capacity to provide services to other computers over a network, and a PC is intended for generic use by an individual.

2. How many devices can USB support?

   Answer: The USB standard supports up to 127 devices.

3. Which has a faster transfer rate, FireWire or USB 1?

   Answer: FireWire has a bandwidth nearly 30 times greater than USB 1.

4. How does Bluetooth communicate?

   Answer: Bluetooth uses randomly chosen frequencies within a designated range and hops or changes from one to another on a regular basis.

5. What types of filesystems will you find in the Windows environment?

   Answer: FAT and NTFS

6. What is the difference between NTFS and NFS?

   Answer: NTFS is used with Microsoft operating systems; NFS is used with Linux and Unix operating systems.

7. What does an incident response team do?

   Answer: An incident response team is responsible for containing damage and getting computer systems back up and running properly after an incident.

8. Approximately what percentage of organizations report intrusions?

   Answer: Only 25 percent of the respondents in a recent survey who experienced computer intrusions reported the incidents to law enforcement.

9. Can an employer search an employee's designated work area or desk?

   Answer: Circumstances might permit a supervisor to search in an employee's desk for a work-related file, but the supervisor usually will have to stop at the employee's purse or briefcase.

10. Search and seizure laws are guided by which amendment?

    Answer: The Fourth Amendment

Chapter 3

1. What are two general ways in which computers are involved in security violations?

   Answer: First, a computer can be used in the commission of crimes or violations of policy. Second, a computer can be the target of an attack.

2. What is computer evidence?

    Answer: Any computer hardware, software, or data that can be used to prove one or more or of the five Ws and one H of a security incident (i.e., who, what, when where, why, and how).

3. What is an incident response team?

    Answer: A team of individuals trained and prepared to recognize and immediately respond appropriately to any security incident.

4. What is real evidence?

    Answer: Any physical objects that you can bring into court. Real evidence can be touched, held, or otherwise observed directly.

5. What is documentary evidence?

    Answer: Written evidence, such as printed reports or data in log files. Such evidence cannot stand on its own and must be authenticated.

6. What is demonstrative evidence?

    Answer: Evidence that illustrates, helps explain, or demonstrates other evidence. Many times, demonstrative evidence consists of some type of visual aid.

7. What is a subpoena?

    Answer: A court order that compels an individual or organization to surrender evidence.

8. What is a search warrant?

    Answer: A court order that allows investigators to search and/or seize computer equipment without providing advance warning to the equipment owner.

9. What is the chain of custody?

    Answer: Documentation of all steps that evidence was taken from the crime scene to the courtroom. All steps include collection, transportation, analysis, and storage processes. All accesses of the evidence must be documented as well.

10. What is admissible evidence?

    Answer: Evidence that meets all regulatory and statute requirements, and has been properly obtained and handled.

Chapter 4

1. What is the first common task when handling evidence?

    Answer: Evidence identification must begin before you can begin the collection and analysis process.

2. Which type of hardware is never of interest to an investigation?

    Answer: All hardware is of potential interest to your investigation.

3. When attempting to prove that an individual used a computer, what clues might computer hardware provide?

    Answer: Fingerprints can directly relate a person with a computer.

4. In addition to hard disk drives, where else might data containing evidence reside?

    Answer: Removable media is a common hiding place for data. People trying to hide data often equate portability with security.

5. Should handwritten notes be considered in a computer forensics investigation?

    Answer: Yes. People naturally write notes of all kinds. You will likely find clues about how a person uses a computer by looking at the notes around it.

6. What is the primary concern in evidence collection and handling?

    Answer: Preserving evidence and ensuring that it does not change after it is collected is the primary concern during collection and handling. Tainting evidence destroys credibility and makes evidence inadmissible in a court of law.

7. Can you analyze a system that is intact and running?

    Answer: Yes, you can analyze it with specialized forensic tools.

8. What happens when a PDA's battery runs down?

    Answer: When a PDA's battery runs down, all data stored in the PDA is lost.

9. What device prohibits any changes to a hard disk drive?

    Answer: Write blockers (both hardware and software) stop all write operations that will change the contents of a drive.

10. How can you prove that you made no changes to a disk drive during analysis?

    Answer: Create hash values before and after analysis, and then compare the two. If the hash values are the same, the images are the same.

Chapter 5

1. Why do you need to be careful about the utilities you choose to use for disk imaging?

    Answer: Courts often accept evidence collected by tools that have been used in past trials. You should be prepared to testify to the authenticity and reliability of the tools that you use, otherwise the evidence may not be admissible.

2. What is an HPA?

    Answer: Hardware-protected area. An area created on a hard disk specifically to allow manufacturers to hide diagnostic and recovery tools. It is a hidden portion of the disk that can't be used by the operating system.

3. How does a mirror image differ from a forensic duplicate?

    Answer: A forensic duplicate contains the data in a raw bit stream format, whereas a mirror image does a bit-for-bit copy from one drive to another.

4. How can you verify that in imaging the source media, the original media is unchanged?

    Answer: This is done by both CRC and MD5 confirmation. These methods ensure that the copy procedure did not corrupt the data.

5. Name a tool that can be used to image the data in the memory of a PDA.

    Answer: Palm dd (pdd) is used for a Palm PDA. SAVEFS is used for a RIM Blackberry wireless PDA.

6. What does the Netstat utility do?

    Answer: Netstat displays the active computer connections. This information provides the investigator with a list of what protocols are running and what ports are open.

7. When collecting evidence, which do you want to extract first: the information in memory or on the hard drive?

    Answer: You should collect evidence on a system beginning with the volatile and proceeding to the less volatile; therefore, memory data should be collected before hard drive data.

8. Why can choosing the method used to shut down a suspect computer be a difficult decision to make?

    Answer: If you disconnect the power cord, you risk losing data, especially on Unix computers. If you shut down the computer through the normal shutdown method, you risk running destructive programs that will delete data upon shutdown.

9. If you need to boot a suspect computer to make an image copy, how should you do it?

    Answer: You should boot from a controlled boot disk and then create a bit stream of the hard disk using a disk-imaging utility.

10. Name three programs or utilities that can be used to collect forensic images.

    Answer: The dd utility, EnCase, SafeBack, Access Data's Forensic Toolkit (FTK), ByteBack, ILook Investigator, Maresware, SnapBack DatArest, WinHex, Grave-Robber, Incident Response Collection Report (IRCR), and Legal Imager and reaSsembly Application (LISA)

Chapter 6

1. What set of rules and conventions governs how computers exchange information over the network medium?

    Answer: Protocol

2. Name some factors that motivate criminal activity.

    Answer: Anger or revenge, financial gain, sexual impulses, and psychiatric illness

3. As a Word document is written and changed, these changes are tracked and produce a type of evidence that is called what?

    Answer: Metadata

4. What types of file should arouse your suspicion when you are examining data?

    Answer: Files with strange locations, strange names, or dots; files that start with a period (.) and contain spaces; and files that have changed recently

5. Why should you look at the header of an e-mail?

   Answer: The e-mail header shows the path the message took from the very first communication point until it reached the recipient.

6. What is steganography?

   Answer: A method of hiding data that encrypts the original plaintext information into a digital image

7. What method can you use to determine if the extension of a file has been changed to avoid suspicion?

   Answer: Signature analysis

8. If you are investigating a case that involves the Internet and pictures, what three areas could reveal the Internet habits of the suspect?

   Answer: Temporary Internet Files folder, History folder, and the Cookies folder

9. What is a dual-boot system?

   Answer: It is a system that can boot to more than one operating system. In essence, one operating system is hidden from the other.

10. Name three types of trace evidence.

    Answer: Slack space, swap file, metadata

Chapter 7

1. What is a password?

   Answer: A password is a word that provides authentication that the user is who she claims to be.

2. What is the process of getting someone to carry out a task for you?

   Answer: Social engineering

3. Are more complex passwords stronger or weaker than simpler passwords?

   Answer: Although a complex password is stronger, the likelihood that a user will do something (for example, write it down) to weaken it is greater.

4. What method should you first use to get a password?

   Answer: Ask the subject for the password.

5. What type of password attack tries passwords from a predefined list?

   Answer: Dictionary attack

6. Which type of password attack uses passwords from a list and then tries variations on each element from the list?

   Answer: Hybrid attack

7. What is an algorithm for encrypting and decrypting data?

   Answer: Cipher

8. What term describes an encrypted message?

   Answer: Ciphertext

9. Which symmetric encryption algorithm is based on the Rijndael cipher?

   Answer: Advanced Encryption Standard (AES)

10. Which symmetric encryption algorithm uses 56-bit keys?

    Answer: DES

Chapter 8

1. Which utility, originally created for the Unix platform, copies and converts files using two basic arguments (if and of)?

   Answer: The dd utility

2. Which software suite provides an Enterprise Edition that specifically supports volatile data analysis on a live Windows system?

   Answer: EnCase

3. Which disk imaging software operates as an extended DOS command shell?

   Answer: DriveSpy

4. What are two common algorithms used to create hash values for drive images?

   Answer: MD5 and SHA

5. Which forensic software suite integrates the dtSearch engine in its searching function?

   Answer: FTK

6. What two software suites are free?

   Answer: TCT and TSK

7. What are two of several vendors of forensic computers?

   Answer: Vogon and Digital Intelligence

8. After creating an image of a drive, what must you do to ensure the copy matches the original?

   Answer: Calculate a hash of the image and compare to the original.

9. You have many factors to consider when choosing appropriate forensic software. Name two.

   Answer: Answers can include expected types of investigations, operating system needs and preference, background and training, budget, and status (law enforcement or private organization).

10. Which utilities provide comprehensive forensic functionality?

    Answer: EnCase and FTK

Chapter 9

1. What set of rules states the General Provisions Governing Discovery and Duty of Disclosure?

    Answer: Federal Rule of Civil Procedure 26

2. What are some of the items of information that a forensic examiner might be requested to provide under Rule 30(b)(6)?

    Answer: Quantity, types, and locations of computers in use; operating systems and application software and dates of use; file-naming conventions and location saving directories; backup disk or tape inventories and schedules; corporate computer use policies; identities of current and former employees responsible for systems operations

3. Why is a template recommended for reports?

    Answer: A template can provide uniformity in all your work.

4. Where can you find out how to properly document and sample log sheets?

    Answer: Use the National Institute of Justice document titled "Forensic Examination of Digital Evidence: A Guide for Law Enforcement," Appendix C.

5. When should you consider using diagrams as a method of documentation?

    Answer: A jury might not understand the workings of computers and networks; therefore, you might want to use pictures or drawings to get your point across.

6. Why should you videotape the entry of all persons into the crime scene?

    Answer: Taping the actual entrance of a forensics team into a crime scene area helps to refute claims that evidence was planted at the scene.

7. Why is it important to be cautious when you are transporting evidence from the crime scene to the lab for analysis?

    Answer: Electrostatic discharge (ESD) can kill your computer components. Electromagnetic fields created by magnets and radio transmitters can alter or destroy data during transport.

8. When formulating a concise report, what are some items you should consider?

    Answer: Understand the importance of the reports. Limit the report to specifics. Design the layout and presentation in an easy-to-understand format. Understand the difference between litigation support reports and technical reports. Write clearly, provide supporting material, explain the methods used in data collection, and explain the results.

9. Why are timelines of computer usage and file accesses important when processing computer evidence?

    Answer: It is important to document the accuracy of these settings on the seized computer to validate the accuracy of the times and dates associated with any relevant computer files. The current time and date should be compared with the date and time stored in the computer.

10. What are some items that your report should contain?

    Answer: Name of the reporting agency and case investigator, case number, date of the report, list of the items examined, description of the examination process, and results and/or conclusion.

Chapter 10

1. How does an expert witness differ from a regular witness?

    Answer: An expert witness can provide an opinion. A regular witness can only attest to facts.

2. What condition should exist before you appear in court as an expert witness?

    Answer: You should receive a summons or be asked to appear by the client. When you appear in court you will be asked to justify your expert status.

3. Will your resumé validate you as an expert witness?

    Answer: Generally, no. Validation of expert status requires more details than most resumes contain.

4. What condition exists when you have personal or business reasons to find in favor of one party over the other?

    Answer: Conflict of interest

5. What is the process of taking testimony and reducing it to written form for admission into court?

    Answer: A deposition

6. What term describes the process of opposing counsel asking questions to cast doubt on your testimony?

    Answer: Cross examination

7. Why should you bother dressing up when going to court?

    Answer: Conservative dress conveys an image of confidence and competence.

8. What are the three components of communication?

    Answer: Sender, message, receiver

9. Should you be explicit in your testimony?

    Answer: Only be explicit enough to answer the question. Don't add any commentary unless specifically asked or required by the question.

10. What should you do when you see that you are losing your audience?

    Answer: Something different! Ask for a break, change the level of your explanation, try a different analogy or approach, or use different inflection. Do something that will break the monotony and return the audience's attention to you.

Appendix B

Forensics Resources

This appendix lists various sources that will be helpful in your computer forensic investigations.

Information

Computer Forensics, Cybercrime and Steganography Resources: http://www.forensix.org/links
Department of Defense Cyber Crime Center: http://www.dcfl.gov/
Department of Justice Computer Crime and Intellectual Property Section: http://www.cybercrime.gov/fedcode.htm
Electronic Crimes Task Force: http://www.ectaskforce.org/
FBI National Computer Crime Squad: http://www.emergency.com/fbi-nccs.htm
National Institute of Justice: http://www.ojp.usdoj.gov/nij/sciencetech/welcome.html
National White Collar Crime Center: http://www.nw3c.org/
NIST Computer Forensics Tool Testing Program: http://www.cftt.nist.gov/

Organizations

Digital Forensic Research Workshop: http://www.dfrws.org/
High Tech Crime Consortium: http://www.hightechcrimecops.org/
High Technology Criminal Investigation Association: http://htcia.org/
International Association of Computer Investigative Specialists: http://www.cops.org/
International Information Systems Forensic Association: http://www.infoforensics.org/index.asp
International Organization on Computer Evidence: http://www.ioce.org/
Scientific Working Group on Digital Evidence: http://ncfs.org/swgde/index.html

Publications

Digital Investigation: http://www.compseconline.com/digitalinvestigation/
International Journal of Digital Evidence: http://www.ijde.org/

Services

Advanced Data Solutions: http://www.adv-data.com/
Center for Computer Forensics: http://www.computer-forensics.net/
Computer Forensics Inc.: http://www.forensics.com/
Computer Forensics International: http://www.computerforensicsint.com/
Computer Forensics Labs: http://www.computerforensiclabsinc.com/
Computer Forensics Services: http://forensicsservices.com/
Computer Forensic Services, LLC: http://www.computer-forensic.com/
CyberEvidence: http://www.cyberevidence.com/
Data Recon, LLC: http://www.datareconllc.com/
Digital Disclosure, Inc.: http://www.digitaldisclosure.com/
Digital Mountain, Inc.: http://www.digitalmountain.com/
ESS Data Recovery: http://www.savemyfiles.com/
Forensicon, Inc: http://www.great-scott.com/
Forentech, LLC: http://www.forentech.com
Forentech Security Solutions: http://www.forentech.net/
ISA Forensics: http://www.isaforensics.com/
Kroll Ontrack: http://www.krollontrack.com/
LC Tech: http://www.lc-tech.com/
LuciData LLC: http://www.lucidatallc.com/
Midwest Data Group: http://www.forensicdiscovery.com/
Renew Data: http://www.renewdata.com/
Sassinsky Data Services: http://www.sassinsky.com/forensics/
Spinelli Corporation: http://www.spinellicorp.com/compfor.shtml
Technical Resource Center: http://www.trcglobal.com
Tektron Solutions: http://www.tektronsolutions.com/
Tunstall and Tunstall: http://www.datarecoveryservices.com/

Software

AccessData: http://www.accessdata.com/
Computer Cop: http: //www.computercop.com/
dtSearch: http://www.dtsearch.com/dtsoftware.html
EnCase: http://www.guidancesoftware.com
ILook Investigator: http://www.ilook-forensics.org/
Legal Imager and reaSsembly Application: http://www.blackcat.demon.co.uk/lisa/
Mares and Company: http://www.dmares.com/
New Technologies, Inc.: http://www.forensics-intl.com/
SMART: http://www.asrdata.com/
SnapBack: http://www.snapback.com/
Symantec Ghost: http://sea.symantec.com/content/product.cfm?productid=9
Technology Pathways: http://www.techpathways.com/
Paraben Corporation: http://www.paraben-forensics.com

Vogon International: http://www.vogon-international.us/Tools
Avantstar Quick View Plus: http://www.avantstar.com/intradoc-cgi/idc_cgi_isapi.dll?
IdcService=SS_GET_PAGE&ssDocName=QuickViewPlusOverview
Digital Intelligence: http://www.digitalintelligence.com/
DiskJockey File Viewer: http://www.clear-simple.com/
E-mail Detective: http://www.evestigate.com/Computer_Forensic_Training.htm
Hashkeeper: http://www.hashkeeper.org
Intelligent Computer Solutions: http://www.icsforensic.com/products_cat_fr.cfm
The Coroner's Toolkit: http://www.porcupine.org/forensics/tct.html
The Sleuth Kit: http://www.sleuthkit.org/sleuthkit/index.php
Tech Assist, Inc. (ByteBack) http://www.toolsthatwork.com/computer-forensic.htm
ThumbsPlus: http://www.cerious.com/
WinHex: http://www.winhex.com/
X-Ways: http://www.x-ways.net/forensics/index-m.html

Training

Cyber Security Institute: http://www.cybersecurityinstitute.biz/
The DIBS group: http://www.dibsusa.com/
Global Digital Forensics, Inc.: http://www.evestigate.com/Computer_Forensic Training.htm
High Tech Crime Institute: http://www.hightechcrimeinstitute.com/
Institute for Forensic Imaging: http://www.ifi-indy.org/
Intense Schools: http://www.intenseschool.com/bootcamps/security/forensics/
Technical Resource Center: http://www.trcglobal.com

Appendix C

Forensics Certifications

Almost every day we read about some type of computer incident. Computer crime represents one of the fastest growing crime rates in the country, and the need for computer forensics is growing. The landscape of performing proper forensics on information systems is changing from law enforcement only to also include corporate IT and information security professionals. IT professionals now need to know how digital crimes are committed, how to gather the evidence, and how to collaborate with law enforcement as a computer forensics case evolves. While performing proper computer forensics to prevent further damage to systems, evidence can be damaged, lost, or become inadmissible in a court of law. Given this, it is not surprising that several computer forensics certifications are available, and they range in topic from computer crimes against children to file system recovery. If you are interested in becoming a cybercrime investigator, getting a computer forensics certification will certainly add to your credibility. This appendix covers some of the most popular and well-known computer forensics certifications.

The Top Five Computer Forensics Certifications

The following are five of the most popular computer forensics certifications and their websites:

Certified Computer Examiner (CCE): http://www.certified-computer-examiner.com

Certified Computer Crime Investigator (CCCI): http://www.htcn.org/changes.htm

Computer Forensic Computer Examiner (CFCE): http://www.iacis.com/html/training.htm

Certified Information Forensics Investigator (CIFI): http://www.iisfa.org/certification/certification.asp

Professional Certified Investigator (PCI): http://www.asisonline.org/certification/pci/pciabout.xml

Advanced Information Security (AIS)

The Security University Advanced Information Security (AIS) certification is a hands-on computer security certification created for the network IT and security professional. The program combines coverage of key information security topics, tools, and technologies with perhaps the best overall hands-on, lab-oriented learning and testing program around. To obtain AIS certification, security professionals must complete eight courses, including six tools-oriented classes on topics such as network penetration testing; firewalls and virtual private networks (VPNs); virus analysis, patch management, and incident response; PKI; intrusion detection and computer forensics, plus two management classes on network security policy and architecture security. They must also take and pass a demanding exam. For additional details about this certification, visit http://www.securityuniversity.net/certification.php.

Certified Computer Examiner (CCE)

The Certified Computer Examiner (CCE) certification is the most complete and thorough evaluation process available today for the computer forensics professional. This certification is offered in association with the International Society of Forensic Computer Examiners, the Southeast Cybercrime Institute at Kennesaw State University, the Tri County Technical College, Pendleton, South Carolina, and Sir Sanford Fleming College, Ontario, Canada.

 The CCE certification has been obtained by examiners throughout the world and is becoming the most recognized certification worldwide for both civilian and law enforcement examiners. Civilian examiners include information security officers and managers, IT administrators, consultants, systems and data security analysts, and even lawyers and HR managers.

The initial CCE process consists of a proctored online multiple-choice exam followed by the forensic examination of a floppy disk, the forensic examination of a CD-R disc, and the forensic examination of an image of a hard disk drive. After the online examination has been completed, the applicant can begin the forensic examination of the test media. The forensic examinations are designed to test the forensic knowledge and skills of the examiner.

The primary purpose of this certification is to measure if the applicant understands and uses sound evidence handling and storage procedures and follows sound forensic examinations procedures when conducting examinations. There are reasonable technical issues that must be resolved to recover the evidentiary data. However, most of the grade is based on following sound evidence handling and storage procedures and following sound examination procedures, not simply recovering the data. An 80 percent total average score will be required to obtain CCE certification. The fee for the entire process is around $300. To obtain additional information about the CCE, visit http://www.isfce.com or http://www.certified-computer-examiner.com.

Certified Cyber-Crime Expert (C³E)

The Certified Cyber-Crime Expert (C³E) identifies computer forensics investigators, information technology and security personnel, law enforcement officials, lawyers, and others who must have the knowledge and tools to effectively collect, handle, process, and preserve computer forensic evidence. The certification requires successful completion of the Computer Forensic and Cyber Investigation course, and a practical and written exam. Additional information on the course can be found `http://www.trcglobal.com/`.

Certified Information Forensics Investigator (CIFI)

The Certified Information Forensics Investigator (CIFI) certification is a designation earned exclusively by the most qualified information forensics professionals in the field. The CIFI encompasses multiple domains of knowledge, practical experience, and a demonstration of expertise and understanding accomplished through a rigorous exam proctored under controlled environments. This credential requires adherence to a code of ethics and is aimed at full-time professional practitioners. The certification is vendor neutral. In fact, candidates may choose to sit for the exam without any restrictions other than adherence to the International Information Systems Forensics Association (IISFA) code of ethics and the exam fee, which runs around $500.

The CIFI exam includes six areas in its common bodies of knowledge (CBKs), all strongly related to information forensics:

- ◆ Auditing
- ◆ Incident response
- ◆ Law and investigation
- ◆ Tools and techniques
- ◆ Traceback
- ◆ Countermeasures

The IISFA offers a short, but comprehensive reading list (`www.iisfa.org/certification/readinglist.asp`) to help candidates prepare for the exam. It also provides detailed explanations of the topics, issues, tools, and techniques relevant to the various CBKs. (Check the submenus on the Common Bodies of Knowledge page at `http://www.iisfa.org/certification/cbk.asp`.) The website (`http://www.infoforensics.org`) also offers various resources, newsletters, pointers to training partners, and more. Until the end of 2004, experienced computer forensics professionals also have the option of attempting to grandfather their way into CIFI certification.

Certified Computer Crime Investigator (CCCI)

The Certified Computer Crime Investigator (CCCI) is offered at two levels—Basic and Advanced. Each exam costs around $500.

◆ **CCCI Basic** Requires two years of investigative experience in any discipline (law enforcement or corporate) or possession of a college degree and one year of investigative experience in any discipline, 18 months of experience directly related to the investigation of technical incidents or technical crimes (law enforcement or corporate), successful completion of 40 hours of computer crimes training course(s) provided by an approved agency, organization or training company, and documentation of the candidate's experience derived from the investigation of at least 10 cases.

◆ **CCCI Advanced** Requires three years of investigative experience in any discipline or a college degree and two years of investigative experience in any discipline, four years of experience directly related to the investigation of technical incidents or technical crimes, successful completion of 80 hours of computer crimes training course(s) provided by an approved agency, organization or company, and documentation of the candidate's experience as lead investigator in at least 20 separate cases and involvement in at least 40 other cases as a lead investigator or supervisor or in a supportive capacity.

Information about the CCCI Basic and Advanced certifications is at http://www.htcn.org/.

Certified Computer Forensic Technician (CCFT)

The Certified Computer Forensic Technician (CCFT) program offers two exams, both of which cost around $500. The CCFT is one of two computer forensic certifications aimed at law enforcement and private IT professionals seeking to specialize in the investigative side of the field.

◆ **CCFT Basic** Requires three years of investigative experience in any discipline or possession of a college degree and one year of investigative experience in any discipline, 18 months of investigative experience directly related to computer forensics, successful completion of 40 hours of computer forensics training course(s) provided by an approved agency, organization or company, completion of a written exam for the certification sought, and documented experience derived from the investigation of at least 10 computer forensic cases.

◆ **CCFT Advanced** Requires three years of investigative experience in any discipline or possession of a college degree and two years of investigative experience in any discipline, four years of hands-on experience directly related to computer forensics, successful completion of 80 hours of computer forensics training course(s) provided by an approved agency, organization or company, and documented experience as a lead forensic technician in at least 20 separate cases and involvement in at least 40 other cases as a lead forensic technician or supervisor or in a supportive capacity.

Visit `http://www.htcn.org/` for additional information about CCFT certification.

Certified Forensic Computer Examiner (CFCE)

The Certified Forensic Computer Examiner (CFCE) program is open to active law enforcement officers and others who qualify for membership in the International Association of Computer Investigative Specialists (IACIS). The external CFCE process can be particularly helpful to qualified examiners who cannot attend the annual IACIS training conference. The applicant must submit an application, along with a required fee, to be considered for the process. IACIS reviews the application and is the sole decision maker in the acceptance or rejection of any application, as it deems appropriate. This is a rigorous testing process that consists of the examination of six specially prepared examinations disks and a specially prepared hard disk drive. Each problem disk must be examined, the technical issues must be solved, and a thorough report must be prepared before continuing to the next problem. Candidates are offered one retake of the six disk problems if they cannot resolve the technical issues in the problem. Candidates may not retake the hard disk drive problem. The reports and evidence must be presented to IACIS in a manner that indicates that sound forensic procedures were used to conduct the examination and that the applicant understands the technical issues. Candidates take a thorough written examination at the conclusion of the process. This process and these disks are the same problems that must be completed by IACIS-trained examiners. There is a five-month time limit to complete the entire process. The cost of the certification process is about $675 and is nonrefundable after the application is accepted. Additional information about the CFCE can be found at `http://www.iacis.com/index.htm`.

Certified Information Systems Auditor (CISA)

The Certified Information Systems Auditor (CISA) demonstrates knowledge of IS auditing for control and security purposes. This certification is designed for IT security professionals responsible for auditing IT systems, practices, and procedures to make sure organizational security policies meet governmental and regulatory requirements, conform to best security practices and principles, and meet or exceed requirements stated in an organization's security policy. The CISA examination is offered one time each year in June. Certification requires a minimum of five years of professional information systems auditing, control, or security work experience. Go to `http://www.isaca.org/` for further details.

EnCase Certified Examiner Program

The EnCase Certified Examiner Program offers certifications for those who have mastered EnCase Guidance software. Training courses and a copy of the software are required to gain the certification. This program is reasonably priced at around $150 for the exam, and it is available through Thomson Prometric testing centers. Complete details about the EnCase certification program are available at http://www.guidancesoftware.com.

GIAC Certified Forensic Analyst (GCFA)

GIAC Certified Forensic Analysts (GCFAs) have the knowledge, skills, and abilities to handle advanced incident handling scenarios, conduct formal incident investigations, and carry out forensic investigation of networks and hosts. To obtain the GCFA credential, a candidate must complete a practical assignment that demonstrates his or her knowledge of the subject area. Each candidate must also pass two exams. This is an intermediate-level certification, renewable every four years. It is targeted toward individuals responsible for forensic investigation/analysis, advanced incident handling, or formal incident investigation. GCFAs have the knowledge, skills, and abilities to handle advanced incident handling scenarios, conduct formal incident investigations, and carry out forensic investigation of networks and hosts. The cost is around $250. The GIAC website has links to the other certifications that GIAC offers as well. Complete details about the GCFA are available at http://www.giac.org/subject_certs.php.

Professional Certified Investigator (PCI)

Professional Certified Investigator (PCI) candidates who want to take the PCI exam must first satisfy the following requirements (as stated on the PCI website):

◆ Nine years of investigations experience, at least three years of which shall have been in case management; or

◆ An earned Bachelor's Degree or higher from an accredited institution of higher education and seven years of investigations experience, at least three years of which shall have been in case management. Documentation for education is not needed if eligibility requirements based on years of experience are met. If education is used, the Certification Program Office must receive an official certified transcript before applicants are considered eligible to test.

◆ The applicant must not have been convicted of any criminal offense that would reflect negatively on the security profession, ASIS, or the certification program.

Eligibility for PCI certification and recertification is denied only when an applicant does not meet relevant security-related criteria, when an applicant has violated the PCI Code of Professional Responsibility, or when an applicant has committed an act that would reflect negatively on ASIS and the PCI program. The cost is around $300 for an ASIS member and $450 for a non-ASIS member. The PCI website is located at `http://www.asisonline.org/certification/pci/pciabout.xml`.

Appendix D

Forensics Tools

This appendix should acquaint you with some of the better-known forensics tools that are available on the market. These tools, along with those described in Chapter 8, should give you a great start in figuring out what you need to put into your forensics toolbox.

Forensics Tool Suites

Forensics suites make processing and organizing large case files easier. These tools combine the functionality of many different, smaller applications and provide a common interface from which to conduct an electronic investigation.

Ultimate Toolkit

AccessData Ultimate Toolkit (UTK) is the industry's most comprehensive set of tools for password acquisition and forensic examination of digital evidence. UTK includes advanced decryption; password recovery; full-text indexing and searching; deleted file recovery; e-mail, Registry and graphics analysis; auto-reporting wizards; and more. UTK includes the following AccessData products: Password Recovery Toolkit; Registry Viewer; Forensic Toolkit; 100-client license for Distributed Network Attack; WipeDrive; NT Login Access Utility, and a one-year subscription and maintenance service. The robust toolset of UTK is maximized by individuals who complete the AccessData BootCamp and other AccessData professional training courses on cryptography and forensics. To obtain additional information about AccessData, visit http://www.accessdata.com.

Maresware

Maresware is computer forensics software that provides a set of tools for investigating and analyzing computer records and data.

It is flexible to meet the needs of all types of investigators, analysts, auditors, and information technology (IT) administrators. The software is useful for forensic analysis, data administration, drive wiping, and forensic auditing. It is command-line driven for flexibility, speed, and unattended operation. It can be used to help provide compliance with HIPAA and other privacy of information regulations. To obtain additional information about Maresware, visit `http://www.dmares.com`.

X-Ways Forensics

X-Ways Forensics is the most resource-efficient forensics tool on the market. It offers versatile functionality for the digital evidence collection process. X-Ways Forensics supports case management, automated report generation, direct access to drive images, various data recovery techniques, and other baseline methods of the trade. It also possesses time-saving capabilities such as skin color percentage calculation for all image files found, and it thwarts various data-hiding techniques such as host-protected areas, NTFS alternative data streams, and falsified filename extensions. X-Ways Trace is an accessory that deciphers and displays the browser history and the Windows recycle bin log. To obtain additional information about X-Ways Forensics, visit `http://www.x-ways.net`.

Forensicware

Forensicware Solution from StepaNet Communications, Inc. provides 20 essential tools for the computer forensic investigator. These tools build on and complement acquisition and analysis packages such as EnCase from Guidance Software and Forensic Toolkit from AccessData, just to name a few. Data parsing, file extraction, link file metadata, and file and directory cataloging are just a few of Forensicware Solution's many capabilities. Forensicware Solution makes the job of advanced data recovery easy. To obtain additional information about Forensicware, visit `http://www.datalifter.com`.

Password-Cracking Utilities

Forensics examiners often find encrypted or password-protected files during their examinations. These tools allow you to view the contents of files.

Passware

Passware has released new versions of its password-recovery software packs, Passware Kit and Passware Kit Enterprise. Passware features new modules and now includes the ability to retrieve EFS-encrypted files from NTFS partitions. Peachtree 2004 support, WordPerfect 11 support, QuickBooks 2003 Enterprise support, Outlook Express Key, and Internet Explorer Key now work on Windows 2003 Server. Passware now has the ability to crack 33 different application passwords. This program is simple to operate, and it works! To obtain additional information about Passware, visit `http://www.lostpassword.com`.

ElcomSoft

ElcomSoft password-recovery software was created to deal with files protected through the use of popular computer applications. More than 80 document types are supported: Microsoft Office, Adobe Acrobat PDF, Lotus SmartSuite, Corel WordPerfect Office, Intuit Quicken and QuickBooks, and many more. Microsoft Windows NT/2000/XP/2003 operating systems (encrypting filesystem and user-level security) are also supported. These password breakers are made available to aid computer forensics specialists in dealing with password-protected data during the course of their work. Based on independent tests and feedback from clients, these tools are the fastest on the market, easiest to use, and the least expensive. They are feature rich. To obtain additional information about ElcomSoft, visit `http://www.elcomsoft.com`.

CD Analysis Utilities

At times, forensic examiners need to examine CDs or DVDs as part of their examinations. These tools allow you to locate hidden sessions that had been previously recorded on optical media.

IsoBuster

IsoBuster is a highly specialized tool designed to perform data recovery from optical medium (all CD and DVD) formats. Its approach is unique in that it shows the true and full content of the media. CD and DVD technology are based on special techniques to divide the media into tracks and sessions. Different sessions can contain different content, and it is easy to hide older content from the popular operating systems such as Windows or Mac OS. Furthermore, sessions can contain different filesystems, each pointing to the same or different files in that session or in older sessions. Popular operating systems will pick only one of the filesystems—again, this way it is easy to hide data. Because IsoBuster shows all these different tracks, sessions, and filesystems, investigators get a perfect view of the content on the media and at the same time gain good knowledge on optical media write techniques and data storing. To obtain additional information about IsoBuster, visit `http://www.isobuster.com`.

CD/DVD Inspector

CD/DVD Inspector provides professional software for intensive analysis and extraction of data from CD-R, CD-RW, and DVD media. The product is tailored for professionals in data recovery, forensics, and law enforcement. Building on the data recovery technology in CD/DVD Diagnostic, it adds detailed displays and enhanced media search abilities, improving performance and usability. CD/DVD Inspector reads all major CD and DVD filesystems. When the disc being examined contains more than a single filesystem, all filesystems found are displayed. Reports are available to describe the contents of a disc in several formats, including with or without MD5 hash information. Additionally, CD/DVD Inspector loads a Hashkeeper hash set and compares it to the contents of a disc. This enables the rapid marking of files that contain content so that they can be examined further or excluding files which belong to a hash set of common files. To obtain additional information about CD/DVD Inspector, visit `http://www.infinadyne.com`.

Metadata Viewer Utility

Microsoft Office files, among others, contain a vast array of information embedded inside documents. This utility allows you to examine this data. Often, the discovery of metadata is crucial to a case.

Metadata Assistant

Metadata Assistant is the most popular metadata cleaner on the market today. Payne Consulting Group created the Metadata Assistant in the late 1990s when they discovered that Word documents contain hidden information that could potentially expose their law firm clients to confidentiality breaches. Since that time, hundreds of thousands of law firms, government agencies, banking, oil, chemical, and pharmaceutical industries around the world have started using the product to remove metadata from Word documents and other file types. Metadata Assistant removes metadata from Microsoft Word, Excel, PowerPoint, and RTF files. It includes the added benefit of automatic notification when attempting to send a file as an attachment to an Outlook, GroupWise, or Lotus Notes e-mail message. When a user clicks on the Send button, the Metadata Assistant identifies whether or not a Word document, Excel spreadsheet, PowerPoint presentation, or rich-text file is attached to the e-mail message. The user is asked if they would like to analyze/clean the document with the Metadata Assistant before sending. The document attachment is cleaned and the original document is left intact. To obtain additional information about Metadata Assistant, visit `http://www.payneconsulting.com`.

Graphic Viewing Utility

Processing graphics files without altering the original evidence is one of the most common tasks of the forensics examiner. This tool allows you to safely view graphics files.

Quick View Plus

Quick View Plus accelerates forensics analyses and reduces software expenses by enabling instant file viewing of over 225 file types without requiring the native application. Quick View Plus is a key software solution for numerous organizations, law enforcement agencies, and forensics professionals to aid in their computer forensics work. To obtain additional information about Quick View Plus, visit http://www.avantstar.com.

Forensics Hardware Devices

Processing computer hard drives can be done from standard PC hardware; however, the use of standalone, specialized hardware devices can ease the processing of evidence.

Intelligent Computer Solutions

Intelligent Computer Solutions (ICS) is the technology leader in the design and manufacture of high speed hard-drive duplication equipment, software-cloning solutions, and diagnostic systems. Having developed the hard-drive duplication technology, ICS has gained international name recognition for 14 years of customer service and for providing its customers with cutting-edge solutions.

Intelligent Computer Solutions is a prominent supplier of law enforcement and computer forensic systems to law enforcement personnel ranging from local police departments to federal and international agencies. ICS units are being used today by government agencies in the United States, Canada, Europe, the Middle East, China, Australia, and New Zealand.

The Solo 2 Forensic system is a hand-held software duplication device made for computer disk-drive data seizure. Image capture operations can be performed from a suspect's drive to another hard drive with duplication speeds up to 1.8GB/minute. This is the ultimate toolkit for forensics data acquisition. To obtain additional information about ICS, visit http://www.ics-iq.com.

Computer Forensics Training

It is imperative for computer forensics examiners to obtain training to continuously improve and update their skills. The following computer forensics boot camp is one of the most complete courses available.

Intense School Computer Forensics Training Class

During Certified Computer Examiner - Applied Computer Forensics Boot Camp, students learn the dark side of computer threats and crimes. They also learn proper investigative computer crime prevention techniques. In this digital forensics course, students learn the information needed to develop an effective corporate computer crime policy, and they develop the hands-on skills to implement it. Students are exposed to the spectrum of computer forensics tools and develop their own forensics toolkit to take to the scene of the crime. Additionally, students learn the core forensics procedures necessary for performing thorough investigations on all computer systems and file types, and they begin the CCE certification process in the class. To obtain additional information about Intense School, visit http://www.intenseschool.com.

Glossary

Address Resolution Protocol (ARP) A protocol used on the Internet to map computer network addresses to hardware addresses.

admissible evidence Evidence that meets all regulatory and statutory requirements, and has been properly obtained and handled.

American Standard Code for Information Interchange (ASCII) A single-byte character-encoding scheme used for text-based data.

asymmetric algorithm Another name for a public key encryption algorithm.

auditing The process of keeping track of who is logging in and accessing what files.

backdoor A software program that allows access to a system without using security checks.

ballistics The science of flight dynamics; often used to determine the flight path of weapons.

Basic Input Output System (BIOS) System software that is responsible for booting the computer by providing a basic set of instructions.

BeOS File System (BFS) A filesystem designed for use by the Be operating system. BFS has the built-in capability to work with FAT12, FAT16, VFAT, and HPFS partitions. BFS can also support FAT32 and NTFS after the appropriate drivers are installed.

best evidence rule A rule that requires that the original document be introduced as evidence when you present documentary evidence in a court of law. You cannot introduce a copy except under certain circumstances, such as when the original has been destroyed.

best practices A set of recommended guidelines that outlines a set of good controls.

Bluetooth A standard developed to allow various types of electronic equipment to make their own connections by using a short-range (10-meter) frequency-hopping radio link between devices.

body language Communication using body movements, gestures, and facial expressions.

browser An application that allows you to access the World Wide Web. The most common browsers are Microsoft Internet Explorer and Netscape.

brute force Systematically trying every conceivable combination until a password is found, or until all possible combinations have been exhausted.

brute force attack An attack that tries all possible password combinations until the correct password is found.

cache Space on a hard disk used to store recently accessed data in an effort to improve performance speed.

CD/DVD-ROM/RW drive A drive accessible from outside the computer that is used to read and/or write CDs and DVDs. A compact disc (CD) can store huge amounts of digital information (783 MB) on a very small surface. CDs are inexpensive to manufacture.

chain of custody Documentation of all the steps that evidence has taken from the time it is located at the crime scene to the time introduced in the courtroom. All steps include collection, transportation, analysis, and storage processes. All accesses of the evidence must be documented as well.

checksum A value that can help detect data corruption. A checksum is derived by summing the number of bytes or other criterion in a string of data. At a later time, especially after the data's been transmitted or copied, the same calculation is performed. If the resulting value does not match the original value, the data is considered to be corrupt.

chosen plaintext attack An attack to decrypt a file characterized by comparing ciphertext to a plaintext message you chose and encrypted.

cipher An algorithm for encrypting and decrypting.

ciphertext An encrypted message.

cloning A process used to create an exact duplicate of one media on another like media.

Complementary Metal Oxide Semiconductor (CMOS) An on-board semiconductor chip used to store system information and configuration settings when the computer is either off or on. Batteries are used to power the CMOS memory.

computer evidence Any computer hardware, software, or data that can be used to prove one or more of the five Ws and an H of a security incident (i.e., who, what, when, where, why, and how).

computer forensics A science involving the identification, preservation, extraction, documentation, and interpretation of computer data.

cookies Small text files that are placed on your computer's hard drive when you browse a website. The file contains a simple unique number that identifies you to the website's computers when you return.

covert channels A method by which an entity receives information in an unauthorized manner.

cross examination Questions asked by opposing counsel to cast doubt on testimony provided during direct examination.

cross validation A method used when one variable has the particular status of being explained by using a second method to verify data.

cryptography The science of hiding the true meaning of a message from unintended recipients.

cyclic redundancy check (CRC) A common technique for detecting data transmission errors. Each transmitted message is accompanied by a numerical value based on the number of set bits in the message. The receiving device then applies the same formula to the message and checks to make sure the accompanying numerical value is the same, thereby verifying the data integrity.

dd Copy and convert utility. Originally included with most versions of Unix and Linux, versions now exist for Windows as well.

decrypt Translate an encrypted message back into the original unencrypted message.

desktop A PC designed to be set up in a permanent location because the components are too large to easily transport.

dictionary attack An attack that tries different passwords defined in a list, or database, of password candidates.

direct examination Initial questions asked to a witness to extract testimony.

disaster recovery The ability of a company to recover from an occurrence inflicting widespread destruction and distress.

disk imaging A process used to copy an entire hard drive into a single file by copying the drive's sectors and bytes to a variety of media types.

distributed denial of service (DDoS) attack An attack that uses one or more systems to flood another system with so much traffic the targeted system is unable to respond to legitimate requests.

deoxyribonucleic acid (DNA) A code used within cells of living organisms. Its uniqueness is useful in investigations to link individuals with substances found in specific locations.

documentary evidence Written evidence, such as printed reports or data in log files. Such evidence cannot stand on its own and must be authenticated.

dual-boot system A system that has the ability to boot, or start, and run more than one operating system.

electromagnetic fields   Produced by the local build-up of electric charges in the atmosphere and can be damaging to computer components. They are present everywhere in our environment but are invisible to the human eye.

electronic discovery   The process whereby electronic documents are collected, prepared, reviewed, and distributed in association with legal and government proceedings.

electrostatic discharge (ESD)   Buildup of electrical charge on one surface that is suddenly transferred to another surface when it is touched.

e-mail header   Data contained at the beginning of an electronic message that contains information about the message.

encrypt   Obscure a message to make it unreadable.

expert witness   A person called to testify in a court of law who possesses special knowledge or skill in a specific area that applies to a case.

Extended Binary Coded Decimal Interchange Code (EBCDIC)   A character encoding set used by IBM mainframes. Most computer systems uses a variant of ASCII, but IBM mainframes and midrange systems such as the AS/400 use this character set primarily designed for ease of use on punched cards.

extension checker   A utility that compares a file's extension to its header. If the two do not match, the discrepancy is reported.

fdisk   A utility that can be run from a bootable floppy disk that displays current disk partition information and allows you to repartition a hard disk.

Federal Rule of Civil Procedure 26   Federal Rule 26 states the General Provisions Governing Discovery and Duty of Disclosure. Section (a) states Required Disclosures and Methods to Discover Additional Matter.

File Allocation Table (FAT)   A simple filesystem used by DOS, but supported by later operating systems. The FAT resides at the beginning of a disk partition and acts as a table of contents for the stored data.

file viewer   A utility that provides thumbnail images of files. Such tools are useful for visually scanning a group of files.

filesystem   The operating system's method of organizing, managing, and accessing files through logical structuring on the hard drive.

FireWire   An IEEE-1394 technology that is a high-performance, external bus standard that supports data transfer and multimedia.

floppy drive   A drive accessible from the outside of the computer into which you can insert and/or remove a floppy disk. One floppy disk holds up to 1.4MB of data.

forensic compression   The compacting of an image file by compressing redundant sectors to reduce the amount of space it takes up.

forensic suite   A set of tools and/or software programs used to analyze a computer for collection of evidence.

forensically sound   Procedures whereby absolutely no alteration is caused to stored data so that all evidence is preserved and protected from all contamination.

hard evidence   Real evidence that is conclusively associated with a suspect or activity.

hardware-protected areas (HPAs)   Areas of a hard disk created to specifically allow manufacturers to hide diagnostic and recovery tools.

hash   A mathematical function that creates a fixed-length string from a message of any length. The result of a hash function is the hash value, sometimes called a message digest. Hash functions are one-way functions. That is, you can create a hash value from a message, but you cannot create a message from a hash value.

High-Performance File System (HPFS)   A filesystem designed for the OS/2 operating system. HPFS automatically sorts the directory based on the filename, and it includes the super block and spare block.

honeypot   A specially equipped system deployed to lure hackers and track their use of the system's resources.

hybrid attack   A modification of the dictionary attack that tries different permutations of each dictionary entry.

HyperText Markup Language (HTML)   A web-based programming language used to create documents that are portable from one platform to another.

IDE port   The Integrated Drive Electronics (IDE) port is a system-level interface that allows the operating system to recognize a hard drive as part of the system.

incident   Any violation, or intended violation, of security policy.

incident response   The action taken to respond to a situation that can be recovered from relatively quickly.

incident response plan   The actions an organization takes when it detects an attack, whether ongoing or after the fact.

incident response team (IRT)   A team of individuals trained and prepared to recognize and immediately respond appropriately to any security incident.

input/output (I/O)   Data transfer that occurs between the thinking part of the computer or CPU and an external device or peripheral. For example, when you type on your keyboard, the keyboard sends input to the computer which in turn, outputs what you type on the screen.

International Association of Computer Investigative Specialists (IACIS)   An international volunteer corporation comprised of law enforcement professionals including federal, state, local, and international law enforcement who are committed to education in the field of forensic computer science.

Internet service provider (ISP)   Provides a gateway to the Internet and other online services, primarily as a paid service.

intrusion detection   Software and hardware agents that monitor network traffic for patterns that may indicate an attempt at intrusion.

IP address   An identifier for a computer or device on a TCP/IP network.

Jaz drive   A true, replaceable hard disk. Each Jaz cartridge is basically a hard disk, with several platters contained in a hard, plastic case.

key logger   Device that intercepts, records, and stores everything that the user types on the keyboard into a file. This includes all keystrokes including passwords.

KISS method   KISS stands for "Keep It Simple, Stupid" and is an acronym that reminds us to avoid making things overly complex.

known plaintext attack   An attack to decrypt a file characterized by comparing known plaintext to the resulting ciphertext.

logic bomb   A virus or other program that is created to execute when a certain event occurs or a period of time goes by. For example, a programmer might create a logic bomb to delete all his code from the server on a future date, most likely after he has left the company.

malware   Another name for malicious code. This includes viruses, logic bombs, and worms.

Message Digest 5 (MD5)   A method of verifying data integrity that is more reliable than checksum. MD5 is a one-way hash function, meaning that it takes a message and converts it into a fixed string of digits, which is then used to verify that the message hasn't been altered.

metadata   A data component that describes the data. In other words, it's data about data.

modem   A shortened version of the words modulator-demodulator. A modem is used to send digital data over a phone line. The sending modem converts data into a signal that is compatible with the phone line, and the receiving modem then converts the signal back into digital data.

Netstat A utility that displays the active port connections on which the computer is listening.

Network File System (NFS) Provides remote access to shared filesystems across networks. The primary function of NFS is to mount directories to other computers. These directories can then be accessed as though they were local.

New Technology File System (NTFS) A filesystem supported by Windows NT and higher Windows operating systems.

operating system Acts as a director and interpreter between the user and all the software and hardware on the computer.

packets Unit of information routed between an origin and a destination. A file is divided into efficient-size units for routing.

passcode A character string used to authenticate a user ID to perform some function, such as encryption key management.

password A string of characters used to authenticate a user by comparing the value to a stored value that is associated with a specific user ID.

password cracking Attempting to discover a password by trying multiple options, continuing until a successful match is found.

PC A personal computer intended for generic use by an individual. PCs were originally known as microcomputers because they were built on a smaller scale than the large systems most businesses used.

personal digital assistant (PDA) A tightly integrated handheld device that combines computing, Internet, and networking components. A PDA can use flash memory instead of a hard drive for storage.

plaintext An unencrypted message.

port scanner A program that attempts to connect to a list of computer ports or a range of IP addresses.

private key algorithm An encryption algorithm that uses the same key to encrypt and decrypt.

protocol A set of rules and conventions that governs how computers exchange information over the network medium.

public key algorithm An encryption algorithm that uses one key to encrypt plaintext and another key to decrypt ciphertext.

real evidence Any physical objects that you can bring into court. Real evidence can be touched, held, or otherwise observed directly.

relevant evidence Evidence that serves to prove or disprove facts in a case.

Request for Comments (RFC) Started in 1969, a series of notes about the Internet. An Internet document can be submitted to the Internet Engineering Task Force (IETF) by anyone, but the IETF decides if the document becomes an RFC. Each RFC is designated by an RFC number. Once published, an RFC never changes. Modifications to an original RFC are assigned a new RFC number.

routers Devices used to forward packets.

search warrant A court order that allows law enforcement to search and/or seize computer equipment without providing advance warning to the equipment owner.

searching tool A tool that searches for patterns (mostly string patterns) in a large number of files.

Second/Third Extended Filesystems (ext2/ext3) State-based filesystems used by the Linux operating system.

security policies Specifications for a secure environment including such items as physical security requirements, network security planning details, a detailed list of approved software, and Human Resources policies on employee hiring and dismissal.

Seized A program developed by New Technologies, Inc. (NTI) that locks a seized computer and warns the computer operator that the computer contains evidence and should not be operated.

server A computer that has the capacity to provide services to other computers over a network. Servers can have multiple processors, a large amount of memory, and many hard drives.

signature analysis A filter that looks at both the header and the contents of the datagram, usually referred to as the packet payload.

site survey Notes, photographs, drawings, and any other documentation that describes the state and condition of a scene.

slack space The space on a hard disk between where the file ends and where the cluster ends.

social engineering A method of obtaining sensitive information about a company through exploitation of human nature. Also the process of encouraging someone else to carry out a task (normally requiring more access to a particular resource than you possess) on your behalf.

SPAM Unsolicited "junk" e-mail often sent to a large number of people.

spanning across multiple discs Breaks the image file into chunks of a certain size so the image file can be backed up onto multiple CD recordable discs or other media types.

steganography The process of hiding the existence of a message by embedding it in another message or file. The very existence of the embedded message is unknown.

subpoena A court order that compels an individual or organization to surrender evidence.

substitution cipher A cipher that substitutes each character in the original message with an alternate character to create the encrypted message.

summons A court order that compels a witness to appear in court and answer questions.

swap file Space on a hard disk used as the virtual memory extension of a computer's actual memory.

symmetric algorithm Another name for a private key encryption algorithm.

temporary Internet files Copies of all the HTML, GIF, JPG, and other files associated with the sites a user has visited on the Internet.

testimonial evidence Evidence consisting of witness testimony, either verbal or in written form. Testimonial evidence can be presented in person by the witness in a court or through a recorded deposition.

trace evidence Traces of data either left behind or found with a criminal that can be used to prove that a crime was committed.

traceroute A command used to see where a network packet is being sent and received in addition to all the places it goes along the way to its destination.

Transmission Control Protocol/Internet Protocol (TCP/IP) network A network that uses the TCP/IP protocol.

unerase tool A utility that assists in recovering previously deleted files. In some cases, files can be completely recovered. At other times, only portions of the file can be recovered.

Universal Serial Bus (USB) A connectivity standard that allows for the connection of multiple devices without the need for software or hardware.

user ID A string of characters that identifies a user in a computing environment.

virtual FAT (VFAT) Also called FAT32, an enhanced version of the FAT filesystem that allows for names longer than the 8.3 convention and that uses smaller allocation units on the disk.

virus A program or piece of code that is loaded onto your computer without your knowledge and is designed to attach itself to other code and replicate. It replicates when an infected file is executed or launched.

voluntary surrender   Permission granted by a computer equipment owner to search and/or seize the equipment for investigative purposes.

war dialing   Uses an automated software application that attempts to dial numbers within a given range of phone numbers to determine if any of those numbers are actually used by modems accepting dial-in requests.

WinHex   A universal hexadecimal editor used in computer forensics, data recovery, low-level data processing, and IT security.

wireless access point (WAP)   Network device that contains a radio transmitter/receiver and that is connected to another network. A WAP provides wireless devices access to a regular wired network.

workstation   A desktop computer that has enhanced processing power, memory, and capabilities for performing a special function, such as software or game development.

worm   Similar in function and behavior to a virus, with the exception that a worm does not need user intervention. It takes advantage of a security hole in an existing application or operating system and then finds other systems running the same software and automatically replicates itself to the new host.

Zip drive   A small, portable, high-capacity floppy disk drive developed by Iomega Corporation used primarily for backing up or archiving PC files.

Zip file   A single compressed file that contains a complete set of programs or files.

Index

Note to the reader: Throughout this index **boldfaced** page numbers indicate primary discussions of a topic. *Italicized* page numbers indicate illustrations.

Symbols and Numbers

TELL US WHAT YOU THINK!

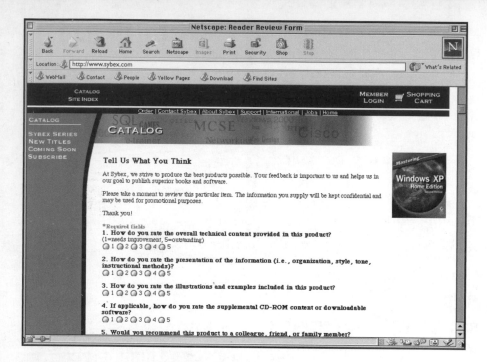

Your feedback is critical to our efforts to provide you with the best books and software on the market. Tell us what you think about the products you've purchased. It's simple:

1. Go to the Sybex website.
2. Find your book by typing the ISBN or title into the Search field.
3. Click on the book title when it appears.
4. Click **Submit a Review.**
5. Fill out the questionnaire and comments.
6. Click **Submit.**

With your feedback, we can continue to publish the highest quality computer books and software products that today's busy IT professionals deserve.

www.sybex.com

SYBEX Inc. • 1151 Marina Village Parkway, Alameda, CA 94501 • 510-523-8233